Samuel Dana Horton

The Silver Pound and England's Monetary Policy Since the Restoration

Samuel Dana Horton

The Silver Pound and England's Monetary Policy Since the Restoration

ISBN/EAN: 9783337417758

Printed in Europe, USA, Canada, Australia, Japan

Cover: Foto ©Suzi / pixelio.de

More available books at **www.hansebooks.com**

THE SILVER POUND

AND

ENGLAND'S MONETARY POLICY SINCE
THE RESTORATION

TOGETHER WITH THE

HISTORY OF THE GUINEA

ILLUSTRATED BY

CONTEMPORARY DOCUMENTS

By S. DANA HORTON

A DELEGATE OF THE UNITED STATES OF AMERICA TO THE INTERNATIONAL
MONETARY CONFERENCES OF 1878 AND 1881

LONDON

MACMILLAN AND CO.

1887

TABLE OF CONTENTS.

	PAGE
PREFACE	ix
INTRODUCTION.—On Certain Meanings of the Word "Standard" .	xxi

CHAPTER I.
THE THREE STANDARDS.

§ 1. The National Instrument of Valuation . . .	1
§ 2. The Standard of Desiderata	3
§ 3. The Greater Standard of Value . . .	6

CHAPTER II.
THE FALL OF PRICES AND ITS CAUSE.

§ 4. The Rise in the Value of the Sovereign	10
§ 5. The Cause of the Fall of Prices	13
§ 6. Quantity-Theories and the Indo-European Conflict of Coinages .	20

CHAPTER III.
ENGLAND'S RESPONSIBILITY AND ENGLAND'S INTEREST.

§ 7. England's Responsibility for the Outlawry of Silver	28
§ 8. England's Interest in the Reinfranchisement of Silver . .	31
§ 9. Scruples touching the Intervention of the State . .	33

CHAPTER IV.
TRANSCENDENTAL SINGLE-METALLISM . 40

CHAPTER V.
A LESSON OF HISTORY: THE MONETARY CRISIS OF 1696.

§ 11. The Recoinage of 1696, and its bearing upon the Questions of To-day	64
§ 12. The Disorders of the Time and their Remedy . .	70
§ 13. Locke and the Ratio of $15\frac{1}{2}$ to 1 . . .	73
§ 14. Newton on Silver and Gold .	87

Chapter VI.

A LESSON OF HISTORY (*Continued*): THE DESCENT TO GOLD.

	PAGE
§ 15. The Rating of the Guinea and Pistole in England	94
§ 16. The English Monetary System and the Originality of the State-men of the Recoinage . . .	109
§ 17. The Guinea at 21 shillings .	117

Chapter VII.

A LESSON OF HISTORY (*Continued*): THE ABANDONMENT OF THE SILVER POUND.

§ 18. The Arguments of Lord Liverpool	125
§ 19. The Anti-Silver Statutes—Lord Liverpool's Scheme . . .	143
§ 20. The Monetary Theories of Sir William Petty, of Joseph Harris, and of Sir Robert Peel	165

Chapter VIII.

SILVER BEFORE ENGLISH PUBLIC OPINION.

§ 21. The Status of Silver in England since 1816	183
§ 22. International Concurrence in the Past and in the Present .	192

Chapter IX.

NOTABLE ARGUMENTS AGAINST INTER-METALLIC PEACE.

§ 23. Certain Theses of Professor Erwin Nasse . .	200
§ 24. Silver Outlawry and the Manual-labour Classes . .	203
§ 25. Lions in the Path of the Reinstatement of Silver .	206
§ 26. A Dilatory Plea	212

Chapter X.

A MONETARY BALANCE OF POWER . 217

APPENDIX.

THE HISTORY OF THE GUINEA,

Illustrated by Contemporary Documents.

CONTENTS.

NO.		PAGE
1.	An Order for the Coinage of Guineas, December 24, 1663 .	229
2.	The Statute of Free and Gratuitous Coinage, 1666 (Extract) .	230
3.	The Mint Indenture of Thomas Neale, 1686 (Extract) . . .	233
4.	Silver before the House of Commons, April, 1690.	234
5.	Report of a Committee in Favour of Debasing the Coin, March 12, 1694-5	236
6.	Petitions concerning Guineas at 30 Shillings, February, 1695-6 .	238
7.	The Bank of England and the Guinea in Camp before Namur, July, 1695	240
8.	Statutes relating to Coinage and Currency of Guineas (1696):—	
	A. The Guinea at 26 Shillings	243
	B. Suspension of Obligation to Coin Guineas	244
	C. The Guinea at 22 Shillings	246
	D. Repeal of Statute Suspending Obligation to Coin . . .	247
9.	Action of the Treasury touching the Currency of the Guinea, October, 1697.	248
10.	Letter of the Commissioners of Excise Touching the Rating of the Guinea in 1694-6, July 22, 1698	249
11.	John Locke and the Ratio of 15·58 to 1 :—	
	A. Order of Reference to the Council of Trade, Sept., 1698	250
	B. Report on Lowering the Guinea	250
	C. Orders to the Government Officers not to take Guineas for more than 21s. 6d.	253
12.	Instances of Contradiction between Statements of Doctrine in Locke's Writings on Money, 1690-1698	255
13.	A Private Letter of Locke touching the Recoinage, March 30, 1696	257

viii   *Contents.*

No.		PAGE
14. "Memoirs of the Great Recoinage," MS. by Hopton Haynes		258
15. Reports Relating to the Coinage, MS. signed by Sir Isaac Newton, 1700-1702:—		
	A. Report Touching the Currency of the French and Spanish Pistoles in England, January 20, 1700-1	261
	B. Report concerning the cutting of Counterfeit Money	262
	C. Report Touching the late Change of Ratio in France, September 28, 1701	263
	D. Report Touching the Rating of the Guinea, etc., 7 July, 1702	264
	E. The Value of Gold in Proportion to Silver in Several Parts of Europe	267
	F. Proposals for Preserving and Increasing the Silver Coin of this Kingdom, July 7, 1702	270
16. Order in Council, Lowering the Currency of Louis d'ors and Pistoles to 17s., Feb. 5, 1700-1		272
17. Minute of Orders to the Mint Officers, Feb. 12, 1701		273
18. Sir James Steuart and Adam Smith on the English Standard, 1759		273
19. Biographical Notice of Lord Liverpool		275
20. Report of the Committee of the Privy Council on Coins, May 21, 1816		278
21. The Proclamations of the New Currency, 1817		281

HISTORICAL MATERIAL—MISCELLANEOUS.

22. Contraction in 1818-1822		287
23. Alexander Baring (Lord Ashburton) on the Silver and Gold Standard in England		288
24. The Restoration of Silver before the Bank of England in 1828		291
25. A Silver Discussion in 1837		294
26. Sir Robert Peel on the Standard of Value, May 6, 1844		297
27. Monetary Treaties in the Past		302
28. State Papers relating to the Policy of Monetary Union, 1878, 1881, 1882		306

PREFACE.

A THEORY and a statute[1] are on trial. The constituency of the theory has been world-wide, and the statute is a British statute, but the law is no respecter of persons; the issue cannot be evaded—whether England does well to obstruct the orderly establishment of the world's Money, by maintaining the Disinherison of Silver?

In slow progression her rulers approach the final hearing of this cause: In 1876, a Select Committee of the House of Commons on the Depreciation of Silver; in 1878, and in 1881, Delegations to represent the British Empire in the International Monetary Conferences at Paris; in 1885, a Royal Commission on the Depression of Trade and Industry; in 1886, a Royal Commission on Gold and Silver: successive

---

[1] Section XI. of "an Act to provide for a New Silver Coinage, and to regulate the Currency of this Realm," 56 Geo. III. c. 68 (June 22, 1816), is as follows:

"And whereas, at various times heretofore the Coins of this Realm of Gold and Silver have been equally a legal Tender for Payments to any amount, and great Inconvenience has arisen from both those precious Metals being concurrently the Standard Measure of Value, and equivalent for property; and it is expedient that the Gold Coin made according to the Indentures of the Mint should henceforth be the sole Standard Measure of Value and legal Tender for Payment, without any Limitation of Amount, and that the Silver Coin should be a legal Tender to a limited Amount only, for the Facility of Exchange and Commerce:

"Be it therefore enacted, That from and after the passing of this Act, the Gold Coin of this Realm shall be and shall be considered and is hereby declared to be the only legal Tender for Payments (except as hereinafter provided) within the United Kingdom of Great Britain and Ireland," etc. etc.

steps in diagnosis of general economic malady, which point at least toward active measures of cure.

A world is waiting for decision—or for solution of the problem of cure—a world not as once, cynical or indifferent, but now expectant, and one may almost say, anxious.

The following work is a contribution to the argument and to the evidence in this cause.

The immediate occasion of its preparation was an invitation, with which I was honoured in 1885, to address the British Association for the Advancement of Science on "the British Standard of Value." The request came from the Committee of Section F (Economic Science and Statistics) for the meeting in Aberdeen, September, 1885. Professor Foxwell did me the kindness to select and read portions of a lengthy address. That discourse has been revised and enlarged, and the accompanying documents of proof and justification, so far as they bore upon events in the present century, have received some reinforcement. The researches into the history of the earlier period [1] embraced in my survey, were made in 1881 and 1882, and were a direct continuation of earlier explorations in forgotten fields of monetary history, the results of which were put in print, respectively, in a treatise on "Silver and Gold" (1876), in a Discourse on "The Monetary Situation" (1878), in a partial Documentary History of Monetary Policy, accompanied by notes and explanatory essays, which was annexed to the Report of the Monetary Conference of 1878, and in an open Letter to Professor Jevons, entitled "Sir Isaac Newton and England's Prohibitive Tariff on Silver Money," in 1881.

The results of inquiry, purely historical, into the past and

---

[1] For facilitating them, it is my agreeable duty to express my indebtedness to my former colleague in the Monetary Conference of 1881, the Hon. C. W. Fremantle, Deputy-Master of the Mint.

present of the English Standard, and of an examination of controlling general theories, or principles of monetary legislation, are here presented in their bearing upon the Disinherison of Silver. The reason of this joinder of subjects is apparent: for those active measures of cure for existing evils, to which allusion has just been made, can be none other than the Reinstatement of Silver to its former position as Money, by joint action of nations; and the connection between this proposal and the attitude of England toward Silver, is plainly vital. This is true not merely because other nations regard such joint action as impracticable unless England takes proper part in it, but because if England's omission to join is politic, in England's interest, then doubt is cast upon the wisdom of the proposed joint action on the part of other nations. This proposal has been outstanding ever since 1878. It was formally enacted by the Congress of the United States in that year, and presented to the nations in a Monetary Conference in Paris; and it was repeated by France and the United States jointly in 1881. The most important subject in the history of English Money is thus the most pertinent phase of the great monetary question of the age.

The present pertinence of this historical inquiry is further enhanced by the peculiar need of securing precision—and, especially, of guarding against overstatement—in making the demand of present reform known to the English public. In this direction much is, of course, to be gained by placing the desired future modifications of English law into their due perspective and relation to English doctrine and English law —both as they have been, and as they are to-day. There is also much to be gained in point of precision, through an improved nomenclature; for words are good servants, but bad masters, and the words "Gold Standard" and "Bimetallism," which seem to be in the ascendant in popular discussion, leave much to be desired in point of clearness. While using the word "Standard" in the following pages, as an inevitable portion of English speech, I have endeavoured to restrict its power of misleading, by a rigorous course of definition,—an original analysis of its meanings, coupled with historical examples of their application.

This analysis and definition become the basis of a classification of Money as an object of state policy; and, by devising or adopting distinct terms or names, I have endeavoured to individualize certain cloudy and wandering notions which have much obscured the field of vision. It rests in the discretion of others to grant that co-operation which is needed to naturalize these distinctions in the terminology of Money.

It will, I believe, become apparent that by this method, beside obtaining a guarantee for present clearness of discourse, I have succeeded in throwing light upon opinion and action in the remoter past, and have established a certain order and continuity in the comparison of monetary policy at different periods of history. A salient instance will advise the reader of the importance of this course.

The contrast between Single Standard and Double Standard plays the most important part in modern discussion. Here, in fact, is the line of battle along which the opposing forces of Babel-tongued controversy have been arrayed.

Nevertheless, the facts which I shall set forth, show that in spite of authority on either side, in spite of decades of conflict and myriad outpourings of thought in print and speech, this antithesis is quite fallacious. Indeed, as I shall show, the English Monetary System was for centuries *a Single Standard and a Double Standard at the same time.*

Now as I read the story of the past, mistakes parallel to this are found, upon critical examination, to be, historically, the efficient cause of the present state of the law and opinion which support the Exclusion of Silver in England. The

"Treatise on the Coins of the Realm" of Lord Liverpool (1805), the Act of Parliament of 1816, the views of Sir Robert Peel (1819-1844), and the work of Metrical Coinage Reform, which, in the decade 1857-1867, fixed the later fashion of thought, are to an important extent, *so far as they support the Exclusion of Silver*,—successive steps in a gradual accretion of error; or in the building up of a structure, a goodly part of whose beams and pillars are errors of theory resting upon errors of fact.

In their origin these errors of fact chiefly relate to events and ideas connected with that older System of the Silver Standard and Dual Money, which was formally replaced in 1816. Indeed, a gulf seems to have separated the present century from the knowledge of earlier times; as if the memory of the monetary past had been swept away by the tide of Paper Money (1797-1821); only so much being saved as was contained in Lord Liverpool's "Treatise on the Coins of the Realm."

In the following pages the effort is made to establish the lines of historical communication thus broken, to take up the work as Lord Liverpool left it, in 1805—to examine the claims of his treatise[1] to the position it has held as the Institutes, if not also the Pandects, of English Monetary Right—and, so far as may be, to supplement its defects by new evidence and argument.

The direct bearing of these investigations upon the practical issue of to-day—namely, whether Parliament shall put an end to the Disinherison of Silver—will depend, for each reader, upon the importance which he ascribes to the efficient causes of the order of things under which he lives: for—so far as I can estimate the probability—this order of things never would have existed but for these errors of fact.

---

[1] The citations throughout this work refer to the edition of 1846.

It was in the conduct of that older System of the Silver Standard and the rated Guinea, that the main principles of monetary legislation were established in England. The dedication of this volume is but an expression of the estimate I place upon the work of those who did most to give those principles strength and consistency. That these elder counsellors of England found room within England's borders to deal with the Duality of Metal and Unity of Money upon a plan which, in their narrow field, recognized the international elements of the monetary problem, is an assurance that their enlightenment—to the vindication of which it is my privilege to contribute—will in due time be emulated in a world-wide field by their successors in that office.

It is but justice to the various monetary writers, past or present, from whose conclusions I have here to express my dissent, to admit that my position is based not merely upon new argument, but also, to some extent, upon new evidence, which fortunate researches have enabled me to discover; to the benefits of which—as giving what in a Court of Law would be ground for a new trial—my opponents are equally entitled with myself.

It is also fitting that I should draw the reader's attention to certain documents which form part of this evidence. That this volume presents to the public a reprint of Monetary Reports from original manuscripts in the hand of Newton, and that it also contains a Report signed by Locke, and the authorship of which is fairly to be ascribed to him, assures it an interest which is quite independent of anything else it may contain. The same remark applies in a different degree to an appeal from the Governors of the Bank of England, sent from Antwerp in July, 1695, to the King of England, then in command of the armies besieging Namur, which reveals a monetary and financial situation of peculiar interest.

In thus setting forth the later course of history, in which the English Law-maker has been called upon to deal with Money, I have sought to regard the various practical situations thus described, in the light of various leading truths or principles, whose existence, or whose relative importance, are not unlikely to be ignored.

This distinctively practical point of view has been overshadowed to a greater extent than is generally supposed, the more usual course having been to regard Money chiefly in its character of a broad debatable ground of economics, rather than as an established institution of the state, or as a concrete object of legislative amendment, at the hands of a majority. To this cause is perhaps to be ascribed the fact that in some minds there is a certain unwillingness to accept the elementary thesis that Money is an integral part of the province of Government, and that the duty is incumbent upon the State to regulate this institution with a view to the general weal; and the same remark will apply to the consequences which grow out of these truths.

Among the objects of Monetary Legislation none are more important than those which have been slighted in the refusal of England to give adequate co-operation with other nations in arresting the chaotic course of events, caused by the Outlawry of Silver; in producing which, England has been the prime mover.

Through this course certain elementary desiderata of monetary policy have been neglected, namely, stability in the value —the average Purchasing Power—of a National Money, and the maintenance of parity between it and other Monetary Systems.

To the evils of the economic situation in England since 1873—a reduction of the ratio of profitable activity in various departments of production and of exchange, and an iniquitous revolution of pecuniary conditions through the general depreciation of vendible things—England's consent to remove the ban against Silver, offered the one practicable and legitimate means of prevention or of cure.

It should be needless to observe that these evils could not have been entirely prevented, and that they cannot all be cured. Nor is human knowledge equal to the task of divining the precise percentage of harm which could be averted, any more than a Board of Health can ascertain the exact figures of mortality which can be prevented by some wise plan of sanitation. This fact has never been held, in England, to warrant the rejection of measures to promote health; that is to say, health in the purely physical sense. Economic health, however, has stood on a different plane.

Among the obstacles to action on England's part in the direction referred to, inertia, heedlessness, and perhaps, in some instances, a sordid and short-sighted self-interest, form an array which can only be dispersed or won over by agitation; but, of course, the obstacles with which a book can deal are only those which take the form of articulate opposition.

If we count among the latter the natural disposition to "stand by the old Standard," or "the existing order of things," it is germane to prove, as is done in the following pages, that it is not the Gold Standard which is the object of attack, it is merely the Exclusion of Silver. There need be no "change of the Standard" in the truest sense of the word. The Gold Standard can be maintained: Gold can remain the Standard Measure of Value, the controlling Money, without excluding Silver. To object that this idea is novel is merely to prove that it is important.

An important place in the field of academic contention is occupied by the doctrines of Unity of Standard and of non-intervention of the State. The latter, in the form of an alleged incapacity of Parliament, is quite disposed of by proof that

England is really the home of artificial regulation of Money, so that the principle which is alleged to be "artificial" is in reality "natural" to English statesmanship. The results of its application having been approved by the experience of centuries, there is something peculiar in the effort to call a halt at this particular time.

Touching the doctrine of Unity of Standard, some suggestion has already been made of misapprehensions which have had currency with reference to the elder form in which it appeared, and it is my privilege to deprive it of the chief guarantees of authority which have been allowed to recommend it in this century, among which is the name of John Locke. In its latest form of an ascription of mysterious sanctity to Gold Coin, it is an indirect offshoot of the agitation in favour of extending the Metric System. It was quite natural for adepts in the exact sciences to fix their attention upon a coin as a physical weight and measure, and to avoid that other arduous field of study which deals with the institution of Money, and with the economic effects of political action relating to it. Through this breach came error; for the important class of learned men interested in this enlightened movement were, unconsciously, enlisted in favour of an impracticable aim; and in the pursuit of an impossible Unity of Material, the disruption of an actual and beneficent Unity of Money was encouraged.

This, however, is but an evanescent fashion of thought. How slight its hold is on England can, perhaps, most simply be shown by the fact that Sir J. F. W. Herschel preferred the Silver Standard to Gold, and a Binary Standard to either. That one of the first names of the century, the greatest man of science, since Newton, who has been Master of the Mint, could utter this doctrine in 1853, in London, while in office, publicly, before a Royal Commission, shows that the roots of the doctrine which flourished at the Monetary Conference of 1867 are very near the surface.

"But surely," it will be said, "those wise statesmen who established England's system were not wholly at fault in the Exclusion of Silver." Certainly not! They were dealing with facts as they then were, not with facts as they are now. And the world went very well then, comparatively speaking. Lord Overstone's doctrine that a metallic currency will take care of itself, could safely enough be relied upon, so long as other nations took good care of England's Money by keeping the peace and par between the Metals. Neither he nor Sir Robert Peel nor Lord Liverpool contemplated laying a general embargo on Silver; nor did the law which was actually adopted in 1816—still less did the scheme that Lord Liverpool proposed—bar the door to an extended monetary use of Silver in England.

Detailed consideration is further given to some of the current objections touching that joint action of nations which awaits England's concurrence: and to the means which are used to obscure the view of the entire practicability of this work of economic sanitation: the restoration of permanent order—in which all have an interest—in the place of chaos, in which no one has a serious interest.

To the Memory

OF

SOMERS, MONTAGUE, NEWTON, LOCKE,

MONETARY COUNSELLORS OF ENGLAND.

INTRODUCTION.

ON CERTAIN MEANINGS OF THE WORD STANDARD.

SOME OF THE VARIOUS MEANINGS ATTACHED TO THE WORD "STANDARD," WHEN USED IN MONETARY DISCUSSION.

No. 1. The fineness of Money-metals, or proportion of pure metal to cheap alloy.

No. 2. The fineness prescribed by law for a coin.

No. 3. The weight prescribed by law for a coin.

No. 4. The National Unit of Account, regarded as a denomination, name, or title, as distinguished from what may, at various times, be its body or substance.

No. 5. The National Unit of Coinage, being the body and substance of what I call the Unit of Account.

No. 6. The Full-Legal-Tender Money of a country.

No. 7. The kind of such Money chiefly in use (the chief coin in use).

No. 8. The kind of Money, the manufacture of which is free, and which maintains or controls the par of the Moneys of a country, or with which the other kinds of Money are kept at par.

No. 9. The Monetary System of a country, in general terms.

The application of these distinctions to law and fact in England's monetary history will occupy not a few pages of the following work, and full comparison will be made of the meanings here distinguished with ideas and forms of statement current in modern days.

In the meantime, it will, perhaps, serve the reader's convenience, if an illustration be given, drawn from actual facts of to-day, but remote from the field of present controversy; which requirement can be met as follows :

ILLUSTRATION.

THE KINGDOM OF HOLLAND.

What is the Dutch Standard ? It is, according to

Meaning

No. 2. Nine hundred and forty-five thousandths.

No. 3. 9.45 gr. of Silver, and .6048 gr. of Gold, to the Gulden.

No. 4. The Gulden.

No. 5. The Silver Gulden (at least, as I understand the matter : I am not informed of any statute explicitly withdrawing this character from the Silver Gulden, though, by the suspension of its coinage in 1875, it has been thrown into what I may name a state of suspended animation).

No. 6. Silver and Gold.

Meaning

No. 7. Silver.

No. 8. Gold.

No. 9. Nondescript; the "Limping Standard." To describe the Money of Holland adequately, it is necessary to state that the Coinage of Gold is free for all; that Silver Coinage is now a right of the government, the exercise of which is suspended; coins of both metals are Full-Legal-Tender; there is a great stock of Silver-coin; very little Gold; but all Moneys at par with Gold.

Speaking only in general terms, then, Holland has, all at the same time:

        No. 5. A Silver Standard.

        No. 6. A Silver and Gold Standard.

        No. 7. A Silver Standard.

        No. 8. A Gold Standard.

        No. 9. A Limping Standard.

ERRATA.

Page 35, line 1, *for* " page v " *read* " page ix ".
,, 46, ,, 18, *for* " page xv " *read* " page xxi ".
,, 80, ,, 1, *for* " the preceding " *read* " a preceding."
,, 93, ,, 21, *for* " by the " *read* " by."
,, 101, ,, 22, dele " *late*."
,, 108, ,, 16, *for* " 1698 " *read* " 1699."
,, 108, ,, 21, *for* " 15.^{9} " *read* " 15.^{93}."
,, 110, ,, 12, *for* " 14.^{418} " *read* " 14.^{48}."
,, 112, ,, 10, *for* " dearer " *read* " more valuable."
,, 124, ,, 16, *for* " weighty " *read* " mighty."
,, 132, ,, 24, *for* " No. 8 " *read* " No. 5."
,, 135, ,, 16, *for* " object " *read* " ground."
,, 143, ,, 23, *for* " the man " *read* " a man."
,, 156, ,, 18, *for* " seigniorage " *read* " brassage."
,, 174, ,, 4, *for* " No. 7 " *read* " No. 6."
,, 174, ,, 5, *for* " No. 6 " *read* " No. 7."
,, 190, ,, 32, *for* " shall not be " *read* " shall be."
,, 199, ,, 2, *for* " 1886 " *read* " 1887."
,, 248, 253, 272, *read* " Return March 11."

CHAPTER I.

The Three Standards.

§ 1. The National Instrument of Valuation.

To the mind of Ricardo it appeared an axiom that "commodities measure the value of Money, as Money measures the value of commodities."

This proposition, so self-evident to a mind like Ricardo's, seems not to be self-luminous to the degree desirable for the practical management of the business of government; to many minds, like other truths of monetary science, it lacks the glow of inherent obviousness. Were this not the case, it would be superfluous, in approaching the very important and very practical question which is the subject of our discourse, to explore the recondite foundations above which, as upon solid earth, the practice of nations and the languages of men are wont to proceed in dealing with the subject of Money. But, as human nature is constituted, such exploration is, unfortunately, a crying need. Upon the generation now living has fallen the duty of rebuilding a monetary structure that has been visited by earthquake. Though this duty strains the strength of the interpreters of science, there is no escape from it; the present generation owes it to itself, for its own present happiness and good name, and not merely as a benefaction to posterity, to meet and solve the problems in its path.

At such a time, reasoning upon standards of value, whether

standards of the value of commodities or of the value of Money, needs all available support to establish, not merely the security of its foundations vertically, if I may borrow the figure, but also to determine the strain in each direction which its pillars are able to sustain; that is to say, to make special precaution against misunderstanding.

Hence the importance of first clearing the ground of terminology, of establishing the sense in which words are to be used, of which the reader of these lines has seen a recognition in the introductory pages of this work.

Passing beyond the list there given of meanings of the word "Standard," to consider the sense of the phrase "British Standard of Value," we shall find it, in its turn, a compound, open to analysis and separation into outlying thoughts. But in completing a survey of the subject, which I hope may serve as a rough map of the labyrinth of Money, I am not unmindful of the penalties imposed by laws which I respect, upon him who shall seek to disturb a land-mark; nor am I lacking in sensitiveness to a truth, which I was once glad to unearth, like a diamond, glittering with the polish of Mirabeau's wit, namely: "That it is not worth while to search out a new definition of Money in order to introduce another error into the world."[1] I shall not attempt to give a definition of Money in the ordinary sense; the views I present are essentially practical. I shall assume that a Monetary System exists; that its maintenance is a duty of the State; that the function of a "standard of value" is of great importance. I seek merely to gain certain general points of view from which the various conditions favourable to the adequate fulfilment of that function can be discerned in due perspective.

A consideration of the conflict and confusion, to a part of which I venture to hope the list of meanings of the word "Standard" affords a clue, may perhaps lead some minds to

[1] "Observations Préliminaires sur le Rapport du Comité des Monnoies," etc. Paris, 1790. Document of the Conference of 1878, p. 297.

welcome the phrase " National Instrument of Valuation," as a useful alternative for " Standard of Value " in the concrete sense, and so as a servant of correct thought. I shall in the next pages note the lines of classification through which we distinguish two other Standards of Value, quite distinct from the National Instrument of Valuation ; to which, claiming the right of an explorer in these fields, which, though old, are ever new, I have ventured to give names, calling them " The Standard of Desiderata " and " The Greater Standard of Value."

§ 2. THE STANDARD OF DESIDERATA.

Those commodities, of which Ricardo was speaking, which are to measure the value of Money, must be selected commodities.

If this be not the case, each vendible thing will be on an equality with all other vendible things, in measuring the value of Money. Beagles are vendible in England, but if a dog-epidemic and a turn of fashion should quintuple the price of beagles, no one would think that the purchasing power of the sovereign had fallen, while if wheat should rise to many pounds sterling the quarter, a convulsion would ensue, in which the whole world would share.

What, then, is the basis of selection of these commodities which are to be united to form a just measure of the value of Money? What is to fix their relative standing? Is it quantity (weight, bulk, or number), or the number of times they are exchanged before being consumed, or the length of time they are in use, or their relative importance, as necessities of complex modern life? Are materials to be counted both in their raw, and in their manufactured, state? Are land and wages to be taken into account? Is the prevalent rate of interest at all entitled to be considered? On determining which, or whether all, of these factors are to enter into the result, in what exact numerical strength are they to marshal themselves?

Evidently, whatever the ground of selection, this new *tertium comparationis* is a mental product of statistical lore and of computation, a conglomerate of things desired, a conventional, artificially compounded, body of heterogeneous objects which men desire to buy; it is for this that I have thought " Standard of Desiderata " an appropriate name.[1]

It seems plain that in order to attain an ideally correct composition of this measure—after some preliminary questions of selection are settled—a combination must be sought of what I may call averages; an average community, or an average man; an average of his or their desires; and some plan of equalization must be devised in order to eliminate the disparities between the qualities of various things succeeding each other in use, or arising from the growth of new needs, the creation of new objects, or from a change of demand for them in the transformations of time.

I am not aware that this work has been done:—no convention has yet seriously sought to establish this conventional standard : the organic law of a Standard of Desiderata is still a desideratum. The subject seems to lack its devotees, though the memory of much that has been achieved already, encourages the belief that such devotees will appear in time.

At this point I must present an humble disclaimer. I have no practical contribution to make here to the lore of " Index Numbers," which is the peculiar name through which the Standard of Desiderata seems to be best known to-day. I have no message to give here touching the composition of this Standard, the chemistry of this sun of the monetary firmament.

It is, however, germane for me to make, in passing, my

[1] A Chapter of a Treatise on " Silver and Gold " (Cincinnati, Robert Clarke & Co., 1876-7) bears this title.

Galilean profession of faith by saying, " it is the sun, and the world of Money turns round it." As is the sun in the heavens a fact, although its composition be the problem of every age, so, if I may borrow the comparison for these humble uses, the monetary sun shines to-day as it has shone in the past, though we should wait till the XXth century ere a worthy catalogue be made of its elements. It marks, in fact, the inevitable dividing line, or point of departure, of movements the general character of which (whether dimly or clearly) is perceptible to every intelligent citizen. To the layman, as to the economist, its general position is known; it is spoken of in the counting-house as well as in the study. Whoever speaks of Expansion or of Contraction, of a General Rise or of a General Fall of Prices, of the Purchasing Power of Money, of Appreciation [1] or of Depreciation of Money, is, whether consciously

---

[1] The words "appreciation" and "depreciation" applied to Money (to a Standard or to Money-metal), have of late years occasionally been the objects of a fallacy-breeding use, which it is perhaps worth while to mention.

The plain meaning of appreciation is the rise, let us say, of Gold relatively to things vendible, which takes place as prices fall; depreciation is that fall of Gold which takes place as prices rise. The fallacious use I speak of, comes from the effort to appropriate the words for certain special instances of rise or fall of prices; so that, for example, they shall only be used when the speaker thinks the change has been produced by certain special causes, or when he thinks it is permanent, or that it is progressive.

This use is, in my judgment, unscientific and indefensible, because it diverts from two useful words their natural signification—of a Rise or Fall of the Purchasing Power of Money, and offers in exchange no clearness of opinion as to the points just referred to; but in place of such clearness, erects a blind, or masked defence against understanding. If any-one is of opinion that some special order of prices has been neglected in the account which goes to form an " Index Number," or that certain causes have been at work which deserve to be specially mentioned, or that the present is but one stage of a certain process, it is an obvious remark that he has but to say so; and that he can hardly say so to any good purpose by undermining the plain common-sense meaning of "appreciation" or "depreciation."

or not, speaking of a Standard of Desiderata, however formless his idea of its constitution.

The question of adjustment, therefore, of equivalence between the Actual, and the Ideal, Standard of a country, is always in order, as a matter of scientific interest, though seldom rising into the range of attention as an element of political calculation. Our subject cannot be fully, cannot be adequately, discussed, without raising the question—how closely does the British Instrument of Valuation, the body of Money used in Great Britain, adhere to a " Standard of Desiderata?" In other words, how far does the Gold coin of England, which, by reason of the Law of 1816 (re-enacted in substance in 1870), affords the sole " Standard Measure of Value" fulfil, on an average over proper periods of time, the most important functions of a Measure and of an Equivalent?

§ 3. THE GREATER STANDARD OF VALUE.

We have seen that it follows from Ricardo's axiom, that the stability of the legal, and hence customary, instrument of valuation, the Money of a country, is merely another term for the constancy of the general level of prices expressed in it.

But this level of prices, in England, how exclusively is it under British jurisdiction? How much more so than is the level of the sea that washes Britain's shores? In time of calm the English Channel may easily be regarded as independent of the Northern Ocean or of the Bay of Biscay, and they, in their turn, of all the continent-embracing seas; but thought dispels this forgetfulness of fluidity and of gravitation, which make the sea-level one and continuous the world around. Is it a violent statement to affirm that there is an analogous oneness and continuity in the world's Money, though the sea of Money has its colours, the yellow, the white? To my view, at least, the mass of Gold coin in England has been, is, and remains a tract of sea that keeps its local level (as compared with things vendible), because of the lateral support of circumjacent tracts of Money.

English valuations, whatever the legal material for the Standard in England, are sempiternally dependent, laterally, upon foreign Moneys, as well as, vertically, upon that tract of coin upon which the English arms are displayed.

We thus disengage the idea of a Standard of Value in a broader sense, which I have called the "Greater Standard," as the sum total of National Instruments of Valuation, the Money of the world. Of this Greater Standard, the distinctively British Instrument of Valuation is but a part. In an important sense, therefore, these British valuations are indirectly expressed in terms of the Greater Standard of Value.

We note further that, inasmuch as no nation can own more than a fraction of all existing Money, the centre of gravity of each local-national monetary system must be outside of the nation that uses it. The perfection of far-sighted policy, then, is to be realized only by keeping the National Instrument of Valuation in accord with the National Standard of Desiderata, and this can only be done by a favouring adjustment of the Greater Standard of Value, the Money of the world.[1] In its wider range, therefore, monetary policy is essentially a matter of foreign, as well as of domestic policy; a policy always holding in view the adjustment of foreign tracts of Money, if I may so strain the word, as well as the condition of things at home; or if we express it in a more practical way, a matter of adjustment of complex international relations looking to the maintenance of a certain stability of averages of price.

It must be well observed that the statement just made, while entitled to the dignity of a "principle," and worthy to hold guidance of legislation in the rare instances when mone-

---

[1] "Silver and Gold," Chapter VI., and "Monetary Situation" (1878), Chapter I., § 3, "That Money is an Institution not of one nation, but of the world."

tary laws are to be passed, yet claims attention in our argument here as fact.

It is indifferent to what extent, in any century, Englishmen, whether connected or not with Parliament or Bank, or Treasury, or Exchequer, have apprehended this truth I am seeking to set forth. The point to which I ask attention is that the truth existed. This foreign and lateral support of Money has always been in place. Was there ever, I ask with confidence, a time when the withdrawal of this support would not have meant disarray for England's valuations; that is to say, when a failure of the mines or a demonetization of either metal, or similar interruption of normal supply and demand outside of England, would not have introduced disorders into England? I think not. Now, this foreign and lateral support did not exist solely "by the grace of God." No "law of nature" was in force for its benefit; it was not there by virtue of gravitation, nor of cohesion, nor of chemical affinity; it was there because men so willed, and laws were made accordingly; and thus it appears that England was beholden to these men who willed the things that were for her benefit, and made the laws which maintained the security of her valuations.

I venture to think there is here a general truth, pointing backward over past centuries, as well as forward to the future, which deserves a permanent place, and a place of honour, in the learning or doctrine of Money.

Upon the practical importance of a recognition of this truth I have already indicated an opinion. Whether England in the past was aware of this interest of hers, is a question for the curious; but that she should be clearly conscious of it to-day is a matter of the first importance.

So long as the constitution of the world's Money was favourable, so long as the Greater Standard of Value was so adjusted as to promote justice and prosperity for Englishmen, the practical statesman could safely leave things as they were, so far as the immediate present was concerned, and perhaps could safely take the current reasoning on the subject for granted. The utility of recognizing the truth in question rose to the first rank only when the precedent of centuries was abandoned, when the constitution of the world's Money became unfavourable. But the truth is not dependent upon the utility, and can be more easily seen in its due perspective from the standpoint of the past. To-day the Greater Standard of Value, through ill-advised tampering with important classes of national instruments of valuation, has in fact fallen into a pitiful state of mal-adjustment. The further course of this work will throw light upon the extent of the harm done.

In the meantime we may conveniently note here that this Greater Standard of Value, upon which the valuations of England have always been dependent, is a Compound Standard. The world's Money—its Measure of Value and Equivalent for Property—is Silver and Gold. It always comprised—it still comprises—*both* the precious metals. As for the future, I can safely challenge to-day—so far has conviction proceeded —the sincerity of foresight to discern a future when it will not comprise both metals. When, indeed, is Silver to cease everywhere to be Money, Full-Legal-Tender Money, freely-coinable Money? Whatever Englishmen have done, or may do, the Standard of Value in which they have had, have, and will continue to have, the heaviest stake is in large part Silver.

CHAPTER II.

THE FALL OF PRICES AND ITS CAUSE.

§ 4. THE RISE IN THE VALUE OF THE SOVEREIGN.

THAT the British Instrument of Valuation, the Standard Measure of Value and Equivalent for Property, has expanded of late years in value—that is to say, in purchasing power—is a fact so generally known that we can without further preface ask for the accredited estimates of the extent of the rise. Those directly in view at the date when this work was substantially written (1885) will be presented, with an indication of the subsequent course of prices, but without details. As for a date to be compared with 1885, 1875 offers itself as a natural term of comparison. Without going into recondite questions of the average duration of "a business," or of an investment, it will be admitted that we shall have an idea "how things stand" if we compare the state of affairs of ten years ago with those of to-day, and that, in any case, it would be a mistake to neglect a decennial period, entirely, for one either longer or shorter. As authority we can interrogate Mr. Giffen, in his article in the " Contemporary Review " of June, 1885, and can conveniently compare two current and accepted approximations to the Standard of Desiderata which are set forth by him.

According to the method of Mr. Newmarch, the "Index Number" for 1875 is 2,778; for 1885, 2,098. Mr. Giffen's own Index Number for Exports gives ($65.^{51}+8.^{87}$) $74.^{47}$ for 1875 and ($65.^{50}-5.^{95}$) $59.^{55}$ for 1883; his Index Number for

Imports gives $(81.^{16}+.^{25})$ $81.^{41}$ for 1875 and $(81.^{16}-9.^{43})$ $71.^{73}$ for 1883; to which figures an allowance must be added for a downward movement to 1885.

We have, then, from the method of Mr. Newmarch a fall of $(24.7°/_0)$ $24°/_0$ in round numbers, while exports and imports show a fall of several per cent. more than 19 and 12 respectively. It may safely be assumed that the figures of Mr. Newmarch, devised to represent the value of Money in England, are more likely than either imports or exports to be near the Standard of Desiderata for the whole country, and we can therefore accept, for the temporary purposes of our discussion, a fall of $24°/_0$ in average prices, a rise of $24°/_0$ in the value of the Pound Sterling, between 1875 and 1885. For the years since 1885 the same authorities indicate a further rise.

We can picture to our eyes the importance of this rise, if we observe its effect upon debts current during that period; the National Debt, for example, regarded as a principal sum, has in a certain sense increased its weight upon the shoulders of the British tax-payer between 1875 and 1885, by nearly 200 millions sterling; an amount nearly equalling the Franco-German war fine. Of course I do not make this assertion on my own authority; it is merely an application to Mr. Newmarch's figures of the precedent set by Jevons in an important work on a kindred subject.

Whether these figures are strictly accurate or no, the broad fact is ascertained, the rise in the value of Gold is a serious rise. Is it still in progress? In 1885, Mr. Giffen saw no reason why the fall should be at an end. He thought it might go on; in fact, it was probable that it would go on, and, as we see, his forecast was correct. Has England before her a further subsidence of prices, a further upheaval of the value of Gold? Having myself made parallel forecasts in 1876, and since, which have been justified by the event, I feel I can inquire with some confidence, how the further degradation of Silver can fail to produce a further fall of price. It would therefore seem to lie in the hands of the Royal Commission on Gold and Silver to decide whether England is to suffer a further subsidence of prices, a further upheaval of the value of Gold.

What, then, does this mean—for the interests of men—a rise in the value of Gold, the controlling Money of the Occidental world? To answer the question rightly, we must realize that Valuation, Appraisement in Money, is, so to speak, a condition of modern thought. Man is as inevitably an appraising being as he is a political, or a social being. Labour and Property—what does man know of them to-day, except as he sees them through the medium of Money; and what is there else but labour and property within the range of material interests?

The round world and they that dwell therein are appraised for taxation; both the lives of men and the surface of the earth figure in business calculations as investments; in every obligation, in every investment, the past and the future meet each other; from the cradle to the grave, debit and credit are, as it were, an air that is breathed by civilized man.

A rise in the value of Gold means a dislocation of the land-marks of the property of men,—and so the rise of Gold is a wrong. But it is far more than this, it is a wasting disease of that economic body which is formed of the men who toil with hand or brain.

The world of business, of enterprise, of investment, may well be likened to a sensitive organism, which requires complete health and vigour in all its various parts for its highest activity; and the motive for exertion of individuals, which is the continuing cause of this health, and vigour, and activity, is the hope of receiving greater money-value than was given: and it is the difference between first-cost and sale-price which makes the organism of business move. When prices rise, there is always an encouragement to activity. But when all the prices at which sales are made, are falling, then the force which rules the producing and exchanging world slackens;

there is, relatively, less movement, less production, less consumption, less success in business; there is embarrassment and idleness; there is a prolonged crisis; or, what we familiarly call "hard times." The rise of Gold, then, means what may be called, monetary malaria invading the health of nations, a plague of Money.

It is true that optimism still walks in high places, and in apparent observance of the duty of cheerfulness, has assumed the tone of Candide, as if all were for the best, and this were the best of possible monetary worlds.

But as the years go by, this patient world grows restive; the continuance of suffering arouses question whether optimism is not here and there a cloak for interest, and whether the recipe of patience be not serving mainly to defer a diagnosis which may, to the discomfiture of the elder physicians, be followed by cure.

§ 5. THE CAUSE OF THE FALL OF PRICES.

What is the cause of the fall of prices? Evidently, the Anti-Silver-laws of the Western Nations are the primary, the efficient, and the removable cause.

Of course casuistry and special pleading can find full exercise in the game of hide-and-seek between causes and conditions. It would be but a dull and barren age, which, after having set on foot an inter-continental outlawry of one of the Money-metals of man, should make default of sophistry in self-defence! In the earlier days of the Anti-Silver-movement, which broke ground actively in 1873-4, when protest was made against a policy which obviously tended to provoke a check of confidence and shrinkage of values, the stereotyped answer did duty in well-nigh every Occidental language, "the fall of prices is a mere normal reaction from a period of inflation." For convenience of discussion we may call this "Cause A."

But, as time has gone on, and contraction marches apace, the serviceableness of this argument wanes; it is necessary for the apologist of Anti-Silver-laws to find some other means of rebutting the testimony which incriminates him, and so the defence proceeds upon lines which may be briefly stated as follows:

CAUSE B. New processes of labour, inventions, etc., which cheapen production, are elevated into a cause for the fall of prices.

CAUSE C. New methods of business, the elimination of middlemen through the facilities of inter-communication and of transportation, are elevated into a cause.

These causes deal with the past fall, and, if we may judge by the use sometimes made of them, are assumed to have come into play just in time to be substituted as causes in the place which, but for them, Anti-Silver-laws might perhaps have been permitted to occupy.

Another cause is at hand to provide for the desired counter-movement which is to check the fall: Postal orders, cheques, telegraphic transfers, clearing-houses infinite, etc., are to economize cash, set it free, and stop the contraction. This we may call "Future Counter-cause D."

Of course with this ample set of causes, and marshalling the facts of their entries on the scene in the manner suggested, it is possible to piece together an arrangement, so to speak, of the play of Hamlet with the part of Hamlet left out; and so to present the Anti-Silver, Gold-favouring, monetary war of the last decade as a pastoral-symphonic entertainment. But in justice to all disputants in the monetary arena I must hasten to say that, so far as I know, no one—not even the most irretrievably committed politician—is chargeable with all the extravagance in thus ignoring fact, of which I have endeavoured to give a combined picture. There is no such expanse of malice aforethought. In fact, forethought is rare; for cause and counter-cause are not infrequently put side by side, as if they could work together, though one works toward a rise, the other toward a fall. It is only certain instalments of fact that one disputant, and then perhaps only partially, ignores, while another perpetrates an hiatus in another direction.

In general, however, it is to be noted that (at least so far as I know), no responsible disputant, however valiant he may be in self-defence, has accepted the full burden of proof which has lain from the first as a public challenge before him, namely, the burden of proving how it was possible that the Anti-Silver, Gold-favouring policy could, under existing circumstances, fail to produce a rise in the value of Money. Looking at the subject from the end nearest to us, we can ask, who is there among the champions of Gold to-day, who will take upon himself publicly to deny that, in his opinion, had Germany, in taking Gold at 15½ after Sedan, maintained her free coinage of Silver, the investments of the Western world would have been spared one most potent factor of disorganization?

Now these are the mighty tasks which the champions of demonetization ought to be coping with, if what seems to me their usurpation of law is to maintain itself before posterity.

I submit that a general demurrer lies to the entire genus of argument we have been considering.

We start with the demand for a stable Standard of Value, as commerce asks for a level sea—not an absolute plane, of course—for of that we have neither precedent nor promise: winds and waves and tides are there, tides annual and tides decennial, obedient to the lunar attraction of human moods—but, on the whole, on the average, a level sea. This is the demand of science; this is *good Money;* a just "Measure," an honest "Equivalent," to use the words enshrined in the Statute of 1816. To whom is this demand addressed? Primarily to the State. It is the function of the State to establish and maintain, as far as is practicable, a good Monetary System. And such a Money was in fact provided by the monetary constitution of the world as it was down to 1873. It was to the State that appeal was then made in order to outlaw Silver from its traditional position as Money. Without the law there would have been no outlawry; without a law the outlawry cannot be cancelled.

Now arises before us the duty of estimating the character, the influence, of this governmental policy affecting Money, which made the breach in the monetary constitution as it was down to 1873: the Gold-favouring side of which policy we may, for the sake of brevity, leave at one side for a moment, calling it a movement to get laws and regulations adopted in order to outlaw Silver in the chief Money-using nations. What was this revolutionary policy to do for the nations in question? This was, and is, the only practical thing under discussion, the only thing involving *action* on a large scale; this, or of course with it, the counter-proposition, to replace outlawry by reinstatement; which are two sides of the same question, distinct acts, in a word, of the corporate and conscious free-will of nations; the outlawry having taken place to a considerable extent, the reinstatement being urged as a measure of public policy. This, I repeat, was and is the only important practical monetary question before the nations.

Now this outlawry of Silver reduced the customary increase of the metallic stock by which the business of the world had long profited; and this reduction was made just at a time when national demands arose for cancellation of Paper Money or for covering it with metal. It was sure, by dislocating the par between Silver-countries and Gold-countries, to derange the inter-metallic business of the world, and by depreciating Silver to depress the Gold-price of things in Silver countries. Such a movement must *prima facie*, other things being equal, tend to contract Gold-prices.[1] Having thought, and said

---

[1] Of course in saying this I bind myself to no rigid quantity-theory; of this I shall speak later. (See page 24.)

in print, the equivalent of this since 1876, I may be allowed to adduce this forecast of mine as evidence of the obviousness of the view now set forth.

If "other things" are not "equal," if counter-forces are at hand to neutralize this tendency, which occupies the ground with such overwhelming force, they must come forth, prove themselves, show that they can overbear the presumption, and sustain the burden of proof.

Such being, then, the state of the case, let us assist at the arraignment and trial of an imagined Defendant, the Demonetizer of Silver. He has admittedly been instrumental, as we have seen, in setting agencies at work which tend artificially to contract prices, and to enhance the value of Money. The effect has been produced. He is accused of stealing from that average of prices which makes the practical measure of values and equivalent for property of civilized man. The crime is a grave one, and self-preservation is a law of nature. Men expert in criminal practice are at hand, under whose prompting he pleads "not guilty." The trial proceeds, consisting entirely of the defendant's testimony; the other facts being admitted.

Evidence is introduced to show:

CAUSE A. That some of the prices were decaying:

CAUSE B. That some of them were claimed by inventors:

CAUSE C. That some of them were being carried off by railroad and telegraph men.

And further, the deponent saith not. The defence rests. That is all! To show that Defendant did not commit the offence charged, counsel rely on evidence *to the effect that some-one else committed another offence.*

The ancient and well-invented "bull" of the witnesses who sought to prove a Defendant's innocence of stealing by swearing that they did not see him steal, has at last appeared in the flesh. So fatal is the Nemesis that pursues science when she is untrue to her better self!

But this order of argument, which, as we have seen, has so long been tolerated by educated opinion, does not yet appear before us in all its native simplicity. A few strokes more are needed to lay it bare. We must observe that the greater the inroad upon prices which Causes A, B, and C can be held to have set on foot, the higher does the Anti-Silver-policy rise in the scale of incompetence, the more flagrant the blunder of it. It has intensified, aggravated, disaster, when the duty of the state was to remedy, to relieve. Controlled by the Demonetizer, the State, which should act as physician to the suffering economic body, has devoted itself to reinforcing, artificially, the natural agencies that were working evil: instead of antidote, it has given more poison.

Having disposed of this inversion of sense, we can now proceed to assign a fitting place to Causes A, B, and C, and to Counter-Cause D. To the thinker they offer most important fields of observation, and to the monetary statesman they are vital elements of the problems with which he has to deal. What annual increment, for example, is necessary in order to maintain constancy of prices? This is a question for science, "What is desirable?" What increase is practicable, and, at the same time, safe, is another question. Each question deserves an answer, though it may get none.

Without attempting to enter upon the matter fully here, I take space to note, in passing, certain points with which the investigation of this field will necessarily deal.

1. I have elsewhere shown ("Silver and Gold," 1876-7) that the experience of England between 1844 and 1874, indicates that the habits of Money-using are such that prosperity implies a considerable and constant increment of metallic stock, in excess of the growth of population.

2. The agencies which we have reviewed, in so far as they set free cash which would otherwise have to be held in a specified employment, have, while tending to reduce the prices of certain classes of articles, the secondary effect, other

things being equal, of contributing a certain quota, however small, toward expansion.

3. The manifold influences which affect the expansion of credit—the habit of using credit compensations rather than cash payments—the extension of operations into the future, which enlarges the field in which such compensations can be arranged and the figures they can attain—all these are peculiarly susceptible to the impulse arising from monetary operations of great magnitude, of which governments alone are masters.

4. Alterations in the quantity of Money are competent to intensify, or to neutralize, the practical effect in average prices, of any and all influences which are exerted by the ordinary operations of business; the limit to their force is only the practical one, of the amount added to, or subtracted from the stock with which the hypothesis starts, due allowances being made for the element of confidence, as, for example, for the quality of the money, and the mode of its appearance or disappearance.

It will be found that these considerations unite in establishing the unwisdom of the policy of outlawing Silver; its condemnation *a priori*, independently of late specific experience: a condemnation from the point of view of 1871, as well as of 1887.

If we look closely at A, B, C, and D, we shall note of the latter three, that they are of perennial stock. Any effort to represent them as appearing from the clouds, just in time to relieve the Outlawry of Silver from this sentence of condemnation, is doomed not only to failure, but perhaps even to ridicule. I say this with all respect for a number of distinguished gentlemen—citizens, respectively, of at least five different countries —whom I have in mind, but do not name.

"Now when I shall compare the prices of things at this day with those of ancient times— . . . the proofs would be very disputable . . as for example . . Cloth,

Linen, Leather, and such like would have the like variety of prices through the same causes, viz., difference of seasons, diseases, war, and through other causes, as through Impositions laid on them, *new inventions whereby the Manufacture may be more easily and speedily made*, engrossing of them, false making of them, want of workmen,"—p. 103. (The italics are mine.)

Whence comes this quotation? The book was written about 1650! It is Rice Vaughan's "A Discourse of Coin and Coinage" (1675).

I venture, in fact, to allege without offering detail of proof, save a passing allusion to the extension of the railway, telegraph, and cheque systems, in late decades, which I can assume to be within the reader's knowledge, that Causes B, C, and D, were active in important degree, on one side or the other, while prices were rising after 1850, while prices were comparatively steady, between 1868 and 1873, while prices have been falling since 1873, and that as regards A, in so far as it was a real tide, it tended not to exhaust itself in an ebb, but to gather force for a returning flow; which cannot well be said to have occurred.

For the rest we can close this Section by recommending to whom it may concern, Counter-Clause D, as a cucumber, more likely than any in the field, to yield sunshine.

§ 6. QUANTITY-THEORIES AND THE INDO-EUROPEAN CONFLICT OF COINAGES.

These charges against the Anti-Silver-policy which are contained in the preceding Section, having been repeated in substance in various forms yearly since 1876, I have gathered some experience of the difficulty of guarding against misinterpretation in setting forth views on this nebulous subject.

Among other points it is incumbent upon me to make clear

that I have affected no retrospective prophecy touching the entire field of economic phenomena since the battle of Sedan, and each and every portion of that field. I therefore call attention to the fact that I do not aver that no rise in the value of money would have occurred, if there had been no governmental Outlawry of Silver; I merely say that no rise would have occurred approaching that which year after year has justified forecast, by being ascertained as fact; and that, while some panic corresponding to that of 1873 must have occurred, yet it never would have reached the actual acuteness of that panic, nor would the following years have been marked by the persistent depression which has been cumulatively ascertained.

I desire also, with a similar end in view, to record a protest against a rigorous application of certain phrases which are sometimes adopted in treating of the subject, which seem to me to require peculiar caution to insure their usefulness. I refer to "Scarcity of Gold" and "Gold-famine." Certainly as popular term, analogy or simile, these expressions are natural, appropriate and useful; but for the purposes of scientific precision they leave much to be desired. In one sense there is always Scarcity of Gold. Who ever had as much as he wanted? In another sense there is never scarcity. Anyone who can give the proper equivalent can get Gold. Famine means lack of the average food, the "ration" for the support of life. The quantity-theory in matters of nutrition is, therefore, absolute, resting on unalterable fact; but there is no ration of Money indispensable to economic life. Famine, if it go far enough, means death; but a dearth of Money means no such thing; bankruptcy, repudiation, a fall of prices, no matter how far, are not absolute death to the economic body. In a famine there is no substitute for food. But in a dearth of the metals, men have been content with other materials or with credit, and barter has always its range of practicability. Between good Money and bad Money, between stagnation of business and prosperity, between progress and standstill or retrogression, between impoverishment and enrichment, the difference is essentially one of degree.

Beside this, in a society suffering from this "scarcity" or "famine" of Money, a disposition and possibility are always at hand, ready for a new departure, a new equilibrium of prices; good Money, stable Money, at a new level as compared with vendible things. In the monetary field everything is relative. When people talk of famine or scarcity of Gold, they merely mean scarcity at a former price.

As compared with "scarcity" and "famine" the word "contraction" has certain advantages; but I know of no one word which can be said completely to epitomize a definition of the effect of Anti-Silver-laws, the dislocation of the Par of the two kinds of the world's Money.

But monetary debate need not be niggardly in words. If one word, or phrase, or sentence, will not do, the situation is well worthy of a paragraph or of a chapter. The public should by this time have learned patience. Dealing constantly with numbers, compelled to form an opinion at every turn as to the importance of this or that "quantity," liable to have his conclusion endangered by the temptations of numerical analogies which are rigid and insensible to the changing moods of Money-using men, the domain of the monetary thinker is, though apparently near, really quite remote from the range of customary apprehension. If we turn to the details of practice, we find that the practical questions for the monetary legislator are always questions of the amount of Money, and at the same time of the quality or character of the Money, for which provision is to be made through the instrumentalities of government. In deciding these questions, the legislator, starting as he must from a given condition—an actual quantity and quality of Money in the hands of citizens, or with reference to which the existing law of his country has been framed—naturally seeks guidance for any new action that may be proposed, in considerations touching the efficiency, or circulation and use, of Money, touching the relations between the quantity and quality of the cash of his country, and the valuations in which the citizens are interested, and touching the effect of a diminution or increase of this quantity, or change of its quality, upon prices, upon the activity of business, upon existing Money obligations, upon prosperity, upon social development. It is through this labyrinth that thought and action must go hand in hand. Surely " pardon must be granted to" number, as well as to " novelty, of words when they serve to illuminate such an obscurity of things."

After laying down the reservations and limitations thus set forth at length, it is safe to assert that to reason about Money, and ignore questions of quantity, is to insure losing one's way. To have a quantity-theory of some kind is inevitable.

The generally recognized principle is that " prices are in the inverse ratio to the quantity of Money." This, however, is but a statement of a " tendency." To follow this tendency into detail of practice, that is, to take note of the various counter-forces that modify results *pro tanto*, is matter for volumes in which to set forth what is known, and will be matter for more volumes, when the unexplored regions of the subject shall have been surveyed.

That the Silver and Gold coming from America in the XVIth century raised prices in Europe is a common-place of the books.

It is germane to note in passing that Adam Smith's notion of the *modus operandi*, the stress lying on the cheapness of production of new Gold or new Silver, has now—I think I can at last safely say—been superseded by recognition that the active force lies in the *quantity* added to the existing stock; it is chiefly the quantity added, not the cost of adding it, that affects prices, excepting in so far as the process of adding, itself absorbs a portion of that quantity. The same observation applies to the use of credit, which, I doubt not, has wrought its share of the rise of prices in a similar way. Through these considerations we attain a glimpse into the gulf that separates Money from commodities in general.

Returning to our principle, we find that one of the counter-principles has been well established, viz.: that an issue of convertible notes did not raise prices in proportion. In other words, it was an effect as well as a cause, a concomitant of a instinct and separable increase of Money-using business. So a check of that unknown x, the normal increment of metallic stock required to maintain stability of average prices, and to maintain at the same time the normal increase of exchanges, which is the concomitant (cause or effect) of "prosperity" and "progress"—this check may not lower prices, but only make a corresponding contraction of use of Money. Similarly, an overplus may produce new business to absorb it, and not raise prices.

The quantity-theory, then, cannot legitimately be confined within the cast-iron frame of the generalization first above stated, but must be broad enough to embrace counter-principles of which I have given a hint—and capable of accepting the new truths that shall come from the broad region of the unknown.

I think it will be found that the better minds, whether writers or men of affairs, are in substantial harmony about this matter, though their utterances may not be exhaustive or explicit, and though they may not agree as to details. I know of no one who rejects *in toto* the view above set forth, excepting now and then a crude or eccentric schoolman, or some mere partisan.

The dangers of pinning faith to one "tendency," binding one's practical conclusions in some given case to the strict terms of numerical ratio, may rise more clearly in the mind when such questions as the following are considered:

(A.) How much of the fall of prices is directly traceable to absence of cash which should have come into existence, and did not make its appearance at all, or should have been made to circulate freely, and did not?

(B.) How much of the fall of prices can be held due to mere apprehensions, timid forecasts, fears?

(C.) How much of the fall of Occidental Gold-prices is due to the conflict or collision between Gold-based Monetary Systems and Silver-based Monetary Systems?

(D.) To give a special case of the latter question (C): How far would gold-prices have fallen in Europe, if India had not existed, or if such a state of affairs had obtained that the specific grinding and crushing conflict between India's Silver-values and Europe's Gold-values could be eliminated from the question? Of course, the hypothesis imports a violent stretch of the imagination, but this is necessary if one seeks to divide and classify and measure complex agencies which go to produce an important event.

(E.) What would have been the effect of a largely increased output of Gold, in the past decade—

1. Upon Gold-prices in Europe?
2. Upon Silver-prices in India?

(F.) What would have been the effect of a largely increased output of Silver—

1. Upon Silver-prices in India?
2. Upon Gold-prices in Europe?

In presence of these interrogations, it will, I hope, be plain that if one wishes with a word to characterize the situation, the word "contraction" covers more ground than the word "scarcity," or the word "famine."

We can now approach with more confidence some phases of the question of Indian competition, or better, of the Indo-European conflict of coinages. Of late years Gold-prices have gone down before Silver-prices, instead of Silver-prices rising to a new level with Gold, or, instead of the two meeting half-way. To use the figure of fable, the Occidental Gold Standard has proved the pot of earthenware, while the Oriental Silver

Standard proves to be the pot of iron. So much has been settled by the experience of the last few years.

I shall present the point which seems to me of chief scientific importance in this connection as a criticism of what I shall name the ordinary mercantile view, and of the Anti-Silver-view, of Indian competition.

To the farmer in Minnesota, as to the retired scholar, whose reading excludes the teaching of the Monetary Unionist, this competition is competition, like any other.

To the wheat-dealer, acreage in India, bushels in Liverpool, are the chief thing; India, or Australia, or Russia, it is a matter of quantity for sale, and nothing else.

To the retired scholar this competition, whatever its peculiarities or effects, is a "natural" event, a normal conflict of wealth-getting men.

To this I have replied as follows: Both of these views leave out of account the one novel and most important element of the situation; important from the practical, and from the scientific, point of view. *It is statute and decree, arbitrary and official, that are primarily responsible for the phenomenon; the fall of prices is the result of a conflict of coinages, rather than of a competition of individual men.* This is not in any proper sense a "natural" event, a normal conflict of wealth-getting men; any more than confiscation would be a natural event, or attainder against the rich a normal conflict of wealth-getting men.

Occidental wheat- and cotton-growers are interested in, or affected injuriously by, acreage in India, and bales or bushels in Liverpool, only in the second line: first in order is the price. It is but a small matter to the interests centreing in Chicago or Savannah that so many bushels or bales come from India; it is everything that they come at their present price. If they should come, every one of them, at the normal price which arbitrary laws have done away with, and which absence of those laws might restore, they would produce a moderate effect compared with that which is now exerted. As it is, they come strong in the strength of a grand army, of which they are but the vanguard. The immensity of this market of supply for wheat and cotton, all standing at Silver-prices, and at Asiatic-prices, looms up behind the actual imports, and enforces the drag on the prices of all Occidental stocks, tending to bring all down to the scale imposed by the artificially reduced Gold equivalent of Indian Silver prices; for no scheme to control the market can be carried out.

The specific loss of the Western Nations through the dislocation of the par between Asiatic and European Money imports no corresponding gain to Asia. The conflict of monetary systems is, to an important degree, analogous to a collision, and affects the business of the world somewhat as a series of earthquakes would affect the orderly pursuit of happiness in a busy mining or manufacturing region.

How far this "contraction" of prices would have occurred had the annual increment of total metallic Money-supply been greater, is a problem which must await solution. How far the phenomenon is specifically due to the habits of an Asiatic people, is also curious matter for meditation. The whole subject has a profound interest for the entire constituency of the Occidental Gold Standard.

One thing is evident: no mere palliative will meet the disease. No half-measure will avail. No measure short of restoring a fixed par between Silver and Gold, at a rate as near as possible to that which formerly obtained, will meet the requirements of the time.

CHAPTER III.

England's Responsibility and England's Interest.

§ 7. England's Responsibility for the Outlawry of Silver.

That England has the casting vote to carry or defeat a measure for concurrent regulation of the Money-metals, is a proposition that brings its acceptance with it.

This power which England wields is of double origin, due in part to the influence which England's example exerts over the feeling, the confidence, the imagination, the interest of the rest of the world, the leaders of nations, and the business community upon whose support laws must rest; and in part to the actual physical strength, so to speak, of the monetary battalion which England can marshal to join in this great undertaking, of reinstating Silver to parity with Gold. If minds are not wanting to whom a Silver and Gold Union, even with England, the World's Clearing House, at its head, suggests doubts and fears, how far beyond them must these doubts and fears cast their gloom, when a Union is contemplated in which England is not to join?

A brief review of the course of the Anti-Silver-movement will throw strong light upon the influence of England's example.

The Anti-Silver-movement set on foot by Germany is, in its origin, distinctly and avowedly an English idea. The line of its transmission to Germany is direct. To J. G. Hoffman, the Monetary Counsellor of Prussia in the early decades of this century (a prominent co-worker with Stein and Hardenberg in her regeneration), London was a monetary fairy-land over which Lord Liverpool ruled as a magician. To him the prestige of England's example bore somewhat the same relation to that of other nations that the commerce of the Spree or of the Upper Seine bore to the world-encircling commerce of the Thames. Both by the general influence of his admirable works, in which he declared in favour of the Gold Standard for Prussia, and as the preceptor and inspirer of one who has devoted the studies of a laborious life to monetary researches, Hoffman's influence has remained a power.

This pupil was Adolf Soetbeer. As the official adviser of the Associated Chambers of Commerce of Germany, Soetbeer directed an agitation in the decade 1860-1870, which paved the way for, and made possible, the legislation of 1871-3. In Soetbeer's cause, the wise and the unwise were linked together. Side by side and as of equal, or indeed of paramount, importance with the unification of the various systems of German coinage, long the object of worthy aspirations among German thinkers, Soetbeer promulgated, with the sanction of the council of economists, *ex cathedra*, the English idea of outlawing Silver. And here the circuit of influence was completed, for it was the prestige of England that insured the acceptance of this doctrine, in a business world which had known only the Silver Standard. The result it is needless to recapitulate here. It was when Germany put herself in the train of England that the task of maintaining the parity of the world's Moneys against the combined attack of two Chief Powers, proved too great for the Bimetallic Countries. Their coinage of Silver was first limited and then stopped, and the Bimetallic Union ceased its operation.

In the studies which the consequent chaotic condition of Money has since forced upon the thinking world, the past experience of England has necessarily been a favourite object of consideration. Did England prosper and take the lead among nations by reason of the Exclusion of Silver, or was it rather in spite of it, as Lord Beaconsfield said in 1873? Gradually the view gains acceptance that though neither he nor others knew or intended it, Lord Liverpool's teaching produced a system of aimless revolution, of organized disorder.

If the Exclusion of Silver was compatible with a good Monetary System from 1820 to 1873, it was, as I have shown, because of the comparative stability of the value of the sovereign. But the demonstration is also clearly within view, that in the decades that have passed since 1816, the British sea of Gold-prices owed its comparative permanence of level to the lateral support of circumjacent oceans of Silver and Gold, held as they were in unbroken fluidity by the self-adjusting action of laws of alternative coinage on the Continent. As I have elsewhere shown, the Great Transhipment of British Valuations from Paper to Gold, the Resumption of Cash Payments (1816-1823), owed its share of statesmanlike achievement to the law in other countries, which kept the Silver-price of Gold from rising. So likewise, in the second crucial test of the Monetary System which outlawed Silver, the Gold inundations from California and Australia, the English Standard is equally indebted to the law in other countries, which kept the Silver-price of Gold from falling.

So long as France, with the huge metallic stock held by her and by her satellites, maintained the free coinage of Silver, so long the revolutionary tendency of the Anti-Silver-theory was held in abeyance, and its character veiled from the ken of most monetary thinkers.

But now this unconscious balance of power, which made the local experiment of the scheme of excluding Silver a temporary success, is broken. The revolutionary Outlawry of Silver has done its perfect work in the monetary disorder of a decade, at the end of which the far-seeing now look forward with earnest apprehension.

The world is waking to the fact that something must be

done. What is to be done? There is but one best thing to do. It is to keep the two Moneys of the world at par. This can alone be done by joint action of nations, such as that proposed to the nations by the Conference of 1878. It rests with the common sense of the nations to heal the fracture—and to reintegrate the Greater Standard of Value, in which Great Britain has so great a stake—by a new and enduring, because conscious and intended, balance of power. What part is England to take in this new construction? Is she to wait, in the hope that other nations will unite to form a Union without her, and re-establish the Money of the world in secure equilibrium for her benefit, as well as their own, without her coöperation? What is to be gained by waiting? What is to be gained by refusing coöperation?

§ 8. ENGLAND'S INTEREST IN THE REINFRANCHISEMENT OF SILVER.

Does a perception of England's interest in the Reinfranchisement of Silver, on the part of the leaders of English opinion, or of the accredited rulers of the country, imply an intellectual, as distinguished from a moral, effort, to which the minds in question are not at present equal?

This very practical question it seems safe to answer with an unqualified negative. It seems safe to venture the assertion that every business man in England, who has the means of forming an opinion, is already preparing to recognize the truth. We need not take counsel of the future, nor ask what tasks may lie before England in Africa, or in Asia, for which a settlement of the world's Money on a firmer basis would give material support. Restricting attention to what is present and close at hand, we can confidently inquire, would anything give more relief to the investments of England of to-day, than that the present course of shrinkage should be arrested, that the rupee should return to its former stability of ratio to the sovereign, and that confidence and the sense of prosperity should replace depression?

Certainly, wherever they are, in any adequate sense, understood, the British people seem in a favourable mood to welcome what can hardly fail to be recognized as a universal change for the better. The future is very dark. Who, indeed, thinks he sees the end of the shrinkage of property valuations, and of the consequent disorganization of the machinery of production and of exchange? Do those interested in foreign trade and Silver-values find relief in forecast of the future? In an address at Manchester (July 26, 1885), Mr. Goschen said there was no hope of knowing what to think of the insecurity of trade with Silver-using countries, until the question of the "Bland Bill" should be settled; and he concluded that the uncertainty may increase. And yet this is hardly the last chapter of this book of the future which commerce is to read. What will come after the question of the Bland Bill shall have been settled? What will Holland do? What will Germany do? Nay, what will India do? Indeed, what will other countries not be compelled to do, if England still holds aloof? Is there, in fact, any prospect of escape in the future from uncertainty as to the measure of values between, or in, Silver-countries and Gold-countries, except by this very restoration of the former equilibrium between Silver and Gold which is now proposed? Absolutely none! The Trustees of Nations, who are like officers on watch in a stormy sea, may study the chart and the sky, and look ahead as far as they can: there is no comfortable living in that sea: the sooner they make for the port of Monetary Union the better.

But there is authority upon the point now before us which Englishmen can hardly fail to find important. I refer to the attitude of Her Majesty's Government, both under the premiership of Lord Beaconsfield and under that of Mr. Gladstone. It was the interest of England which in the Council of Nations of 1878 arrayed England against the further demonetization of silver, and in 1881 (after all due diplomatic reservations had been made), in favour of a formal reinstatement of Silver in a Union of Nations. In 1881, it having become apparent that no important measure of remonetization was to be looked for without concurrent action on the part of England and of Germany, both of these Powers showed their readiness to offer inducements in order to engage the Powers which had called the Conference (France and the United States), to enter, with others, upon the Free Coinage of Silver. Unfortunately for England as well as for other Powers, the inducements offered were not regarded as commensurate with the consideration to be given in return. And so the affair rests. The solution of a problem which, while it embraces the whole world, gives practical relief to the interests best entitled to British support, to the productive forces of the realm, the makers of its prosperity, is in England's hands.

§ 9. SCRUPLES TOUCHING THE INTERVENTION OF THE STATE.

Other pages of this work set forth with some precision the conflicting contentions, which have played their part in the battles that proceed in the upper regions of theory, touching the power of the State; the power that is, and the power that ought to be. I shall here briefly present some practical considerations bearing upon the subject.

As to the general proposition, which will be examined more closely in the following chapter, that it is the duty of the State to maintain good Money, I doubt whether there are responsible disputants who would commit themselves unequivocally against it. Nor are there many who will undertake to deny that the paramount quality of good Money is stability of value, or that the more important signification of stability of value lies in stability of average purchasing power.

That for those who hold these principles, the monetary conditions which have obtained of late years in England, legitimately raise the question of applying a remedy by amendment of the law, is too obvious to need argument. It is not, therefore, to support the general proposition that inquiry is called for: it is against certain special circumstances, exceptions, reservations, saving clauses, strained scruples, and punctilios of opinion, that refutation must proceed.

It will clear the ground for discussion if we set in order, and in due perspective, the array of facts with which the proposed reform attempts to deal, not entering into detail, but regarding merely the general scope of the law, and the accepted principles of administering it. These primary facts are, I regret to observe, even to-day, after all the mental work that has been done in this field, far from being commonplaces of knowledge. It has happened to me, for example, quite lately, to be under the necessity of informing an American monetary theorist (an economic teacher of notable influence), that the Gold sovereign was Legal-Tender in England. *Errorem vidi tantum!*—proof positive of the incompleteness of an education based upon such economic works as have been available for men now no longer young.

It was this very "good Money," of which we have been speaking, which the Legislators of the Kingdom sought to establish, in framing the present Monetary System of England. I do not merely aver by this, that the present Monetary System under which three generations have lived, and until lately, prospered, in the British Isles, and which, whether as offering a Means of Payment, or a Standard of Account, has enjoyed, and still enjoys, a broad supremacy in the calculations of the whole world, was presumably intended to establish justice and to maintain truth. I mean that, in fact, the legislator who framed the Law of 1816, with the frankness of an age unperverted by overstrained theory, told, quite plainly, what he meant, and that he meant no less than this—in framing the Law of 1816. The new Pound Sterling of Gold was to be a "Standard Measure of Value," and if the reader should turn to the Statute (see above, page v), he will observe that the idea is present that the Gold coins were to be the "Equivalent for Property."

Now the words "Standard Measure of Value," (and, similarly, "Equivalent for Property"), are an aggressive assertion of a claim to that stability and permanence of value, that is to say, of Purchasing Power, which is the essence of a *just* measure, of an *honest* equivalent. At the same time I am free to contend that, whatever their legal force, the words are descriptive of a law which ought not to need to be written. But we are dealing with a delicate question—the degree of diligence demandable from the state: and fallacious doctrine is rife, which devises excuses for negligence: and it is therefore quite to the point to remark that no inertia, no indifference, no plea of prescription, or apology for supineness, can wipe these words from the Statute Book, nor should the adroitest pleading lodge in any competent mind a misconstruction of their meaning.

To guard against possible exaggeration I desire to record my view that proper fulfilment of the duty of the State, imports no levity nor haste in changing a Monetary System, once it is founded; no keeping it, so to speak, upon the workman's bench, for uninterrupted tinkering in pursuit of a microscopic ideal.

A settlement is a settlement: *de minimis non curat lex* is a rule of practical sagacity, framed in view of the practical limitations of governmental action. That a nation should set the machinery of legislation at work to correct a great evil, does not commit that nation to inexpedient activity in repairing small evils. Indeed, both the practical business man and the economist might join hands with the jurist in recognizing that conservatism rises, in a sense, to be a positive, rather than a negative principle, where a Monetary System is to be dealt with.

But these considerations impose the rule of prudence, not of timidity. The present seems an appropriate time to recall that, throughout England's history, great reforms have, from time to time, appeared in the light of a restoration of rights and benefits fallen into disuse, and that the possession of a good Monetary System is an imprescriptible right of the English freeman. *Nullum tempus occurrit regi:* there can be no statute of limitations to bar the reformation of the Money of the realm. To affirm, therefore, that the Anti-Silver-law of 1816, or its successor, the Coinage Act of 1870, is on trial to-day in England, is merely equivalent to stating that there are Englishmen living, who feel no inability to confront the problems of statesmanship which the changes of time have brought upon them for solution, and to do it in the spirit which has, through former decades or centuries, actuated a worthy line of monetary statesmen and reformers.

Such, then, is the general scope and purpose of the law: it is there upon conditions, upon good behaviour, *donec bene se gesserit,* or as if by the old-time tenure of Knight-service to render loyal aid to the people-sovereign of the realm.

Proceeding further to look closely at the practice, or custom of administration, we shall find that the exertion to be undertaken by the State, if it is to perform what I allege to be a duty, is, in quality if not in extent, far less an exhausting exercise of power than that to which the State is already inured. It is a curious fact, repeatedly illustrated in the history of monetary policy, that, in an acute crisis, well-nigh everyone recognizes the preservation of the Purchasing Power of Money as a legitimate object of the most strenuous exertion on the part of the State. To take instances from England's history —the Cabinets that suspended Cash Payments in 1797, that suspended the Bank Act in 1847, and in 1866—before what law did they bow?

Salus populi suprema lex.

The safety of the people in what respect? Was it not the interest of the people *in maintaining stable Purchasing Power for the Money of the country,* which was then the supreme law?

I am ready to affirm that such was the fact, and though the contention be regarded as novel, I have no fear that it can be gainsaid.

From one point of view the crisis, in each case, appeared as a depreciation of values threatening to increase in acuteness, and thus to extend its calamitous influence upon the finances of the community—upon the fabric of obligations through which the business of the country was enabled to proceed. The values, and the obligations, were expressed in Money, all of them existing, for what? That the enjoyment of property and the production or exchange of wealth, might proceed in safety. Now, the so-called "real" wealth or property of the country or of its citizens, the existing matter or material, the lands and tenements and goods and chattels, remained without change—it was afterward what it had been before, and the capacity to render services was unimpaired. Wherein lay the crisis? In the calculations of business men, touching the Money-value of property and services.

If there had been no depreciation of values, the owners of property could have had all the "Money" they needed by means of sale or upon credit. But if the owners of property could have had all the Money they needed, could the crisis have occurred at all? Certainly not!

The difference, then, between the crises of 1797, 1847, and 1866, on one side, and, on the other side, of the decade now closing, is, in important phases of the matter, a difference in degree; the first mentioned crises being acute, intense, but very short, the latter making up for its comparative mildness by a phenomenal duration, by the cumulation of distress, and by uncertainty of its reaching an end.

If precedent, then, is to have any weight, we can securely set aside objections to the intervention of the State by citing, not merely the statute of 1816 itself, but the action of the British government in 1797, in 1847, and in 1866.

And the list of precedents can be extended if need be.

What, for example, was the outcome of the testimony of the cloud of witnesses whose evidence was distilled into such finished products of decision as the Resumption Act of 1819 and the Bank Charter Act of 1844? Wherein lies the justification for the general prohibition of the issue of demand notes signed by an association other than certain specified names? Is not the answer to be found in the department of prices, of the Purchasing Power of Money?

It will also, I believe, become quite apparent that the chief proposition pending for amendment of the British Monetary System bears a character which ought peculiarly to commend it to a race of conservative instincts.

We have not to deal with anything comparable, for example, with the demonetization of Gold which was proposed thirty years ago, when no less a personage than Richard Cobden conveyed to England Michel Chevalier's messages of alarm at the Gold Discoveries. The proposition is merely to restore to Silver throughout the world the general position as Money which it held down to the year of Grace 1873.

The change urged upon England was, and is, a conservative and restorative change; maintaining the national body in pristine vigour, and removing nothing important except disease; a legitimate amendment of the law to conform to altered circumstances, preserving all its spirit, and so reforming the letter as to bring the law into conformity with conditions which were not in view at the time it was framed.

The former maintenance of an equilibrium between the two Money-metals can, in fact, be regarded as the work of a trust administered by certain nations for the benefit of all. Changes occurred which compelled the abandonment of this trust: a trust in which England, as the chief Money-using nation, was, it is safe to affirm, the chief beneficiary. The essential aim of the proposed amendment then, so far as England alone is concerned, is actually to restore to England advantages which, under her then existing system, she enjoyed down to 1873, but which she has now lost; and the local changes she is called upon to make in order to secure these benefits, are but a modest quota to a general fund of change, to be contributed by the commercial nations as a body.

In support of these views, a triple order of evidence and argument will be offered in the following chapters. I shall first inquire into the nature of the theories or principles of governmental conduct which are mainly responsible for the great monetary disorders prevalent throughout the world.

England's history will then be interrogated by a review of action and opinion in England relating to Money since England's Money passed, with the Restoration of Charles II., under what may be called distinctively modern conditions. After summing up the results of this inquiry, I shall endeavour to confront the salient arguments advanced in opposition to the establishment of equality between Silver and Gold by joint action of nations.

CHAPTER IV.

Transcendental Single-Metallism.

To attempt a general roll-call of all the manifold forces which united to produce, and which still maintain, the present monetary dead-lock of Christendom, is here a task beyond our scope.

It is chiefly to what—following further the simile of an army—I may call the general-staff of theory, that I ask the reader's attention; for here are to be sought the central inspiration, direction, and leadership of the Anti-Silver-movement.

Touching the causal connection between great political events, such as that with which we have to deal, and what is called "theory," there may well be a debatable ground of opinion. Certainly instances are not wanting where an elaborate theory appeared, in many senses, as an afterthought. But in the events which led to the partial Outlawry of Silver dogmatic teaching declares itself quite plainly as an effective source of political action on a great scale.

An age like the present, which makes mighty strides in improving means of transit, of transport, and of communication, can hardly fail to make like effort to facilitate the operations of exchange; and, accordingly, no sooner had that tide of activity set in which was the concomitant and, in some measure, the result of the great Gold Discoveries, than ideas of simplifying the means of exchange began to show new life.

Unfortunately the learning of the time was unequal to the demand made upon it: defective dogma gained control of the forces of civilization, and out of these defects of dogma proceeded a policy destructive rather than reformatory, tending to self-mutilation rather than to health. Endeavours to enlarge the domain of the Decimal System, and to bring the weight of the coins of different nations into simple numerical relations, quite absorbed the activity of those who sought to improve the means of exchange in the decades 1850-1870. These commendable objects were thus raised to a false position; and inasmuch as the duality of Money-material seemed a barrier to progress in either line, the idea took shape of getting rid of one of the metals, and grew in favour, the attack being first made against Gold, and later against Silver. In the field of action good and evil went side by side. With the unification of German Money upon the Decimal System—in itself an event well worthy to accompany the organization of a New Empire—came the attempted Outlawry of Silver, through which the whole measure is, as it were, dragged in the dust of a lame and impotent conclusion. And yet the applause of the learned world was gained in advance for Germany's course. In all respects save the selection of the precise weight given to the new Gold Unit, the "Gold Marc," the action of Germany was the natural sequence of the conclusions of the first great International Monetary Conference of 1867. It was a special scheme of Monetary Unification which was thus enabled to

> "Get the start of the majestic world.
> And bear the palm alone "—

and this scheme is now in control of Occidental Monetary Law.

In setting forth that portion of it which I conceive to be error—the theory which is directly responsible for the Anti-Silver-movement—I shall endeavour to outline its logical structure with a certain sharpness, and to expose it in open daylight by incisive criticism.

Lest I be supposed, in so doing, to be overstating the position of some opponent, I lay stress upon the fact that I am seeking to give a comprehensive outline of theory—to reduce to system, so to speak, a tendency of thought.

In order to accomplish this result, it is essential to be very clear; and not only is it unnecessary, but, in one sense, irrelevant, to inquire precisely how far this or that individual, who bore a part in the general movement which I seek to characterize in its true nature, actually followed his convictions to all their natural conclusions.

This creed, which inspired the Anti-Silver-movement, divides itself into two chief articles, namely :
1. The doctrine of *Unity of Standard*.
2. The doctrine *that the State lacks power to regulate the value of money*.

The idea of Unity of Standard, *in the sense now in vogue*, can perhaps be most properly, as well as vigorously, characterized as an excrescence, or by-product, of metrology, of the science or art of measuring.

The history of its appearance points to this; for, as I have indicated, the Anti-Silver-mania, as a conscious passion, is a direct outgrowth of the movement for "International Coinage." I doubt if an advocate of demonetization proclaimed his doctrine before the advisers of Louis Napoleon began their endeavour to obtain for the "Gold franc" that pre-eminence which the metre had rightly won in another field. The Congress of the Nations which, in 1867, gave official sanction to the English Single Gold Standard as the objective point of monetary reform for all countries, was thus, in many regards, rather a Metrological, than a Monetary, Conference.

That so subordinate a matter as Metrology should be giving laws to so important a matter as Money, is curious testimony to the unconscious parsimony of science, which, as the ages pass, perfects itself only when it becomes particularly necessary to do so, or rather, which gives to truth a majority only when self-defence requires it.

So long as Alternative, or Optional, Free Coinage of the Money-metals, in a strong body of nations (France and her allies), held the balance between Silver and Gold, making each, respectively, good Money in the Single Standard Countries—a régime which ruled the Monetary World till our day—so long did the error of chaining Money to metrology remain apparently, and for the time really harmless. With the coming of the revolution in the standing of the metals which so deeply interests our generation, the scene changed, and science set to work to repair its errors, in searching for the means to cure the evil which that revolution brought in its train.

The peculiar error I seek to analyze is openly exposed in the current terminology of government; it is but the scholastic expression of the familiar view which brackets Coinage, Weights, and Measures, into one phrase.

Certainly a coin is a weight, and coins of the same name ought to be, and to remain, of the same weight. Money, which, for the senses at least, may be looked on as composed of coins, is a measure. Plainly, Coinage, for some purposes, must consort as naturally with Weights or with Measures, as Weights do with Measures, and Measures with Weights.

Again, Standard Weights and Standard Measures are established by the State, and Coinage is a monopoly of government.

Of the first, the purpose is to have some fixed portion, so to speak, of gravity, or of the dimensions of space, with which to compare others, so that the citizen may know what a pound is, what a yard is, what an acre is, what a bushel is, or a gallon.

And that is all; if the State keep the Standard Weights and Measures unchanged, or practically so, it has done its work.

So of Coinage, says the metrologist, seeking to enlarge his jurisdiction, *the function of government is limited to fixing upon a quantity of fine Gold or fine Silver, and to certifying copies of it, so that the citizen may know what a pound sterling is.*

A fatal fallacy !

As well say that the state should confine its executive energies to the maintenance of a museum of arms, to show the citizen what war is, or should replace judiciary and police by formal publication of a code of civic conduct, to show the citizen what good citizenship is !

But, before considering the relation of Money and the state, we can most conveniently examine somewhat in detail the measuring qualities of this weight of metal called a " Coin." Its object is to measure, not things physical, constant, eternal, not weight, nor length, nor surface, nor size ; but something non-physical, temporary, variable, subject to the whims of human will—namely, value : and its position as a constant measure of value, that is to say, the permanence of its Purchasing Power is all the time dependent and uncertain, a resultant of the relative quantities of objects and the desires of men.

On considering what has been said elsewhere of the Purchasing Power of Money, it will be seen that there is no single coin, nor weight of metal, which is exclusively the actual measuring body, the *corpus* of the Standard, " Money." The " measuring," in one sense, is done by the total quantity of Money in use, whether this Money be duplicates of the Legal Money Unit, or lawful substitutes for it ; and so, really, by the total number of units, whether principal-units or substitute-units. Following further this comparison with weights, one may say that the actual weight of coins of any kind of use, is inferior in importance to the weight prescribed by law for the Legal Unit, and to the practical effect of provisions made for authorized representations of that Unit. Moreover, the total weight of coins, or number of units, in use, is changing all the time through import or export, melting down or new coinage, issue or retirement.

Of course, to extend in unqualified literalness to a "measure" like this, the analogies of a measure such as the pound, the gallon, the yard, is preposterous.

The Law of Navigable Waters, within certain limits, treats the adventures of a mud-barge on the same principles as those of the Great Eastern. To its august logic Mud Creek and the Atlantic Ocean are the same. So, to the Law of Bailment, within limits, a porter with his truck and a Pacific Railway Company are treated alike. But what should we say of a judge who should be so smitten with literalness as to take the matter seriously, and treat them really alike; give damages of half a million for injury to a mud-barge, and issue a mandamus to a porter, as the president and board of directors of a truck, to execute his decrees simultaneously in San Francisco and New York?

Logically, on ultimate analysis, this is the sense of the one-metal dogma. It not only puts the Pound Sterling on a par with the Pound Troy, but holds as an article of faith that a pound weight is not a pound weight, unless it be made of a certain metal; a quart is not a quart, unless it be measured in a golden cup.

Let us now review the second article of the creed in its full extent, and in line with the first; for the one stands, as we have indicated, in close and indissoluble sequence to the other.

From the doctrine *that the fixation of a chief coin, and the certification of copies of it, exhaust the duty of the state*, it is a short step to the doctrine *that to establish coins of different metals, as of the same value, is to attempt to create equivalence between disparate things, to violate nature, and transcend the power of the state.*

At the entrance to the labyrinth which our discussion must thread, it will prove useful to note that, accepting the hypotheses which we have stated, the logical structure we are analyzing is really at war with itself, and can be subverted from within as well as from without.

The chief coins of our metrologist, of which the state was to certify copies, were to be of a fixed weight of fine Gold, or of fine Silver. It is implied that these coins would be Money. They would both be Money in different States, it is true, but still, Money, an instrument of exchange, a measure of value. But exchange is international as well as domestic. Even in the mind of the most literal mathematician this meaning follows the word. Now this supposed trade in Money-valued goods and in Money, between the Silver-Coinage-System and a Gold Coinage-System means, *pro tanto*, equivalence of value between these same unequal weights of Silver and Gold. Hence it follows that the state can and does bridge the gulf between Silver and Gold.

Proceeding further in our examination of the one-metal dogma, we may usefully compare it with principles of monetary policy based upon such facts and truths as are ascertained and distinguished in our statement of the meanings of the word Standard (page xv).

If we put Meaning No. 5, the National Unit of Coinage, into a maxim which shall prescribe for the State a policy of the same carrying-distance as the one-metal dogma, we shall say:

(A.) *A Unit of Valuation, once adopted, should never be abandoned.*

In what relation does the dogma we are reviewing stand to this proposition? Are they the same in substance; does one include or imply the other?

They may seem to be the same, but that is all.

Proposition A is not the proposition of the one-metallist, or of the Gold-advocate of recent decades. They stand or fall with Meaning No. 6; they ignore or repudiate Meaning No. 5.

The one-metallist says:

(B.) *No State should—or my State must not—make Full-Legal-Tender-Money out of more than one metal.*

The Gold one-metallist says:

(C.) *Full-Legal-Tender Money should be made of Gold alone* (though he sometimes adds, " or of promises to pay gold ").[1]

So far as A is concerned, the idea that a material (and weight) for the Unit, once selected, should not be abandoned, it is evidently a sound general proposition, having for its firm support—within proper limits—those considerations which make constancy and order the attendants of the welfare and progress of peoples.

Has the one-metallist of to-day any claim to the benefits of this proposition? None! His "one-ness" is one-ness of material of which Full-Legal-Tender Money is to be made. The one-ness of Proposition A is one-ness of the material of which the Unit is to be made (and its maintenance at full weight).

A Monetary Unit is one thing; Full-Legal-Tender Money is another and quite distinct thing. Coins that embody the Monetary Unit are, of course, to be Full-Legal-Tender Money; but the legal position of the Monetary Unit may be independent of the material of which other Full-Legal-Tender Money may be made.

There can be a Silver Unit and Gold Money, a Gold Unit and Silver Money, or Gold Unit and Silver Unit with either Gold Money, or Silver Money, or both, in actual use.

The reader will note I am not speaking of what ought to be: I do not say it is desirable that divorce, or separation, in any degree, be made between the Measure of Payment and the Means of Payment, between the National Unit of Coinages, and the Money in actual use in the country. I merely observe as a fact that such separation is possible.

If this statement shall awaken surprise or dissent, certainly

---

[1] We may conveniently note in passing, that Proposition C conflicts with Proposition A in that it proposes or sanctions a general abandonment of old Units of Valuation in other countries than England, concurrently with the maintenance of the modern Unit of 1816, in England.

its usefulness will have received sufficing proof. That the literature of Money has had little to say of Money Units, seemed to me very strange, until I observed that Money—belonging neither to Politics and Law alone, nor to Economy alone, but being a compound of all—has been, in a certain degree, a side-issue for the literary specialists of either of these branches of knowledge. It is here, in fact, that Monetary Science has needed to perfect itself: for that the sagacity of statesmen, and important lessons of the policy of nations, have not been adequately represented in literature, is well proven by the present state of the world—Christendom suffering from an epidemic of monetary disease, superinduced by well-meant, but unskilful medication of the atmosphere of business. It is in the presence of such events as this, that sight is sharpened to perceive the intense practical importance—for the life, liberty, and happiness of men are involved—of the broad general conceptions of the functions of society which are set forth in books. That Money is an institution of civil society, a department of the state, an integral part or province of government, as are judiciary, or police, or army—that it deserves a place corresponding in dignity among the accredited sciences,[1] which fix the tone of the better public opinion touching the proper conduct of public affairs—is a statement of truth which, I fear, still lacks its meed of earnest recognition in regions of scientific authority.

So far as the special subject before us is concerned, it is to be observed that the Money Unit belongs peculiarly to the juristic side of monetary learning; indeed, it is, in my belief,

---

[1] The views here stated were set forth in "Silver and Gold" (Cincinnati: Robert Clarke & Co., 1876-7), in an essay on "The Position of Law in the Doctrine of Money" (London, 1881), and in other publications. [The essay referred to appears also in the Document of the Conference of 1878 (Washington, Department of State, 1879), and in the Document of the Conference of 1881; and translated by Professor de Laveleye as "La Monnaie et la Loi" (Paris: Guillaumin et Cie, 1881), and by E. Koch as "Das Gold und das Gesetz," Cologne, Heimann, 1881).]

best explained through analogies drawn from the law, which will be considered on a later page.[1]

The legal establishment of Money, with a National Unit of Valuation as its central figure, is a feature of all government. In each country, each generation grows up in the domain of such a National Unit.[2]

It will further conduce to clearness if I set forth with some fulness, the fact that this distinction between the Unit and Legal-Tender, between the Ultimate Standard of Valuation and Legal Means of Payment, which I seek to emphasize in Meanings Nos. 5 and 6, in the Introduction of this work, and again in Propositions A and B, now under consideration— lies imbedded in the public law of the modern world. Nothing will, perhaps, more clearly show that this " one-metal," " anti-two-metal" theory, whose noxious outcome we have characterized, is a creature of our time, distinctly modern and revolutionary, an ephemeral product of irrelevant learning, without parentage of statesmanship, or claim of title supported by any prescription in the past.

I venture to affirm that even at the close of the last century there was no nation in which there was not, historically, constitutionally, or legally, a Single Standard in the sense of a National Unit of Coinage. What were the pound sterling, thaler, mark, gulden, rubel, franc, dollar? They were National Units of Coinage, and all of Silver. With due allowance for the occasional admission of what is known as the " Parallel Standard," Silver was "the Standard" generally; the Gold Money—though the degrees of its subordination to Silver were various—was rated by Silver.

To use both metals equally as Money was the general rule:

---

[1] See pages 176 and 177.

[2] There are instances of distinct and explicit tran-shipment (analogous to a re-charter), as, for example, the change from thaler, etc., to mark in Germany (1871-3), and from livre to franc in France.

and though the rates and terms of currency of Gold—in Holland, for example, in the XVIIIth century, and in some German states down even to a late date—are matters which deserve more detailed examination than I am able to give them here, yet, through custom and consent, which were facilitated by the then great relative scarcity of Gold, as well as by its lightness, this general rule was not far from being universal.

No nation prohibited Gold. I know of no instance of demonetization which deserves the name. Each nation struck, or accepted, Gold Money under varying conditions, and at its own rating.

A Dual "Standard" of Money in the sense of Full-Legal-Tender, a Single "Standard" of Money in the sense of Monetary Unit, was thus an accepted policy of States. The question of "the Standard," in so far as it existed, was a mere question of the National Unit of Valuation. It was not a question of using one kind of Money to the entire exclusion of the other, but only which metal should provide the Unit *to which the other must be made to conform in value.*[1]

It is by losing the track of this distinction when flushed with new Gold, fooled by the example of England, and fired

---

[1] Hamilton's Report on the Mint contains, so far as I am informed, the first formal proposition to "let the Unit stand upon the two metals;" albeit his century knew nothing of the doctrine that Full-Legal-Tender-Money must be made of only one metal. It does not appear that, although Jefferson, in this, agreed with his great rival, the law, as subsequently passed by Congress, unequivocally makes Gold a Unit as it does Silver. When a change of ratio came, in 1834, it was agreed without a word—whatever the controlling motive of the choice—that the Gold Dollar, not the Silver Dollar, should be changed. So in France, in our day, the "Standard," in this sense, has been Silver. Thirty years ago, Michel Chevalier scorned the idea of pretending that Gold could give the Unit. A Silver franc, one-fifth of a five-franc piece, is, in his view, what I have called the National Unit of Coinage.

with the dreams of metrology, that intending reformers of Money have led their generation into a slough of defeat.

The Single-Standard Doctrine of to-day has derived its repute from this consensus of the past in maintaining a Single Money-Unit, from the respect felt for the resolution to maintain this "Standard;" a repute to which the modern doctrine has no claim whatever. It is not only not the same doctrine—being really a Single-Metal Doctrine, a Single-Money-ism—but it moves in an opposite direction, it aims at disunion instead of union, disparity rather than parity.

The argument of the friends of Silver-Demonetization, in their books, speeches, and articles innumerable, stands decked in borrowed robes of dignity. Deprived of them, it will, perhaps, be easier for the reader to detect the doctrine of Single-metallism as a mystery, a superstition, a monomania.

One who should put forth speculations upon the desirability of there being but one sex, or should object to a compound gas as an atmosphere for his breathing, or should seek, as a reformer, to excommunicate either anthracite or bituminous coal, would meet with little sympathy in this common-sense world.

Why so? Because no effort is required to recognize the vanity of such speculations. Superlative in absurdity is the first; next comes, one might say, as the comparative degree, the idea of discovering a new element to serve as an atmosphere; while lastly, as a positive absurdity, comes the scheme of forcibly excluding from use either of the great sources of motive-power for modern industry.

And yet how far is the "mono-metallist," with his one-metal doctrine, which we are reviewing, free from exposure to the *reductio ad absurdum* which must haunt the mono-sexuist, the mono-fuelist, the mono-gascist.

Is it less true that there *are* two Money-metals, two metals in the maintenance of which, as Money, the world, and, in its degree, each nation of it, have an interest, than that there *are* two sexes, or two kinds of coal, or that the earth's atmosphere in which human life proceeds *is* a compound of two gases?

These interwoven dualities and unities are all facts.

The absurdity I combat belongs, then, to the same family as these I am imagining; the difference is that in the one case, there is a small absurdity, in the other cases there are larger ones. It is easy to see the larger; it takes more trouble to recognize the smaller in its true character.

It is the half-truth, half-error, of national independence; the fact that, technically, formally, a nation is independent in the choice, and in the regulation of its Money, which conceals the unreality of the mono-metallist's dream.

This independence of decision, this freedom of will, is not merely limited, but is neutralized by a dependence of motives, and by the impossibilities of achievement.

In essentials, the devotee of the Gold Standard, from the point of view of that past in the—conscious or unconscious—contemplation of which he lives, is no more justified in looking down upon, or ignoring, Silver, than was the student of chemistry from Arkansas justified, who, after some experiences in the laboratory, expressed a contemptuous opinion of oxygen gas.

Can the self-confidence of an individual, or of a generation, produce greater effect upon Money than upon oxygen?

The alleged Single-Metal System which England has enjoyed since 1820, was, and is, a Single-Metal System only in a limited sense; it never was monometallic in the full and truer sense of the word. Gold performed its functions in England in the satisfactory manner so often referred to with praise, by favour of the maintenance of Silver and Gold in other countries.

Without repeating here the argument presented in Chapters I. and III., we may conveniently illustrate it by reference to the situation in which Europe now finds itself. Europe enjoys the Gold Standard to-day—that is, the Gold Standard in senses Nos. 7 and 8 of the Introduction; but does anyone allege that for Europe "Money" is monometallic, made of Gold alone; in other words, that Europe in its business transactions, its monetary conditions, its valuations, is indifferent to, or independent of, any Money-material other than Gold ?

Who would be so bold ?

The question can be negatived independently of the hundreds of millions of Silver Money in the banks, strong-boxes and pockets, of Europeans.

Waiving the past, why is the world of Gold prices to-day in a tremor about the future ?

Because of the conflict of Monetary Systems; because of the questions, what is to be the Silver-price of Gold in Asia, or the Gold-price of Silver in Europe; because of the dread that Silver will cross the ocean here, and that, in inevitable reaction, Gold will cross the Ocean there ! It is not a question of goods that troubles the European world : it is a question of their price; and their price is a resultant of complex forces, in which the present relations of Silver and Gold Money play to-day a rôle perplexing and damaging, if not destructive, to the orderly progress of production and distribution of wealth.

Where, then, is the unapproachable solitude, the inexpugnable stability, the inviolate one-ness of "Money" for Europe?

It does not exist. Money is still made of two metals.

After fifteen years of ravages of the anti-two-metal policy in the leading States, man has progressed no further toward his one-metal ideal than to make his two-metal Money a source of anxiety and damage to him, instead of unbroken benefit. The monometallist world is as obstinately tied to a duality as that of the mono-sexuist, the mono-fuelist, the mono-gasoist. So far as the *genus homo* and the planet *terra* are concerned, the Gold-Unitarian's ideal is really non-ideal; it requires extraneous support : it is perfect only on crutches which are not of its own substance, and, in fact, belong elsewhere.

The crutches exist no more as they once existed. The

Single Gold Standard on crutches, as it was before 1874, is a lost cause, obsolete beyond hope.

To advocate it to-day, is to dream of a time when all other nations but one's own shall have adopted such laws as will maintain the excellence of the dreamer's chosen metal as a local standard of value; so that when there is an extraordinary demand (as in 1810-1823), they shall give him his metal at a fixed price, and when an embarrassing supply comes (1850-1860), they shall hold up the market for his benefit; possibilities which belong to a golden age that disappeared from the earth when the par of Silver and Gold was broken.

An unconscious Monetary Balance of Power once existed, and has perished. While it lived, maintaining Gold as good Money by itself, and Silver as good Money by itself, it was a simple matter for each nation to regulate its own one-metal Money in seeming or supposed disconnection with other systems of Money. This state of affairs is at an end. By force of events of sinister import, the problem for Monetary statesmanship has become positively, instead of negatively, international. Formerly it was important to do nothing to disturb an existing Balance of Power; now it is essential to be active, to do something to restore, to re-establish, and to maintain a Balance of Power.

The Balance of Power as it was (in all respects, unconscious, and, in a sense, involuntary) cannot be restored; the aim of reform must be a conscious, intended, Establishment of Money by the chief nations, based upon valid considerations, with mutual guarantees.

There is still another sect of devotees of the Single Metal whose peculiar form of belief merits notice. They are those who deny that they are Single-metallists, who say they believe in Silver, and believe in Gold, but do not believe in a fixed ratio between them.

They are like men who should say: We are not mono-riparians; we are willing that men shall dwell on either side of a broad river; but on condition that no bridge be built across it. We are not single-gauge men; we are willing that narrow-gauge and broad-gauge railroads be built; but we are unalterably opposed to any facilities for trans-shipment. We are not mono-fuelists; but we insist that a man shall make his choice, once for all, between hard coal and soft coal. We are not mono-sexuists; we admit that there are two sexes; we accept their peculiar relations as a fact, and tolerate the consequences; but we are in unalterable opposition to legal marriage.

Minds that can please themselves with such contentions are in some respects even more closely cribbed than the Gold-enthusiast in the toils of the creed we are reviewing; though it is the second article, the limitation of the power of law over Money, which here is salient.

The assertion that, as a matter of fact, the law *does not succeed when it tries*, here, goes hand in hand with the assumed principle that the law *ought not to try*, to affect the value of money; and both the assertion of fact and the assumed principle are put forward to sustain opposition to laws for maintaining the two metals in parity.

But, as we shall have occasion to show on other pages, the actual power of the State to maintain parity and concurrent use of money of the two metals, is amply established by the experience of nations. This fact established, the mere authority need not be discussed in detail. Of course the considerations presented throughout this work necessitate and justify the desired exercise of power.

It may, however, be observed in passing, that the mere existence of paper-notes, whether full, or partial, legal tender, or not legal tender, offers a refutation of both assertion and principle in their broader application; while the observation that, in fact, five-pound notes are usually at par with fifty-pound notes, supplies an effective analogy with the maintenance of a par between Silver-coin and Gold-coin.

Before proceeding with our analysis, it may be well to insure an agreement between the reader and myself, upon the meaning of words, by explaining that the views I express touching the power of law to regulate the value of Money are chargeable only with referring to the range of subjects here under consideration; and that, in speaking of what "the law can do," I assume the benefits of a presumption, to which I am well entitled, namely, that, in any specific instance for which I am to be held as a guarantor, the act of the corporate will of a nation whose power I affirm to be sufficient, shall be wise law: in other words, I presuppose, at least, what the jurist calls "ordinary diligence" on the part both of the law-making, and of the law-executing, power.

This point, though a matter of form and use of words, is not unimportant.

To some minds imagination may not unnaturally present the idea of regulating the value of money by laws, under a magnifying glass, as the *fiat* of an autocracy out of alignment, or bereft of contact with the society it seeks to rule: and hence a *fiat* which the individual will not, may not, or should not, obey. The struggle of generations in both Continents between "Specie" and "Paper" has made it easy to fall into this line of thought.

Hence it is not out of place to fortify my *caveat* by an illustration; observing that the task set before the nations of our time, of driving in harness, abreast, the two "shining coursers of exchange," has its analogies with the prosaic and trivial task of driving a span of horses of good flesh and blood. Of a skilful driver I am permitted to say, "He can drive that span where he pleases," and am not thereby committed to any transcending of the powers of nature; I am not chargeable with meaning that the place "where" driving can be done is in fact a "wherever," without limit; that the horses will fly through the air at the driver's will, or tunnel the earth by pure propulsion of hoofs. Against this, my averment is guarded by a shadowy cohort of presumptions: gravitation, inertia, cohesion, habits, etc. etc., all are presumed: in a word, our ideas remain at the surface of the earth, as do the horses and driver. And so it is with my contentions touching the power of law: they are not in the air. The *fiat* of sagacity and the *fiat* of incompetence are very different things, and it was of the former I was speaking.

Returning from this digression to our issue, it is plain that to cite historical instances of failure to maintain parity or concurrent use of the two metals, is germane for one who, admitting what wise laws may do, is careful to oppose what he believes, and thinks he can prove to be, an unwise law. But this is not the contention we are confronting; that contention is that the mere existence and experience of some unwise laws ousts the jurisdiction, and disproves the power, of the State.

In thus stating the proposition, I give it the advantage of whatever reason there is to support it; and so divest it of the visionary air with which it often appears in public. But in order to be able to affirm in defence of Anti-Silver-laws, that Anti-Silver-laws are natural, but Pro-Silver-laws are unnatural, it is necessary to be visionary, either on a large scale, or on a small scale; either so far to ignore the nature of Money as to fail to recognize it as an institution of the State, or to remain unconscious of the actual range of activity required of the State in connection with the institution. The incongruity of the appearance of the idea in England will be quite apparent when it is realized that England is the home of artificial regulation of Money;[1] and that when Englishmen indulge in visionary system-building in this direction, they are really " disabling the benefits of their own country."

If this rule is to prevail in monetary matters, should it not also prevail in reference to judiciary, or police, or army?

[1] See Section 9.

Upon such principles, the appearance of a corrupt judge, a cowardly policeman, an incompetent general, should suffice to wind up the history of Civil Society, and to relegate mankind to a state of nature—presumably congenial to the philosophy we are seeking to expose in its true character.

The question of authority in the special matter of the Unit of Valuation, viz., whether two or more materials shall separately and equally be invested with the character of Money-Unit, must be regarded from the standpoint of expediency, of practical policy, and is no more to be rightfully excluded, *per se*, on principle, by mere dogmatic limitation of what is called the sphere of government, than are optional contracts, or judgeships of concurrent jurisdiction. Now there is certainly in a statutory option to treat Substance A, Substance B, or Substance C, at discretion, as an embodiment of the National Unit of Account—nothing which is subversive of the objects for which the state exists. It is, I am aware, not uncommon to regard such an arrangement as this as something in its nature peculiarly artificial—as compared with that of the Single-Unit; but this view arises largely from the failure to apprehend the essential artificiality of the Single-Unit itself.

This artificiality can be shown in clear light by every-day facts which are within sight of every business man, and hence without profound inquiry into the true relations of the State to Money. If we ask, for example, what is the real Standard in England, we shall find theorists of the first repute in England who hold the English Standard of Value to be $123.^{7\,10}$ grains of Gold $\frac{11}{12}$ fine. Others would say that it was the sovereign, a coin of that weight and fineness. As between the manufactured article, the coin, and the material, standard bullion—which though it has passed through many processes of labour, may be treated as raw material—there is, in the *nature* of things, a difference, a considerable difference. Now, a most notable feature of English law, is the effort to remove, to annul, to neutralize this difference which lies in the *nature* of things,—a procedure on the part of the Law of England which, in the light of the economic doctrine we are dealing with, must appear *artificial* in the highest degree. The law relieves the owner of bullion from the great expense involved in the manufacture of coin, and puts the burden of these expenses upon the Tax-payer, a proceeding which obviously gives an artificial value to Gold bullion.

An analogous means of artificial equalization is provided by English law for the coin. The sovereign should, as we have observed, be of a certain weight and fineness: but the art of coinage being unable to attain the ideal weight and fineness, the statute artificially makes equal before the law, coins which are naturally unequal. The coin which weighs $122.^{500}$ grains, or is $.^{91464}$ fine, is by law, a sovereign, and Legal-Tender for a Pound Sterling, just as if it were $123.^{27447}$ grains $.^{91466}$ fine. But beyond this we have a further instance of the artificial. How much are $123.^{27447}$ grains of gold $11/12$ths fine *worth* in pounds, shillings, and pence?

Most readers will be surprised at the question, and perhaps none will be prepared for the answer: the point being, strange to say, a novel one.

The following statement of the average price of Gold is taken from a Return made by the Bank of England to the House of Commons. The ounce of Gold—equal *in weight* to £3 17s. 10½d. of ideal coins—was worth in

	£	s.	d.		£	s.	d.		£	s.	d.
1827	3	17	6	1832	3	17	9¼	1837	3	17	9
1828	3	17	6¾	1833	3	17	9¼	1838	3	17	9¼
1829	3	17	9¼	1834	3	17	9	1839	3	17	11
1830	3	17	9¼	1835	3	17	9	1840	3	17	9¼
1831	3	17	10¼	1836	3	17	9½	1841	3	17	9

Another statement from the same source [1] gives four quota-

---

[1] The first statement is from a Return on the Public Debt, 18 August, 1842; the latter from App. 8, Rep. Banks of Issue, 1840.

tions of £3 18s. as the price for 1839. We have, then, the difference between £3 17s. 6d. and £3 18s.,—that is to say, 6d. per oz., close to 2/3 per cent.—as the range of fluctuation in the price of Gold as measured by the English Gold Standard.

Since the Bank Act of 1844 made it the duty of the Bank to pay £3 17s. 9d. per ounce of Standard bullion—the three half-pence of difference being supposed to cover the benefit given and received—the price of such bullion, not coined, has, I believe, remained unchanged. This is, of course, *at the Bank*, for in *any other place* the question of use in that place, or of transportation to another place will necessarily enter into the calculation of its value.

Recognizing then the necessity or the wisdom of these three distinct regulations, which, though necessary and wise, are in their nature artificial, we shall find that between the System which maintains One Unit and Legal-Tender, and the System which maintains Two Units and Legal-Tenders, there is, properly speaking, no difference in kind: at least from the point of view of naturalness, or of artificiality.

We shall also find that the difference in degree, is rather apparent than real. How much more is it an interference with the natural order of things to maintain 100 million Pounds of Gold and Silver coin in England, than to maintain 100 million Pounds of Gold; to give gratuitous coinage to one and the other metal rather than to one: to fix a tolerance of weight and fineness for a sum total, partly Gold, partly Silver, than for the same sum in Gold alone: to establish a fixed price for an amount of bullion, partly Silver, partly Gold, rather than for the same amount of Gold alone? Whatever difference there may be, if it be against the Dual Standard, is of course to be charged to the account of the policy, or, the expediency of such an establishment.

Touching this question of policy or expediency, we may mention among the controlling elements of practical decision upon a proposition of putting, or keeping, " the Unit in the two metals," the following:—

1. The necessity that a State should act as but one member of a community of independent nations which exercise jurisdiction over Money, each State having, so to speak, but a limited property in its own Money-stock, and an undivided interest in the stock of all.

2. That the stock of intrinsic Money and available material for Money in the hands of man, is composed of Silver and Gold, in relative quantity somewhere near sixteen tons of Silver to one ton of Gold, while the prevalent rate of equivalence maintained for the world through the law of Alternative Free Coinage in the former Bimetallic Union, down to 1873, was $15\frac{1}{2}$ to 1.

We have now briefly analyzed, and characterized by comparison, the doctrine of one-metallism, and are, I humbly conceive, entitled to judgment against it.

When such judgment shall have been entered in the minds of a working majority of men of intellect and learning, who are the leaders of opinion in England, then the work of rebuilding what has been destroyed, the enlightened regulation of the world's Money by concurrent action of Europe and America, will begin in earnest, and will attain speedy fulfilment.

Then the doctrines which have marshalled the hosts of Christendom to the Outlawry of Silver—the creed which rules the world to-day in the existing monetary dead-lock of nations and by favour of inertia, stays the hand of statesmen from putting an end to it—will pass to the limbo of "creeds outworn," to be remembered only as a suicidal superstition.

But to the student of history this survey must seem incomplete and unsatisfactory unless some explanation is found of the ascendency which such a compound of fallacy has gained over the minds of a generation.

Such explanation has already been suggested in what has

been said of the introduction of the Anti-two-metal system in England in 1816, and its maintenance since that date.

As the chief financial, industrial, commercial, monetary power, England's policy, sound or unsound, has for the heedless world a perilous prestige. The broad empire of fashion embraces sterner things than dress. The Gold-Standard, or Anti-Silver-movement, is but a form of Anglomania, which events have combined to magnify into continental proportions, and which, unlike many forms of Anglomania, has lacked any sound justification in England for its origin. In other chapters, a review of modern monetary policy in England will put to the test the justice of this assertion.

But granting that the example of England is the efficient cause of existence and of authority for the one-metal crusade, there has been present, it seems to me, a prevailing cause of popularity, which has wrought wonders in advancing the ascendency of the Gold-Standard theory.

This error, which would restrain the state from securing permanent parity between the metals of which man's intrinsic Money is made, moves in line with, and seems to make part of, a certain all-embracing, all-inspiring, current of opinion which has almost made the atmosphere of modern progress —namely, the great history-making, policy-creating tendency of the age toward liberty, individualism, and opposing absolutism, interference, too-much government.

Allying itself in outward seeming with such a mission as this, it was easy for error to find its way into the convictions and into the affections of men.

As for the claim of kinship between this tendency of our age and the Anti-Silver theory, if it be worth while to investigate it, the assumption may be briefly characterized by stating it as follows:—

Is it more in accord with the spirit of the XIXth century that the state should perform an admitted and inevitable duty in a slip-shod, hap-hazard, and slovenly way, than to do it with persevering ability and foresight?

The state can, in fact, as we have observed, no more absolve itself from the regulation of Money than from the maintenance of a System of Private Law. Its work must be done in some way, either well or ill.

The error of the monetary disunionist, therefore, differs only in degree, not in kind, from that of one who should fulminate against Courts of Justice, and close his peroration with an appeal that, if we must have Courts of Justice at all, at least let the Judges and the Clerks and the Sheriffs be as incompetent as possible!

That the dominion of the one-metal creed is waning, is generally recognized in all countries.

> "The old dragon under ground,
> In straiter limits bound,
> Not half so far casts his usurpéd sway,"

but still, from time to time,

> "Wroth to see his kingdom fail.
> Swinges the scaly horror of his folded tail."

So long as the enemy shows signs of life, so long must those who with the weapons of truth have checked his activity, and are seeking to repair the ravages he has caused, plant new arrows of refutation between his ribs.

The necessity of doing this is unfortunate; but it is not we who have made the necessity. The reader who needs no reminder of the truth, must give ready pardon to the writer for the time he employs in combating an error which ought to be, and which every philanthropist should earnestly strive to make, obsolete.

CHAPTER V.

A Lesson of History: The Monetary Crisis of 1696.

§ 11. THE RECOINAGE OF 1696, AND ITS BEARING UPON THE QUESTIONS OF TO-DAY.

Having considered, in the preceding chapters, some general questions of policy relating to the maintenance or reversal of that legislative Outlawry of Silver among the Western Nations, of which the English statute is to-day the chief support, and having presented an analysis of the doctrine upon which the English statute rests, we can now conveniently test the correctness of the views advanced, by a survey of the course of monetary events in England, which shall throw light upon the origin of the theory and practice now in vogue. So far as this purpose is directly concerned, it is unnecessary to penetrate to a period very remote: and, in any event, whether the student shall have taken up his burden in Saxon or in Norman age, or under Plantagenet or Tudor, the dates 1666 and 1696 will, in the end, impress themselves upon his consciousness as the introduction, and the opening scene, of a new monetary epoch, and with these our present study of history will begin.

Among the half-explored regions of monetary history few

periods contain matter of greater interest, or of closer bearing upon the great issue of to-day, than that of which the English Recoinage of 1696 was the centre. In so many regards a turning-point and formative period in the history of Europe, the Whig Revolution which placed the Stadtholder of Holland on England's throne to fight the Stuart, the Frenchman, and the Romanist, offers withal to the student ample and convincing lessons in monetary statesmanship. To the responsibilities of revolution and of foreign war, came the cumulative burden of grievous monetary ills, affecting the foundations of England's economic life; and, through rare favour of fortune, the unexampled crisis found statesmen in command.

"Happily for England," says Macaulay, "there were among her rulers, some who clearly perceived that it was not by halters and branding-irons that her decaying industry and commerce could be restored to health. The state of the currency had during some time occupied the serious attention of four eminent men closely connected by public and private ties. Two of them were politicians who had never, in the midst of official and parliamentary business, ceased to love and honour philosophy; and two were philosophers, in whom habits of abstruse meditation had not impaired the homely good sense, without which even genius is mischievous in politics. Never had there been an occasion which more urgently required both practical and speculative abilities; and never had the world seen the highest practical and the highest speculative abilities united in an alliance so close, so harmonious, and so honourable as that which bound Somers[1] and Montague[2] to Locke and Newton."

"It is much to be lamented," continues the historian,

---

[1] "One of those divine men, who, like a chapel in a palace, remain unprophaned, whilst all the rest is tyranny, corruption, and folly."—From Horace Walpole's "Catalogue of Noble and Royal Authors."

[2] The following is a portion of the inscription upon the monument of

"that we have not a minute history of the conferences of the men to whom England owed the restoration of her currency and the long series of prosperous years which dates from that restoration. It would be interesting to see how the pure gold of scientific truth found by the two philosophers was mingled by the two statesmen with just that quantity of alloy which was necessary for the working. It would be curious to study the many plans which were propounded, discussed, and rejected, some as inefficacious, some as unjust, some as too costly, some as too hazardous, till at length a plan was devised of which the wisdom was proved by the best evidence, complete success."[1]

While echoing the regret to which the historian's study of imagination gives such poignancy, I am compelled to point forward to other, and greater, deprivations: for, in spite of the admirable products of his own research in these fields, there is still far more to be lamented than that of which Macaulay speaks. The record is incomplete in essential

Charles Montague, Earl of Halifax, in Westminster Abbey:—
Brevi etenim hunc virum
Sua in senatu facundia
In concilio providentia
In utroque solertia; fides, authoritas
Ad gerundam Aerarii curam evexit.
Ubi laborantibus Fisci rebus
Opportuné subveniens.
Monetam argenteam
Magno reipublicae detrimento imminutam.
Valori pristino restituit;
Et tantae molis opus
Cum flagrante jam bello diutino
Ut aggrederetur et absolveret.
Ne subsidia Regi Regnoque necessaria
Deessent interim,
Ne fides aut privata, aut publica,
Vaccilaret uspiam
Sapienter cavit.

[1] "History of England" in Macaulay's Complete Works, edition of 1866, iv. 192-3.

points, not merely in reference to details, the lack of which he here deplores. The following pages will, I believe, conclusively show the inadequacy of the current accounts of England's monetary experience, and will further be held to justify the view that history has been erroneously written, so that not only are its more important lessons still to be learned, but the task is incumbent of unlearning the pretended lessons of an erroneous record.

The outcome of this hiatus in literature may, indeed, in time be regarded as quite a master-stroke of the irony of fate: for through this negative means it has become a fable agreed-upon that the devotees of the Single Gold Standard should trace the pedigree of their doctrines to a glorious ancestry: and the dogma of the impotence of legislation to secure the useful employment of both metals as material for Full-Legal-Tender Money, has been allowed to find its sanction in what purported to be the monetary history of the first of Monetary Powers.

It is this dogma, enforced by this example, that mastered the minds of the generation which has carried and now maintains the partial Outlawry of Silver: here is the ground-article of faith of those who thought that the rejection of Silver, the expulsion of one of the Money-metals of mankind, could do no harm, and who still think that its restoration can do good. Such is its transcendent supremacy over the minds of men. I can appeal with confidence to the leaders of Silver Outlawry —Michel Chevalier and Charles Feer-Herzog have passed away, but Esquirou de Parieu, Frère-Orban, and Soetbeer, still,

" Like great Sarpedon, tower amid the field,"

whether the Anti-Silver-movement did not attain its ascendency by dint of the prestige of this dogma; and whether the monetary history of England has not been authoritatively presented as its august sponsor?

It is therefore eminently germane to the argument in support of an amendment of the policy now in control in the

Occidental World, to expunge the errors of that record, so far as may be, and to have the record thoughtfully re-read, as amended.

In presenting the matter in detail, we need not follow rivulets, but can most conveniently approach the main stream and source of doctrine, in Lord Liverpool's "Treatise on the Coins of the Realm." In the form of a letter to the King (printed in 1805), the chief monetary expert of H. M. Privy Council laid down the Law of Money, for his own and for later generations. The formal adoption of the chief features of Lord Liverpool's Scheme of a Coinage System, by the British Parliament, in 1816, under the Premiership of his son, and the maintenance of that system down to the present day, upon the lines, and with the success, elsewhere set forth, give to his book an importance absolutely unique. Here is a treatise upon Money, which, in an important sense, has not only made the latter history of the chief monetary nation of the world; but through this means at a turning-point of affairs it directed the current of opinion and of action, and so set the fashion for the century now current, and imposed its moral rule upon the Western Powers. This book is therefore—if the expression may be used—the Scripture of plenary inspiration for the Anti-Silver faith: or the *Magna Charta Monetaria*, from which is derived, what I can but call the mental slavery of our time to the doctrines of Silver Outlawry. The second edition of it (London, 1846) bears, indeed, upon its title-page—I know not with what authority—a statement which constitutes an avowed claim to this character, namely, that it is a "concise account of all the facts relating to the Currency which bear upon the exchanges of Europe, and the principles of political science."

The theses which Lord Liverpool sustains amid the winding passages of an elaborate but confused argumentation, will be found to include, in substance, some of the ideas which we have analyzed in the preceding chapter—and the experience of his country, in the Great Recoinage of 1696, as well as elsewhere, and the teachings of the chief literary actor in that event, John Locke,[1] as well as those of other writers of note, are presented as, on the whole, sustaining the writer's doctrine. The influence of the doctrinal testimony thus adduced to point the moral of history, in persuading a later generation of the soundness of Lord Liverpool's scheme for a national system of Money, can hardly be over-estimated. What man of greater authority, for example, has ever written on Money than John Locke, who, independently of his purely philosophical reputation, was the "interpreter of the Revolution," which founded anew the constitution and the liberties of England?

It is therefore essential to a thorough and impartial reading of the true lessons of England's experience, to inquire how far these statements are justified?

The facts I propose to prove are these: free and gratuitous coinage of Silver and Gold, each unlimited Legal-Tender, Silver the Unit, Gold rated in terms of Silver in the various degrees allowed by the peculiar law of Legal-Tender of the time, with the power in the hands of the Crown to modify the rating from time to time, as occasion served: such was the system which Locke and Newton and Somers and Montague found, such was the system which they laboured to place under secure guarantees of administrative practice and of legislation.

If this be true, I submit that this experience of England, and the authority of her statesmen, make for the Silver and Gold Standard,—for the duty, as well as the right and power of governments to adopt such measures as may be needed to maintain Silver and Gold in parity and in concurrent use as Money-metals. The following pages will present the evidence which, in my belief, establishes these conclusions.

---

[1] "Certain it is, at any rate, that in nearly all their political action both Somers and Montague were actuated by the principles that Locke advanced, and gave utterance to opinions with which he agreed."—Fox-Bourne's "Life of Locke," vol. ii., p. 311.

§ 12. THE DISORDERS OF THE TIME AND THEIR REMEDY.

The disorder of England's Money, which laid so heavy a burden upon the statesmen of the Revolution, has been brilliantly depicted by Macaulay.

"The Silver-coin," he says, "which was then the standard coin of the realm, was in a state at which the boldest and most enlightened statesmen stood aghast." The failure to take proper measures to prevent the currency of debased, worn, or clipped, and of the old hammered, coins, by the side of the new full-weight milled coins, naturally tended to promote the melting down of all the good coins, and left the bad in circulation. "It may well be doubted," says the historian, "whether all the misery which had been inflicted on the English nation in a quarter of a century by bad kings, bad ministers, bad parliaments, and bad judges, was equal to the misery caused in a single year by bad crowns and bad shillings. . . . The evil was one which daily made progress almost visible to the eye. There might have been a recoinage in 1694 with half the risk which must be run in 1696; and, great as would be the risk in 1696, that risk would be doubled if the recoinage were postponed till 1698." ("History," iv. 184, 194.) As time went on and nothing was done, a general reformation of the coinage had thus been allowed to become first desirable, then important, then a crying need. The "measure was lost," as Locke himself said.

The best coin left was the "guinea," then in the early stages of its appearance in a rôle which proved to be quite unique in the annals of Money. It was coined as a twenty-shilling piece, its weight being fixed by Royal Proclamation of 1663, which lowered the relative weight of the Gold-coins of England by about eight and a half per cent. below the rate which had been established in 1621. Supposed to depend for its material upon the metal which the Royal Company of Adventurers trading in Africa, were to bring from the Gold

Coast, it secured the name of guinea, which is still held by a descendant Money of account. Later, the policy of reducing Seigniorage, which had already found favour with the Councillors of Charles II., was replaced by its total abandonment, under authority of Parliament, which by the Act of 18 Car. II. c. 5 (see Appendix 2), made the minting of the Gold and Silver-coins of the realm gratuitous, as well as free to all comers, native or stranger.

A general rise in the Silver-price of Gold seems to have declared itself not long afterward; and no Proclamation was issued making the guineas obligatorily current at 20 shillings; but in lieu of this, it appears, that the guineas were accepted at something like their current value, which rose to 21s., and then seems to have remained fixed for a long time at 21s. 6d. The agency of the government in maintaining this "rating" through its control of currency in the offices of receipt and expenditure will be discussed on a later page.

Returning now to the condition of the Silver-coin—so well exposed through the vigorous language of Macaulay—it will appear obvious that the progressive fading out of the "Standard" through clipping and counterfeiting, and through the exportation of all the heavier purer Silver-coins, must naturally secure to the guineas, through comparison of them with the decomposing mass of Silver remaining in use, the privilege of acceptance at higher rates. When the deterioration and discredit of the Silver-coins became extreme, the rate of the guinea rose speedily, passing in a comparatively short space from 22 to 30 shillings.

Thereupon came the proposal, "accept the fact of debasement; scale the Silver-coin down;" which seems first to have appeared in the House of Commons in 1690, but later presented itself clothed in the garb of authority, when, in 1695, the Secretary of the Treasury offered a formal report to his superiors, giving reason and detail for a scheme making the Silver-crown a piece of 75 pence instead of 60.

It was upon the state of fact and of feeling thus indicated, that the activity of Montague, of Somers, of Locke, and of Newton was exerted. Each had his own peculiar sphere of influence, Montague and Somers in Cabinet and in Parliament, Locke and Newton in the capacities to be hereafter described.

Of the specific measures which Parliament was brought to adopt, and of the details of execution of the Recoinage, I shall not attempt to speak. The attractive chapters of Macaulay, which I may assume to be within reach of every reader, give the main features of the work. I seek here merely to outline, from the stand-point of monetary policy, events which were within, as well as events which were excluded from, the view of that historian.

Suffice it briefly to say, that times were fixed after which the light coins would not be accepted by the Government at their nominal rate, and after which the use of them should be illegal; that the country gradually brought to the Mint its light Silver-coin, which embraced a majority of the total circulation; that under the able direction of the new Warden of the Mint, Mr. Isaac Newton, the capacity of the mints was multiplied; that the resolutions and discussions of Parliament, beginning in January, 1695-6,[1] with a resolution fixing the rate of admitted currency for the guinea at 28s., followed that coin by several steps to 26s. (this Bill was passed), 25s., 24s., till at length a Bill secured the Royal assent April 13, by which the guineas were fixed at 22 shillings. (See Appendix 8.) Acts were also passed taking off the obligation of coining Gold (imposed by the Act of 1666), and prohibiting the importation of guineas. These Acts remained in force during a few months of the earlier stages of the Recoinage.

On final account, it appears that the operation of recoinage cost the Government a little less than 3 million pounds—in which amount, I suppose, no interest is counted. The im-

---

[1] The legal year then began on March 25.

portance of the measure is well set forth by the following figures. According to the estimates within my reach, the stock of cash in England at William's accession, was, in nominal value, about 3 millions of Gold, and 8 millions of Silver: the ordinary revenue did not exceed 2 millions, the population of England and Wales was about 5,774,000. To these figures must be added whatever percentage is proper to cover the growth and change between 1688 and 1696. As we compare with them an operation which, on the books of the Treasury, came to near 3 million pounds, we become aware of the magnitude of the task. What Legislature or Administration is there to-day in any country, which could face a proportionate responsibility with calmness? Certainly we can absolve the impassioned historian from any charge of strained enthusiasm in his account of it.

The further fate of the new Silver-coin, and of the guineas, will be set forth on a later page.

§ 13. LOCKE AND THE RATIO OF $15\frac{1}{2}$ TO 1.

On both occasions, in 1690-1 and 1695-6, Locke came forth with his scholarly philippics—to the effect, "Silver is the Standard, it shall not be debased."

A brief glance at the general monetary situation of Europe will define more clearly the importance of Locke's activity. The Monetary World of Silver and Gold, then contained but little Gold; for the mines of Brazil had not yet enriched the stocks of Europe. Not only in England but generally, Silver was "the Standard," in senses No. 5 and 7 of the Introduction to this work. Both metals were Money, but the fixed Money, the rating Money, so to speak, was Silver, the rated Money was Gold. Of certainty and stability, either in fineness, weight, or denomination of coins, the world had had little experience, for under what I have called the Seigniorial,

System. Money was subject to arbitrary control, in a wilderness of sovereignties. But in England the Silver Standard, which carried the Pound Sterling, the National Unit—a lineal descendant and successor of the Silver Pound-Weight, the *pund mere hwites seolfres* of Saxon days—had remained, since the reign of Elizabeth, unblemished by debasement, either in fineness, or in weight, and in denomination it could not change.

Within the same period, the Gold had been formally raised four times, in its rate of currency, namely, by Royal Proclamations of James I. in 1607, 1613, 1621, and of Charles II. in 1663, a total rise in sixty years of 32⅝ per cent., while later, as will be set forth in detail in the following chapter, a further rise had been authorized, through the rating of Gold in the Government Offices of Account. With such experience in view, it was inevitable that competent men should feel that Silver was the firm-set base of England's Money.

In laying the foundations of principle in dealing with the coin, Locke naturally—and, I allow myself to say, rightly—brought into prominence the justice and policy of one-ness and inviolability of what he termed the "Measure of Commerce."

How, then, does this doctrine comport with the Anti-Silver-position of to-day, with which we have now to deal? Leaving at one side that Locke's Single Standard was a Silver Standard, fixing our attention solely upon his teaching as to the concurrent use of two metals—for here is the gist of the matter—we have to decide, whether Locke was a one-metallist or a two-metallist? To determine the point, we must necessarily inquire what were his views touching the currency of the "other metal," that is, of Gold.

By statute, as we have seen, the coinage of both Gold and Silver was gratuitous and free.

Now the duration of this statute is phenomenal,—unique, indeed, in monetary history. The continuity of its force was only broken, as to Silver, without formal repeal, in 1798, by partial repeal in 1816, and by further repeal in 1870, while as to Gold—with the unimportant exception noted on page 72,—it has been maintained from 1666 to the present hour. Yet the tenure of this statute was derived from no recognized obligation of superior force. It was not clothed with the dignity of a constitutional provision, or organic compact of the powers of the State; nor was the law originally in form an enactment for perpetuity, or for an indefinite period; it was expressly limited to a short term of years.

The curious reader will find the course of this most important legislation set forth in the Appendix (2). He will observe that of thirteen terms made continuous by re-enactment, three were contemporaneous with the Monetary agitation of which the Recoinage was the centre. The statute was re-enacted in 1685, in 1693, in 1701. Writing as he did in 1690 and in 1695, Free Coinage and Gratuitous Coinage were therefore plainly in Locke's view, as matters in the control of Parliament. Here then was, evidently, a subject concerning which a reformer must needs have an opinion. I submit that in order to relieve monetary literature[1] from the charge of absence of mind, as well as of error, in according to Locke the reputation of being a single-metallist, it is necessary to show at least an effort to prove that Locke rebelled against this coinage of two metals. I know of no such effort. I have no information that the question has ever been thought of by

[1] "I trust, however, that this House will adhere to the present standard,—will resolve on the maintenance of a single standard,—and of Gold as that standard. All the great writers on this subject, Sir William Petty, Mr. Locke, Mr. Harris, and Lord Liverpool, have been decidedly in favour of a single, in preference to a double, standard." From the speech of Sir Robert Peel in the House of Commons on the Bank Charter Act, May 6, 1844. Quoted also in Mr. Inglis Palgrave's important work "Currency and Standard of Value in England, etc." Appendix B. 3rd Report of the Royal Comm. on the Depression of Trade. 1886. P. 321.

See also on Locke as a one-metallist, Jevons' "Investigations in Currency and Finance." London, 1884. P. 332.

anyone but myself, and so in raising it I must give my own answer, namely, that no suggestion of repealing, or of omitting to re-enact, that statute, is to be found in Locke's writings. The partial and temporary suspension referred to above will be considered on a later page.

A careful comparison of Locke's utterances, bearing directly or indirectly on the subject, reveals the fact that his views on the proper legal status of Gold-coin suffered a change, between his first work (1690), and his later publications, when brought face to face with the need of immediate action, and when supporting peculiar pressure of official responsibility, as expert adviser of the Government. There are what I may call three distinct stages of opinion. In his earlier work he advanced the view, that, while Gold should be coined (see Appendix 12) side by side with Silver, which was the standard coin—Money *par excellence*—yet no value, or rating, should be given to Gold coins by public authority, the supposition being that they would, in that event, still circulate as Money, but at their market rate. In his later work, Locke recognized that such rating should be given, "so the value set be under the market price"—alluding, presumably, to the guinea, which was Legal-Tender in the fullest sense at 20 shillings, and which had long been "current" at a higher rate.

No suggestion, however, is made that the "public authority" should abstain from fixing a value upon the guinea, in the sense of sanctioning its currency, either at, or above, its true market value, through accepting and paying it out in the Government Offices of Account. Now from the experience of our day, I do not fear to affirm with certainty, that when a guinea was obligatory Legal-Tender between private citizens for 20 shillings, and was accepted and sought to be paid out in all government offices at 22 shillings, its "currency" at 22 shillings could really be said to be quite firmly, though not permanently, established by public authority.

Still later, in 1698, through a Report, the discovery of which rewarded my research, and which, so far as I am informed, is now first brought to the eye of the modern student (see Appendix 11-B), Locke is shown to have become aware that this acceptance and payment of guineas in Government offices at a certain rate, was really, in effect, a fixation of currency by public authority. It would seem to be, in fact, a more convenient mode of fixation than any contained in the inventory of the King's Prerogative. The Report in question came from the Council of Trade and Plantations. Of this body Locke was then the guiding spirit. The reader will find the detail of proof on this head in the excellent life of Locke, by Mr. Fox-Bourne, who, however, makes no mention of anything corresponding to this Report. It was signed by three members of the Council beside Locke; but I venture to say, that internal evidence, the ideas and the language, as well as the probability established by Mr. Fox-Bourne, warrant its being regarded as the work of Locke.

Here we find a suggestion to change, from time to time, the permitted rating of the guinea in Government offices, and the recommendation for the time (September, 1698), to bring it down from 22s. to 21s. 6d. I have also been able to discover proof that this recommendation was formally acted upon by the Government. Orders were issued (which are reprinted in the Appendix), in consequence of which, a few months later, in February, 1698-9—guineas were taken at Government offices at 21s. 6d. It is noteworthy, that the relative value established by fixing the guinea at 21s. 6d. was, as the Report itself states, "very near as fifteen and one-half to one."

The following extract from the Report sets forth the points of special interest:

"We are humbly of Opinion that it is necessary, Guineas in their common currency be brought down to 21s. 6d. at least; And further humbly conceive that Your Excellencies may fitly do it by giving directions, That the officers of the

Receipt of his Majesty's Exchequer, and all others the Receivers of His Majesty's Revenue, do not take them at a higher rate. This appears to us the Most Convenient way, because it may, at all times, be a ready and easy remedy, upon any further variation that shall happen in the world in the Price of Gold; or even in case this now proposed Lowering of Guineas should not prove sufficient: For it being impossible, that more than One Metal should be the true Measure of Commerce; and the world by common Consent and Convenience, having settled that Measure in Silver; Gold as well as other Metals, is to be looked upon as a Commodity, which varying in its Price as other Commodities do, its Value will always be changeable; and the fixing of its value in any Country, so that it cannot be readily accommodated to the course it has in other neighboring Countries, will be always prejudicial to the Country which does it. The Value of Gold, here at the price of 21s. 6d. a Guinea, in proportion to the Rate of Silver in our Coin, will be very near as fifteen and one-half to one; the value of Gold in proportion to Silver, in Holland and Neighboring Countries, as near as can be computed, upon a Medium, is as fifteen to one; so that by bringing down the Guineas to 21s. 6d. Gold will not here be brought to so low a Price as in our Neighboring Countries; Nevertheless, we are humbly of Opinion that the Abatement of sixpence in the Guinea will be sufficient to stop the present disproportionate Importation of gold; because the Charge for Insurance, Freight, Commission, and the like, will eat up the Profit that may then be made thereby, and hinder that Trade; but if, contrary to our Expectation, this Abatement should prove too small, Guineas may by the same easy Means be lowered yet further, according as may be found expedient."

The questions of policy relating to Gold, upon which this remarkable state-paper throws light, will be considered in their wider aspects on later pages: suffice it here to mark that it completely establishes the correctness of the contentions I have advanced in reference to Locke's position.

That a mind like John Locke's should—at the age of sixty—have passed through the several stages of opinion which I have set forth, is proof of rare sagacity and candour, the teachableness of a devoted servant of truth. At the same time, it must, of course, be admitted that the attendant conflict of statement in his printed works—for no effort seems to have been made to connect any correction with the original statements—may legitimately have given rise to some misconstruction of his position. Both Harris and Liverpool afford instances of this, the latter quoting his two stages of opinion mentioned on page 76 without recognizing that the second was a correction which replaced the first, while both authors are unaware of the latter stage, embodied in the Report.

I must also, in citing Locke as a witness, frankly call attention to a vigour of expression in advocacy of Silver as the "Measure of Commerce," which gives colour to these misapprehensions, and has assisted materially in enabling great men to quote him as a fierce single-metallist.

For example, in a passage of his first work, adverting to the fact that "supposing Gold and Silver to be in value as 16 to 1 now, perhaps the next month they may be as $15\frac{3}{4}$ to 1 or $15\frac{7}{8}$ to 1," he says, "two metals as Gold and Silver cannot be the Measure of Commerce, both together, in any country. Because the Measure of Commerce must be perpetually the same, invariable, and keeping the same proportion of value in all its parts. And so only one metal does or can do to itself. So Silver is to Silver, and Gold to Gold."

For myself, I see no objection to this statement: to accept it, it is merely necessary to ascertain exactly what Locke meant: but it is, perhaps, only fair to admit that to realize what Locke meant by it, implies a study of the history of his time, upon the lines here set forth. An analogous instance of vigorous expression is before the reader's eye in the extract reprinted on the preceding page; for example, where it is said, " Gold, as well as other metals, is to be looked upon as a Commodity." To one familiar with Locke's writings this very phrase, like the reference to the " Measure of Commerce," will, I think, serve as evidence that the Report came from his pen. Now in the latter half of the XIXth century, while one Money-metal is the sole Measure of Commerce in a nation so important as England, the statement that *the other Money-metal is to be looked on as a commodity, like other metals*, has certainly a sharp one-metallic ring to ears attuned to the manifold discords of current monetary doctrine. Experience seems to give clearness of meaning to the phrase. The present Gold Standard Law actually, as administered, effectively makes Silver in England a commodity, a metal and nothing more. At first glance, then, the line seems to have been drawn as closely in the XVIIth as in the XIXth century, between the measure and the things measured, between the one-metal Money on one side, and commodities on the other.

What, then, is the fact? What does the phrase mean?

Is Locke literally committed to monetary laws which shall treat Gold as a commodity like other metals? I remit the query to the reader's activity of search amid the subtleties of monetary doctrine. I am, however, sure that he will in due time concur with me, that Locke is not so committed: for, if he were, it follows in logical sequence, taking the facts as we know them, that he was a multimetallist, equally committed to the coinage of all metals!

The status of Gold was fixed: it was Money in England, as we use the word Money to-day; its free and gratuitous coinage, and Legal-Tender without limit of amount, were rights established by law. Now if, under these circumstances, and starting from this fixed point, we find words current that bear such meaning as to enable one to say, correctly, that Gold was then a commodity in England, and if then we take the further step to which the habit of the XIXth century might lead us, and say that the phrase we analyze implies that other metals are to be "commodities," upon the same footing, it follows that zinc, lead, and tin could claim Free and Gratuitous Coinage and the privileges of a rated Legal-Tender, while iron guineas and copper guineas would bravely dispute the field.

Excluding this absurdity, as perforce we must, no signification is left to the word "commodity" as here used, except as a striking name for an object, which is valued with reference to the chief Money, and, to that extent, stands side by side with "other metals." Now it was inevitable that Gold-coin, although Money, in the sense in which we use the word, should occupy this position in a country where the Pound Sterling was, in the concrete, twenty Silver shillings of the standard of 43rd Elizabeth, and the Gold guinea a piece "running for" so and so many shillings.

Neither, then, as a statement of what is, nor as an indication of what ought to be, does this XVIIth century phrase stand chargeable with complicity in the error, which in our century has mastered the statutes that establish what is, and the doctrine that seeks to comprehend what is, and shapes the current ideas of what ought to be.

From this result of our investigation we may draw a practical lesson to which the form "all that glitters is not Gold Standard doctrine" seems not inappropriate. With this example before us we stand face to face with proof, that to deal summarily with monetary theory is to play with edged tools. Plainly brevity, which is said to be the soul of wit, may also act as a seed of error, for in passing from one mind to another a definition may suffer a slight yet complete change, like that, for example, from sugar to alcohol, and so the harmless over-statement of one mind, losing its vitally constituent atom of unexpressed knowledge, may become the militant fallacy of another.

But, returning to our theme, we shall find, in tracing the course of Locke's speculative work in the field of Money, that his vigour of expression sometimes seems to lead the thinker himself past the limits of soundness, and into contradiction with the position he himself takes, even in the same essay. Instances of this contradiction are presented herewith. (See Appendix 12.)

The explanation is not far to seek. Locke's essays on Money are not academic or scholastic in their purpose, and indeed are hardly to be called systematic treatises. As Locke himself said, in 1695-6, in the frankness of correspondence with a friend (Appendix 13), this subject, which he had "play'd the fool to print about," was not one which he then "relished, or which with most pleasure employed his thoughts."

This was written after his books were printed, and before the date of the report here mentioned. On comparing his monetary writings with his great work on the "Human Understanding," or with the "Discourses on Government," which justified to the learned world of his day the principles of the Revolution, and opened a new era in the science of politics; and on observing the activity of his later years in the limitless field of theology, it becomes evident that the productions first-mentioned belong to the category of occasional and controversial papers. Vigorous, thorough, and learned, as became their author, they are the earnest plea of an advocate on the burning question of the day. Speaking, then, as a practical statesman, Locke is entitled to the benefits of that position, and his work is to be construed as a whole, in the light of the *res gestae*. An effort was on foot, and near success, to engage the statesmen of the Whig Revolution in the career of debasement of Money, which had been a blot upon earlier ages and upon former reigns. Against this Locke set his face, and any little over-statement he may have made is surely rather a credit to his temper than a reproach to his reason.

To conclude in brief, the final outcome of Locke's activity in speculation and action, in monetary affairs, is that his authority makes for the concurrent use of the two metals as Money, and for the power and duty of the state to maintain them in that function.

To-day, the name of Locke is enshrined in monetary literature as the glorious ancestor of the single-metallist doctrine. I venture to think my researches have enabled me to prove that, in fact, he is better entitled to be known to posterity as the original proponent of the ratio of 15½ to 1.

Before proceeding to other matters, we shall perhaps find it profitable to pause for a moment, and look back over the field of doctrine from the point we have just reached. It is conceivable that a reader who has been willing to accompany me through the earlier pages of this work, and who has accepted what is sought to be conveyed, especially by the Introduction, and by the First and Fourth Chapters, may still omit to make thorough application of the results of his survey.

In order to facilitate this effort on the reader's part, without making too great demands upon his time, I ask him to note that any lessons of history I may have discovered, or set forth, serve my argument not merely as precedent or authority, nor as invalidating argument, or precedent, or authority, arrayed against me upon a specific point, but, withal, to prove that what has lately been reckoned, in the civilization of the time, as Monetary Science, is infected in grievous measure with heedlessness and confusion: so that there is an inherent probability of error in practical conclusions based upon that science in its imperfect state. Of these practical conclusions based upon the teachings of reputed Monetary Science, the present legislative Outlawry of Silver is the controlling feature: so that to establish a general presumption of error against this body of science as it was, is to promote a thorough and candid revision of the entire foundation of Silver Outlawry, and of the grounds for continuing it. It is to such revision that we must look for that gathering force of conviction which alone can procure the reversal of this unjust enactment.

How far this revision has already extended—in certain lines—is curiously shown by the matter in hand. The proposition that, in order to make John Locke a sponsor of the Single-Standard, in the sense of the Single-Legal-Tender, it is important to show that he was not in favour of both metals, may seem to-day very simple, very obvious. To-day, after decades of multitudinous activity in the monetary field, when controversy has abounded in many languages—one metal *versus* two metals, single-standard *versus* dual standard—it is, so to speak, "in the air," that a "single-standard man," a single-metallist, cannot be a friend of Free Coinage of Two Metals as Full Legal-Tender.

But this is quite a new thing. It is a novel product of a certain fermentation of spirit, the field of which I am seeking to enlarge. The opinion which to-day is still allowed to rule the world, was constructed quite independently of such nice distinctions. In the original structure of argument for Silver Outlawry they are quite ignored. It is in the defence of Silver to-day that they are incidentally brought to light.

Lord Liverpool was perfectly conscious of the existence and effect of the statute of 1666: he knew that Petty and Locke and Newton and Harris, as well as himself, had lived their lives under laws which kept the Mint open for turning bullion, whether yellow or white, into English Money. Is it to be supposed that his son, the Prime Minister who championed the Silver-coinage Bill of 1816 in the House of Lords, or that the Rt. Hon. Wellesley Pole, the then Master and Worker of the Mint, whose advocacy of it in the House of Commons fills many pages of Hansard, were unaware of this state of things? When they appealed, as they did in their speeches which carried that measure, to Petty and to Locke and to Harris, the greatest English authorities known, and thus satisfied themselves and satisfied others that all the counsel of the wise was in favour of the Bill, were they merely repeating by rote the doctrine which they had learned by ear, without knowledge of the facts that are set forth in the "Treatise on the Coins of the Realm?"

These questions open a fruitful field in the history of opinion: a lesson of no little suggestiveness in the future development of the sciences of legislation, may be found by inquiring whether Lord Liverpool's "Treatise on the Coins of the Realm" acted as a non-conductor to all whom it then concerned, an insulator, which cut off the proper lines of communication by which the XIXth century might recruit itself with the kernel rather than the shell of the experience of the past, and whether the Demonetizers of 1816 were unconscious of the real character and effect of the measure they caused to be adopted.

But whatever the answer, the inheritors of the opinions which found realization in the statute of 1816, those who for two generations have guarded the doors of the Tower Mint against Silver (except as material for tokens) have been quite indifferent to the defects of their title.

The fabric of error is surely, although slowly, being undermined by knowledge; and by knowledge which, as we have observed, has already proceeded at least so far, that to-day the notion that a man cannot be a rigid single-metallist, and yet in favour of Free Coinage of Two Metals, has got a foothold in the general public: it has passed beyond the teaching classes to the reading masses.

If what has been done in this one direction can be done in other directions, the course of undermining will proceed, as did that which once was perfected beneath the rock-ribbed and seemingly inexpugnable floor of Hellgate channel into the harbour of New York, and accordingly a harmless explosion (of opinion ending in repeal) may be expected to follow in time, and new and placid paths be opened for the prosperity of men.

In furtherance of such growth of interest and of instruction among the reading masses, who make majorities in Legislatures, or among those who lead them, the object-lessons of history may have a wide field of usefulness.

A mind which recoils from the subtleties of a dismal science may find a wholesome meaning and suggestion in the spectacle of such a man, for example, as Sir Robert Peel (whose achievements in currency legislation are more important than those of Palmerston, Beaconsfield, and Gladstone combined), speaking with all sincerity, and listened to with that deference with which—on matters disconnected with the question of the Standard—posterity can have no dispute, citing before Parliament in support of the Outlawry of Silver[1] the authority of those elder English masters of Monetary Science, whom he has named, who, as appears in these pages, had lived and died content under laws for the *Free and Gratuitous Coinage of Silver and Gold, which that same Parliament had enacted.*

If the Outlawry of Silver be dealt with according to any recognized code of evidence, this mere fact should render it suspect. The presumptions are against it, the burden of proof lies upon its defenders, when the guarantees are shown to be spurious under which the most notable figure of the century in financial legislation,—leader of England in framing and carrying the Resumption Act of 1819 and the Bank Act of 1844,—gave it his support.

[1] See above, note, page 75.

§ 14. NEWTON ON SILVER AND GOLD.

Macaulay avers in his History that Newton—independently, I suppose, of his public action in reference to the Recoinage—has left no exposition of his opinions touching the currency. The eloquent historian thus leaves out of view the well-known Report of 1717, upon which was based the reduction of the Guinea from 21 shillings and 6 pence to 21 shillings. It would seem, then, that the doctrinal importance of this Report had escaped recognition from the English historian, though, as I have had occasion to ascertain, it was the subject of appreciative comment in France and Prussia more than a century ago. Indeed, I read it first in a German translation, printed at Berlin in 1762.[1]

Researches in the direction of a history of monetary policy have enabled me to bring to the surface some new evidence of the activity of Newton, as well as of Locke, as Monetary Counsellor of England, which I present herewith. (Appendix 15.) Although merely in keeping with already published utterances,[2] special confirmation is given by these documents to the views I have advanced.

The bearing of the Reports signed by Newton as an officer of the Mint, upon the questions before us, can best come into clear light through their parallelism with the position taken by Locke; who was, as we have seen, the distinctively literary member of the quadrilateral of monetary statesmanship of which Macaulay has sounded the praise.

---

[1] The statement on page 168 of my treatise on "Silver and Gold," was based on the erroneous supposition that a tract of Newton's existed which I had not seen.

[2] Beside the Report of 1717, there is a short Report of 1712 in Overstone's "Selected Tracts on Money."

A Report, dated January 20, 1701, is, in substance, a recommendation to lower the rating of French and Spanish Pistoles, which were then current at 17s. 6d. Upon this recommendation I find that action was had through an Order in Council of February 5, 1700-1. (See Appendix 16.) This Order must naturally have operated, either as an instruction, or as the cause of an instruction, to the government officer of account not to take or pay pistoles at more than 17s. Such quantities of pistoles came to the Mint in consequence of this order, that special exertions were called for on the part of the working force. (See Appendix 17.) This whole incident, however (together with an analogous incident relating to the currency of Moidores), is the object of a brief recital in Newton's Report of 1717: and there he states that the phenomenal sum of £1,400,000 was on this occasion coined into guineas.

A Report, dated September 27, 1701, signed by Newton alone, mentions a change of ratio in France, so that the Louis d'or or pistole, at the new ratio, would be worth not 17s., but 16s. 7d., and the guinea £1 0s. 11d. He therefore submits to the Lords of the Treasury the question, whether "the state of the Money in France being unsettled, it may furnish a sufficient argument for altering the proportion of Gold and Silver Monies in England." The implication seems to suggest itself that if the state of the Money in France were not unsettled, there could be no question as to what England should do.

It was also my fortune to discover a Report of 1702, which is stated to be entirely in Newton's handwriting, though signed also by two other officers of the Mint, in which, fifteen years before the famous Report already alluded to, he distinctly recommends the further reduction of the guinea; thus seconding with the authority of practical and professional observation the hint given by Locke as economic adviser of the Treasury four years before.

Newton's abiding loyalty to Silver, as the principal Money of the realm, is further established by the testimony of Cantillon in the famous "Essai sur la Nature du Commerce;"[1] the interview reported by him occurring, if I remember rightly, some years later than 1717. It appears that Cantillon elicited an expression from Newton touching the idea of attaining a change of ratio by raising Silver instead of lowering Gold: a course which had the obvious advantages of debasement, namely, that the holder of Silver would find he owned more pounds after the change than before, while under the plan actually pursued in 1696, 1698, and 1717, the holder of Gold found he had less pounds after than before.

"This objection," says Cantillon, "was laid before Sir Isaac Newton, and all that he could say to it was, that by the established Law of this Kingdom, Silver was the only fixed Coin of the Country, and as such could not be altered." ("Analysis of Trade, etc.," p. 95.) The statement in the French is even stronger: "Suivant les loix fondamentales du Roiaume, l'argent blanc était la vraie et seule monnoie."

In bringing this incident to notice, together with other glimpses of Newton's activity, Professor Jevons applied to Newton's position the excellent phrase, "*Nolumus leges Angliae mutari*"[2]—we will not have the laws of England changed. At the same time it is evident that, inasmuch as the laws of England were laws for the Dual-Legal-Tender—for Gold Money as well as for Silver Money—the currency of Gold is also entitled to the benefits of the phrase.[3] With the evidence now before us, it is shown more clearly than was possible

---

[1] See Jevons, "The Nationality of Political Economy," "Contemporary Review," January, 1881.

[2] The original appearance of the phrase has a curious merit in this connection: "Certain it is that the great and wise men of England in the Parliament of Merton, did not prefer a foreign law before their own, when, motion being made by the clergie that children born before Marriage might be adjudged legitimate, they all made answer with one voice: *Nolumus leges Angliae mutari*."—*Dav. Rep.*, ed. 1762, p. 5.

In some printed discussions relating to the views of Newton certain misunderstandings have arisen, analogous to the misapprehension of the

during Professor Jevons' lifetime, that Newton's conservatism
—beside accepting as it did, side by side with Silver, the
rated currency of Gold, under regulation of the State—was
supplemented by insight into the conditions favourable to the
success of such regulation, and by a desire to promote such
success. Once the great struggle of the Recoinage was
decided, here lay the field of progress and of reform, and here
accordingly was made manifest the enlightenment of Newton
as well as of Locke.

Touching the points of resemblance and of difference
between the open questions of monetary policy in their time
and those of to-day, I have elsewhere presented some studies
(mentioned in the note below), and I shall endeavour herein,
in later pages, to complete the parallel and contrast.

In closing, I allow myself to direct the reader's eye to an
illustration of the historic tendency of monetary situations to
repeat themselves, and of the close kinship among ideas of
progress and of reform. In this Report of 1702, the Investi-

---

views of Locke which has been ascertained in the preceding pages of this work. The difficulty appears to grow out of the disposition to apply the controversial terms of to-day to a state of things quite remote and disparate from that which has produced them, and which, controlling the current use of these terms, limits their fruitful application. The curious reader will find this matter, perhaps, sufficiently presented in the article of Professor Jevons in the "Contemporary Review" for January, 1881, already alluded to, and in a reply to certain points in it by the present writer, entitled "Sir Isaac Newton and England's Prohibitive Tariff on Silver Money" (Cincinnati, Robert Clarke and Co., April, 1881), and in the portions and fragments of an essay on "Sir Isaac Newton and Bimetallism," by Professor Jevons, which was left unfinished by reason of the lamented death of its author. (See Jevons' "Investigations in Currency and Finance," pages 330-360.) Newton's Report of 1717, with the debates in Parliament relating to the fixation of the guinea at 21 shillings, was reprinted by me in the Document of the Conference of 1878, and was commented upon in essays in that Document (see pages 245 and 253). I had previously (in 1876) characterized the fixation of 1717 on the lines here set forth. ("Silver and Gold," page 74.)

gator of Light and Discoverer of Gravitation, in urging the further reduction of the Guinea, brings forth a phrase which deserves to enlighten centuries—"*France has set us an example!*" For myself I offer to Newton for the moral of these words a more heartfelt homage than that I paid on bringing words of Julius Paulus and of Aristotle to the light, and discovering with what depth of insight and felicity of analysis[1] Money, that ever-ancient though ever-novel institution, had been recognized by them in its true nature.

It is like emerging from malarial fog to breathe the air of mountain tops, to pass to the atmosphere revealed by such a phrase as this of Newton's, from the parish patriotism which seeks to treat Money as an institution solely of the speaker's nation, and refuses to recognize it as an institution of the world of Money-using men. Was Newton the less an Englishman, because of these words? I venture to believe that this phrase of his betrays no vagary of the cosmopolite. The gentle sage was none the less a patriot: he was then a member of Parliament, and to him, I doubt not, as to others, France was but the ancient enemy, against whom the allied forces were then preparing war, under Marlborough as Generalissimo. But neither war nor politics could disturb his clear gaze at truth, nor warp the lucidity of his report of what he saw. As a monetary statesman, he placed at the service of his country the same order of dispassionate intelligence, to which nature had yielded secrets that are a cherished possession for ever to his race.

France has set us an example!

The spirit of Newton still has work to do, in the land to which he gave his fame. The world will breathe more freely, when an awakened public opinion shall enable an English Prime Minister to pronounce the equivalent for modern days of Newton's "France has set us an example."

---

[1] See "Silver and Gold," pages 1, 118, etc., and Appendix.

And such words can be said, as these were said by Newton, without prejudice to the venerable maxim *Nolumus leges Angliae mutari*, for conservatism can hardly inure to sustain judgment in favour of the partial experiment of two generations as against the practice of centuries of English law.

Should this page ever meet the eye of one to whom it shall seem strange that a Prime Minister—who must be, of all others, what is called a practical man—should be expected to pay close heed to the opinions of a man of science, the following extract from a famous speech of one who became a famous Prime Minister may convey a fruitful lesson. To others, this extract may serve as a link in the chain of evidence that the errors of policy and of doctrine I attack, owed much of their original prestige and support to a strange perversion of historical truth.

The speech is the speech of the Rt. Hon. Robert Peel in support of the Resumption Act of 1819.

"Sir Isaac Newton," he says, "retiring from the sublime studies in which he chiefly passed his life—from the contemplation of the heavenly bodies—from an investigation of the laws by which their motions were guided—entered on the examination of this subject; [the definition of an "abstract pound"] but that great man came back, at last, to the old, the vulgar doctrine, as it was called by some, that the true standard of value consisted in a definite quantity of gold bullion. Every sound writer on the subject came to the same conclusion . . ."

In reprinting this remarkable fiction I feel bound to say that while no one can believe that the distinguished speaker evolved it out of his inner consciousness, yet I am at a loss to point out the probable culprit.

Perhaps the most notable revelation afforded by the discourse from which this extract comes lies not in the error of fact which the reader has the material for detecting, by comparing the acts and utterances of Newton with Peel's report of their outcome, but in the orator's enthusiasm about "the true standard of value," and in the burning faith with which, like a knight-errant, he runs the gauntlet of very dragons of doctrine in a Quest for "the Abstract Pound."

Is there anything Quixotic, or unpractical in this search? I shall be the last to say so! The only criticism valid in my eyes, belongs to the order of that which I seek to make, namely, that which attacks not inquiry, but defective conclusions reached by inadequate inquiry. If any justification is needed for the labour of analysis to which the Introduction and the earlier chapters of this work have invited the reader, or if evidence is needed to establish the practical importance to practical men of the work of speculative thought in the field of Money, this most notable of discourses in the debates which led to the Restoration of Metallic, in the place of Paper Money in England can most efficiently serve that purpose.

Here we see theory engaged at its work of policy-making. If ever a system was founded on theory it is the system put in force by the "Peel's Resumption Act" of 1819, and it will be found that from the defects of the theory arose the defects in the practical working: that the evils that England has suffered appear just as the transition is made from the *terra firma* of the true theoretical to the quicksands of the unpractical and the visionary.

It is this same speech which contains the passage relating to the question "What is a Pound" which has occupied a place of no little dignity in the political literature of Money in England. In a later chapter the subject and the views of Sir Robert Peel concerning it, will be considered in detail.

CHAPTER VI.

A Lesson of History (*continued*).—The Descent to Gold.

§ 15. THE RATING OF THE GUINEA AND PISTOLE IN ENGLAND.

We have seen that necessity, the mother of discovery as well as of invention, had forced the men whose fitness for the tasks of statesmanship had brought them to the front in monetary affairs, to recognize the need of regulating the currency of Gold. As Locke says in the letter already referred to (Appendix 13), "The business of our Money has so near brought us to Ruin, that till the plot broke out, it was everybody's talk, everybody's uneasiness. . . . . . But now the Parliament has reduced Guineas to two-and-twenty shillings, as well as prohibited the receipt of clipped Money. . . . ."

In dealing with the golden portion of the monetary field I feel constrained to seek to enlarge its importance beyond the range it occupied, so far as I am informed, in the writings which are deemed authoritative in this matter. It appears to me a well-grounded judgment that the rating of Gold was a key to the entire situation in England, before, as well as during, and after, the Recoinage.

In putting forward novel views, which convey what may, perhaps, seem a venturesome criticism upon learning and statesmanship of past times, whether of the XVIIth or of other centuries, I must enter somewhat into detail, in order to justify my position.

The situation of affairs which preceded the crisis of 1696, was a novel one in two distinct respects:

1st. The improvement in the mode of Coinage (of which Macaulay gives a graphic account), the mill and press being substituted for the hammer:

2nd. Coinage being made, of right, free to all, who might choose to bring bullion to the Mint; and at the same time gratuitous, the tax-payers bearing the expense of assaying and of Coinage.

This latter innovation was introduced by the Act of Parliament of 1666. Prior to that measure a charge had been made for Coinage, which varied from time to time. Fifteen shillings to the pound of crown Gold, and two shillings to the pound of standard Silver, were "his Majesty's rates" at Charles II.'s accession: but the charge for coining Gold was reduced soon after, in 1663,—"as an encouragement to the Bringer into the Mint, and soe unto his Majestie in respect of the quantities that thereby may be coined,"—and presently the rate on both Gold and Silver was, as we have seen, abolished by statute. To what extent the Mint—through this law of Free Coinage, which operated as a statutory command and guarantee of diligence in serving the convenience of the bullion-owning public—was made more active in that work, I am not informed; but it is plain that the abolition of all charge for assay and coinage produced a novel facility of turning metal into cash, and so introduced a novel, and not unimportant, element into the calculations of England's business, foreign or domestic. It must also have operated as an encouragement to the further clipping of the Silver and to the exportation of full-weight coins, with which latter points the glowing periods of Macaulay deal very fully.

The contemporaneous facility of pouring Gold into the circulation, at a price which gave profit, perhaps, as great as the clipping of Silver, and yet involved no offence against the law, does not seem to have attracted adequate attention. This operation found a foothold in this new right of Gratuitous and Free Coinage, which was accorded by statute to Gold as well as to Silver, and it was stimulated by two notable features of what may be called the law of Money at that period in England, namely, the currency of foreign Gold-coin, and the arbitrary power of the Government to fix the rate at which Gold-coin, native or foreign, should be accepted and paid in the Government offices of account.

To one who owned Gold, whether it came to him in the regular course of business, or had been brought in for speculative purposes, no desire could be more natural than to have it pass for as many pounds (or shillings) as possible. Whether it was bullion which he proposed to have turned into guineas at the expense of the State, or coin, foreign or native, which he sought to use as it stood, the desire was very natural to have it pass at as high a rate as possible. Great gain was to be made in bringing Gold in, to pass at as high a rate as possible, and in buying Silver at as low a rate as possible, in order to export it. Silver in England could not be the object of a similar operation, for the Unit of Account, the Pound Sterling, was itself of Silver; its "mint price" could not be moved except by formal Act of Parliament for the debasement of the standard. There was, then, a strong pressure of self-interest which operated in favour of Gold and against Silver, to raise the rating of the former in terms of the latter. To this pressure the Government Officer of Account, as well as the individual Money-user, was exposed, and for this interest the license of Government control over the rating of home and foreign Gold-coin was a dangerous instrument; for its working could be gradual, and half-concealed, and would seem venial if attention were called to it. In respect to the intervention of any special private and powerful interest, as, for example, on the part of the Guinea Company, I have no information, and I distinctly disclaim an inference which may suggest itself to the reader's mind, that bad faith was at work—an idea which should be excluded unless it can be proved; and I know no proof.

But it is enough to say, that in this elastic and voluntary fixation of the number of shillings a Gold-coin should be taken for in the Exchequer, lay a natural, powerful, and easy means of disorganizing the Money of the country. Those who sought to raise the rating of Gold might find in the tax-gatherer a support, and in the paymaster an ally. So far as evidence has come to my view, the Government did not withhold such aid.

Of the importance of the practice of the Government, in this matter, it may be worth while to remark that the daily handling of income and expenditure of a nation, implies a monetary agency of unique and dominant influence. If the Government officers received and paid guineas at a certain rate, who would be able or likely to assure their currency at a different rate? If we suppose that symptoms showed themselves in the market of a rise or a fall of the market rate, it remained with the Government *to stand by the old rate, or to change, and fix a new rate;* and so, while, in changing, the Government may easily have seemed to be following the market, it really was also guiding the market, its action being none the less a cause, by reason of being an effect. At the same time it should be clearly observed that, whatever its rate of currency, the influx of Gold into England (see next page), acting necessarily as an increase of demand for it, tended to raise its market-rate compared with Silver, and that its acceptance in England at a high ratio tended further to bring its market-rate elsewhere up to the legal level in England.

It is, in my judgment, safe to assert that a firm hand, guided by a seeing eye, keeping the rating of Gold at a rate which should yield to tides only, but not to waves, of the metal-market, would have maintained the Gold-coin in its place, and have gone far to maintain the Silver likewise.

Looked at as a whole, the change of composition of the Money-stock of England, through exportation of full-weight Silver-coins, and the swelling of the tide of over-valued Gold, was, at the same time, a debasement and an inflation, for which the mode in which the existing law was administered was largely in fault.

As Sir William Petty had said, in 1662, of a like experience early in the century, the country was "pestered with too much Gold," or, as Montague said (1695) in a speech in the Commons, "All Europe sent that commodity (Gold) to this market, and would continue to do so till the Nation should be impoverished, and undone by plenty of Gold." ("Memoirs of Montague," p. 32.)

The following figures tell the story :—

Coinage.	Gold.			Silver.		
	£	s.	d.	£	s.	d.
Under Charles II.	177,253	19	5	3,722,180	2	8
,, James II.	2,113,638	2	8	518,316	9	5
,, William and Mary	443,328	15	6	79,026	9	4
,, William III.	2,975,550	16	1	7,014,047	16	11
,, Anne	2,484,531	8	4	527,467	10	4½

How great a portion of the amounts above given, by reason of being recoined is counted twice, as an element in calculating the amount of Money in use, and how far the recoinage of the Silver, under William III., applies to coinage anterior to Charles II., are matters which seem to have passed beyond reckoning.[1]

A goodly part, then, of these millions of Gold, coined—gratuitously, at the expense of the tax-payer—in the reigns

---

[1] The figure for Silver in Queen Anne's Reign is taken from Snelling's "Silver Coins of the Realm." Ruding gives £207,094 18s. 4½d., and "for Scotland" £411,117 10s. 9d., quoting Folkes.

of James and of William and Mary, represent the speculation of private individuals in English coin, by which the country's circulation was depleted of its original stock of full-weight Silver and filled with over-valued Gold; while the figures for the reign of William III. and Anne, represent a similar attack upon the 7 million Silver Pounds Sterling of the re-coinage.

My contention applies to the entire period, the incubation of the crisis of 1696, as well as the crisis itself, and the following years. To state the point very clearly—though perhaps also very boldly—if a fixation, let us say, if need be, at 21s., had come at the beginning, instead of coming as it did at the end, of the period just placed in view in our table of coinage, the monetary plague, which so darkly shadows the history of that time, would have been shorn of its malignancy. Such a fixation would have cut out at the start the spot of infection which persistently enlarged its inroads upon England's otherwise well-ordered finance.

It was not, then, as it has been customary to suppose, the neglect of the Government touching Silver merely, which was in fault, but also the concurrent neglect as to Gold. It was as important to rate the Gold rightly, perhaps more important, than to recoin the Silver. The trouble was generated by letting the Gold go "up" as well as by letting the Silver go "down;" if it was a mistake to let the Silver-coin go down in intrinsic value, while remaining "up" in nominal value, it was likewise a mistake to let the Gold go up in nominal value, while remaining "down" in intrinsic value. The almost irremediable disorder of the Silver-coins was thus in great measure a result of the easily remediable disorder of the Gold-coins.

The measures adopted to reduce the rate of the guinea, which have already been fully set forth, are, of course, evidence in support of these views. But beside these there are other solemn Acts of legislation which may serve the same purpose. The further legislation briefly described on page 72, formed a provisional arrangement destined to hold Gold-coin and bullion in due subordination. The Act provides (see Appendix 8 B) that between March 2, 1696 (1695-6), and January 1, 1697 (1696-7), the officers of the Mint *should not be obliged* to coin Gold, and that the importation of guineas should be a misdemeanour.

The reasons for the Act, and for the Acts which followed it, are given in their preambles, and will be found of peculiar interest, for they throw the clearest light, both upon what was done, and upon what ought to have been done.

"And whereas great Quantities of Gold have been lately imported from foreign Parts which being coined here as aforesaid into Guineas have been (on occasion of the present ill state of the Silver Coins) taken and accepted by the Subjects of this Realm at very high and unusual rates and prices tending to the great Damage and Loss of the Publick; the Continuance of which practice (unless speedily prevented) will run the Nation vastly in debt to Foreigners for the re-payment whereof the Silver Moneys of this Kingdom must inevitably be exhausted on Terms of great Disadvantage therefore to prevent the further Growth of soe great an evil, be it enacted," and so forth.

We have here a lucid and authoritative statement, which I think illustrates and justifies the principles I have endeavoured to set forth in these pages. The Repeal of this Act, a few months later, supplies material for criticism, and support for our judgment upon the policy actually pursued.

"And whereas the reason of making the said Act was occasioned by the high and unusual Price of Guineas which might in the end be very prejudicial to the Subject. But the price of guineas being now reduced to or near the Standard and Sundry persons being desirous to coin Gold and also to import great Quantities of guineas and Halfe Guineas which will be very beneficial to the Trade and Commerce of this Kingdom. For the encouragement whereof be it enacted," etc., that the former Act be repealed, and that "on or before Nov. 10, 1696, one or more mills and presses be set apart for the coinage of Gold and the same kept in distinct account from the Silver."

In that phrase, "to, *or near*, the Standard," lies the breach by which the enemy entered to take possession. To put the guinea at 22s., was to put it near the "Standard"—that is to say, the proper ratio—but not very near, and by no means near enough. The grand portals were closed, but the postern gate was left ajar.

In connection with these observations upon the policy of Parliament and Treasury, with reference to the rating of Gold, the reader may find an interest in certain other bits of contemporary evidence, which are presented in the Appendix (Nos. 4, 5, 6, and 7). Of one of these papers (which rewarded my search among the Public Archives) I shall make special mention. I refer to a portion of a communication on the subject of the guinea, bearing date Antwerp, 6 July, 1695, from the Commissioners [1] of the Bank of England, then entering the second year of its existence. This letter purports to have been sent to the camp before Namur to be presented to the King, "repeating of our instances to the King that a stop may be put to this mischievous high price of Gold and Guineas in England." What was desired was a "proclamation reducing the price of Guineas to the *par of our neighbours before the late extravagant rise.*" The italics are mine.

The demand for a rating of the guineas according to the "par of our neighbours," is a fitting statement of the outcome of the considerations presented in this Chapter.

It will be seen that this letter of the officers of the Bank also offers material suggestions upon the great issue of the power of law to regulate the value of Money. In further application of the views on this head, which have already been presented, it is germane to ask the very blunt and practical question, whether it is strained supposition to assume that

---

[1] The question is suggested in the Appendix whether the rating of the guinea was not the main motive of this famous visit of the Directors of the Bank to the seat of war, in the course of which the Deputy-Governor, Michael Godfrey, lost his life in the trenches.

such men as the Bank officials must have been—knew what they were about when they sought remedy from "fatal and certain evil consequences" to England and to themselves in a Royal Proclamation. Were they likely to be putting their faith in an empty pronunciamento? I think not. As I have shown, the founders of the Bank of England had in plain view, as matters of every-day observation, forces which were quite competent "to regulate the value of Money," and which the preceding pages have brought in sight. Chief among them was, in my belief, this very control of the Government Offices of Account over the rating of the Gold-coin, of which I have been speaking.

We shall do well to proceed a little further upon this line, taking careful account of the doctrinal importance of the facts we have ascertained, touching the rating of Gold; of the facts, I mean, that are beyond question, and also at the same time of those which I indicate as matter of inference.

I do not know that we shall find better evidence on any of the points presented in Section 9 and in Chapter IV., touching the power and duty of the state, which, to-day, is still the great issue under debate, than is exhibited in the solemnity with which what were by them supposed—with entire sincerity—to be the events of this period, were treated by Lord Liverpool and by Lord Macaulay. It was, apparently, because he was not informed of the orders of the Privy Council (of 1698-9), and of the Treasury, touching the guinea, which are reprinted in the Appendix, that Lord Liverpool, adverting to the Acts of Parliament, forbidding the currency of the guinea above 26s., and above 22s., was able to aver that "when the Recoinage was completed, Guineas fell in their rate or value below the value limited in these Acts, *without any interposition of public authority.*" It was by favour of his unconsciousness of the whole order of fact which I set forth in this chapter—the practical Legal-Tender of the Gold-coin, established by the action of the Treasury—that he was able to say :—

"In very rich countries, and especially in those where great and extensive commerce is carried on ... Gold will in practice become the principal measure of property and the instrument of commerce with the consent of the people, *not only without the support of law, but in spite of almost any law that may be enacted to the contrary.*" (P. 160.)

It was because he was not informed of the existence of these orders, or of the Report of Locke, and I dare say also of the letter referred to (all of which are reprinted in the Appendix) —that Macaulay was able to say :—

"But some of the details both of [the Recoinage Act] and of a supplementary act which was passed at a later period of the session, seem to prove that Montague *had not fully considered, what legislation can, and what it cannot effect.* For example, he persuaded the Parliament to enact that it should be penal to give or take more than 22s. for a guinea. It may be confidently affirmed that this enactment *was not suggested or approved by Locke*. He well knew that *the high price of Gold was not the evil which afflicted the State,* but merely a symptom of that evil, and that a fall in the price of Gold *would inevitably follow, and could by no human power or ingenuity be made to precede, the recoinage of Silver.* In fact, the penalty seems to have produced no effect whatever. Till the milled Silver was in circulation, the guinea continued, in spite of law, to pass for 30s. When the milled Silver became plentiful, the price of the guinea fell; *and the fall did not stop at 22s., but continued till it reached 21s. 6d.*" [1] (The italics are all mine.)

In these utterances the reader may easily recognize the familiar doctrine of the impotence of legislation to affect the value Money, of which so much has been said.

Lacking information of the existence of "the law," both Lord Liverpool and Macaulay seize the occasion to point out— as they suppose—its impotence. What is the motive of this

---

[1] "History," in Works, iv. 202.

haste? Evidently to Lord Liverpool the idea recommended itself as a good argument for Gold; while Macaulay was quite under the charm of that antipathy to interference with individual liberty, and the "natural" course of events which, as I have explained in an earlier Chapter (page 61), is still a prevailing fashion of thought. Such is the power of error of fact to stimulate the growth of error of doctrine. It is, however, but justice to all concerned to accompany this criticism with proof, which shows how natural the error was, how widespread this same misapprehension of the facts has been. This may be revealed by a glance at the following extract which I translate from Abot de Bazinghen's "Dictionnaire des Monnoies" (Paris, 1764). "The Guinea was struck to be worth exactly 20s., or a pound sterling; later, it was raised to 21s. 6d., but *merely by the tacit consent of the Nation without any public law;* it remained at the rate for more than half a century," etc.

Evidently, these errors of fact are uniquely adapted to inspire erroneous doctrines.

To follow our criticism somewhat more into detail, I observe that what Macaulay, repeating the customary phrase, calls the "high price of Gold," was not, if precision be observed, a "price," but rather a rate of currency which the Government authorized. That the historian is mistaken in assuming that Locke did not recognize this, is clearly indicated by the evidence. To the historian's assertion that the Act of Parliament forbidding the currency of the Guinea above 22s., had no effect to bring them down from 30s. to 22s., I venture to affix, at this distance, an interrogation point. I am not prepared with full evidence to the contrary, but merely desire in this way to note that the situation calls for strict proof. The point is distinct from those which we have lately been discussing. The observations of the preceding pages apply mainly to the period anterior to this Act. After the law was passed, it was, evidently, a very great misdemeanour for an official in any government office to take or give, guineas at a rate above 22s.: and it would be difficult withal, to discover any motive for such action. To the individual Money-user, the practice of government officers would serve as an example and as a hindrance to transgression. If it be really true that the Ministry failed to see to it that its own subordinates carried out its measure, we have then to deal with a political, rather than with an economic, event.

That there was no force at work which was competent to overrule the influence of the Government Offices of Account in fixing the rate of guineas, is amply shown by a fact to which Lord Liverpool testifies, namely, that they refused to take guineas for more than 30s., and thus prevented their rising above that rate. (Treatise, pp. 75 and 85.)

It remains now to direct our attention to the peculiar scope of this action of Parliament, and of the Administration, which I have called a "rating" of guineas. In each case the terms of the command were, *not* to take the Gold-coin *for more than a certain sum*. The Gold-coin therefore was not, strictly speaking, made current, obligatorily current, at the rate established.

Twenty shillings remained its rate of currency in the fullest sense of the word, namely, that a tender of coin at that rate was a Legal-Tender of payment in discharge of a debt expressed in pounds and shillings. This status was, however, a creation of the same power in the State as that which regulated the rating in Government offices, for both lay in the jurisdiction of the Crown, subject, as we have seen, to the occasional intervention of Parliament, over which the Crown had its veto. The Legal-Tender-power of the guinea as a 20-shilling piece, arose from its issuance as the equivalent of 20s., by authority of the Crown. It was as an expression of sovereignty, that the Mint Indenture (see Appendix 3), a contract of the Crown, had the force of law.[1]

---

[1] This Prerogative had been confirmed by the Act of Parliament 19 Henry VII., ch. 5, and 5 & 6 Edward VI. ch. 19—the former providing that all Gold and Silver-coins "shall be current for the sum they were

Without entering here upon the question of currency by consent, which I find to be another mode of authorization recognized in the law of the time, it is plain that permission to pass guineas at 22 shillings, coupled with an actual practice of government offices to use them as 22-shilling pieces, tended effectively to legalize and to promote their circulation at that rate. The rule of the Mint Indenture might still control in case of captious dispute about the operation of an offer of Gold-coin in discharge of a debt, though all the while in the actual circulation the coin stood everywhere at a higher level. It was, in fact, by no means self-evident that the rate of 22 shillings was not obligatory; for the question arose in such force as to elicit a resolution of the Commons, that no one was compelled to accept guineas at 22 shillings. The legal effect of the Order of the Treasury stood, of course, below the binding force of the Proclamation of 1717 (of which further mention will be made hereafter), which contained the words "at which rate or rates (21 shillings to the guinea) we do hereby declare the said respective pieces of coined Gold to be current;" yet the practical effect for the time being, of such an order as that just mentioned, if continued and enforced, might be in practice to a large extent the same, the probable exceptions being the supposed case before-mentioned, always rare, of captious dispute about a Legal-Tender in discharge of debt. The main body of the Proclamation of 1717 is to the same effect as the Statute and Orders for 26, 22, and 21¹ shillings, that is, *not* to take guineas above 21 shillings; but it contains, in addition, the above clause, which, thereupon, in the most

coined for;" the latter forbidding, on pain of forfeiture, exchanging Coined Gold or Coined Silver for more than they are declared to be current for *by Proclamation.*

The rate of 20 shillings for the Guinea, provided in the Mint Indenture, had never been established obligatorily by Proclamation, and hence exchanging it at a higher rate had never become an offence. The Government offices were therefore free to take it at a higher rate, as well as the people.

binding form, fixed a limit below, as well as above, and so substituted for the 20-shilling Legal-Tender-rule of the existing Mint Indenture, the new rating of the Proclamation. The Mint Indentures subsequent to 1717, accordingly provided for the same coin as a 21-shilling piece.

A word, in conclusion, touching the ratio embodied in the rating of the guinea as a 22-shilling piece. The ratio is about $15.^{93}$ to 1, if the comparison is between full-weight Gold-coin and full-weight Silver-coin. This ratio is several per cent. above the average market-rate at the time for Gold.[1]

The question, therefore, confronts us, why this high ratio was chosen, for to-day it appears quite obvious that it was so much above the market-rate as to offer a profit for the substitution of Gold for the new Silver-coin then in process of manufacture. The following considerations suggest themselves in answer.

1. The greater part of the existing Silver-coin was under-weight; the new full-weight Silver-coin was a thing of the future; and the actual comparison of coin with coin—a guinea being, in fact, for the time, made equal only to 22 *light shillings*—the actual rate, so to speak, was far below $15.^{93}$ to 1, and taking the average of the mass of coins in use, could only gradually rise to that figure with the completion of the re-coinage, which, in the end, required near three years.

2. Twenty-two shillings was a rate which seems to have been observed for some time in the earlier days of deterioration

---

[1] Professor Soetbeer's Tables of the average ratio of Gold to Silver in Hamburg show the ratio in that market of the years just before, and just after, the fixation of the guineas above recommended, as follows:—

1695	15.02	1698	. 14.94
1696	15.00	1700	. . 14.81
1697	15.20	1701	. . 15.07
1698 . . .	15.07	1702 . .	15.52

How closely this conforms to the general rates on the Continent, I am not surely informed; suffice it to say here that the facts known to me reveal no very important divergence from these figures.

of the Silver-coin, and may well have stood in the public mind as a fair average, or compromise.

3. It was a hardship to many innocent holders to "fall" the guineas at all, and it was natural that the highest practicable rate should be taken.

4. For high ratios, the example of Spain and of Portugal could be adduced, an argument which, at that time, had great authority. It is quite in accord with the then condition of economic knowledge, that these countries, which owned the mines of precious metal, should be regarded as the arbiters of their ratio.

5. Lastly, I observe that it is not probable that the operation of the law of Free and Gratuitous Coinage was well understood; upon this point further considerations will be presented upon another page.

The fixation of guineas by the Treasury in 1698 upon the Report of the Board of Trade, of which a full account is given in Section 13, reduced their rating to 21s. 6d., and brought down the ratio—as found by comparison with full-weight Silver-coin—to 15.5 to 1. The course of reasoning, which was held to justify the rating at 15", had still a certain measure of persuasiveness in supporting the new ratio. The mistake of the time lay in the failure to follow out the recommendations of Locke's report. That report was based upon the idea that the adoption of the new rating would stop the excessive importation of Gold: but it went on to lay down a rule for the future—"but if, contrary to our expectation, this abatement should prove too small, guineas may, by the same easy means [an order of the Treasury] be lowered yet further, according as may be found expedient." This lowering very soon became, in fact, expedient; but it was not discovered to be so. As usual, the monetary interests of the nation which demanded consistent and competent attention, failed to receive it.

The general course of the Government touching the rating of the Pistole, has been indicated in the preceding Section, in connection with the Reports of Newton.

The desire must naturally be to keep the alignment between the rating of foreign coins and that of the guineas: but the path of success in this effort was, no doubt, crossed both by the unwillingness to bring small fractions of the shilling into the figure of the rating, and by the varying quality of the coins themselves. I know of no estimates of the quantity of foreign coins circulating in England, but the amount mentioned by Newton as having been recoined about 1701—which was no less than £1,400,000 worth—certainly shows that they might be an important factor in the circulation.

§ 16. THE ENGLISH MONETARY SYSTEM AND THE ORIGINALITY OF THE STATESMEN OF THE RECOINAGE.

The accredited statement touching the English "Standard" during the past two centuries, gives for the period preceding 1717, the Silver Standard, for the period subsequent to 1717 the Double Standard.

This statement, in all probability, chiefly rests upon the authority of Lord Liverpool, who states (in passages of his Treatise, reprinted on p. 141) that from 41 Henry III. (1257) to 1663, and again, after 1717, the Gold Coins and Silver Coins were equally the "legal measure of property," but that in 1663 the Gold Coins ceased to be a legal measure of property. This account is adopted in part by Sir Robert Peel, as will be seen by reference to the Appendix, page 295.

The necessity has perhaps already become apparent of a radical correction of these statements; and in pausing at the close of a review of the Great Recoinage, to consider the system then existing, and the work of those who administered it, we may conveniently epitomize the past and anticipate the coming pages by a tabular view of the English "Standard" in the entire period.

*

THE ENGLISH MONETARY SYSTEM BEFORE AND AFTER THE RECOINAGE OF 1696.

English Gold and Silver Coins were "Current coins of the Realm;" and from time to time certain Foreign Gold-coins had currency within the Realm in various degrees, though, probably, never called coins *of* the Realm.

National Unit of Coinage.	Government Rating of Gold.[1]	Effective Legal Ratio.	Ratio of obligatory Legal-Tender.	Principal Money in Use.

To preclude misunderstanding, I call attention to the fact that the above phrases have no claim to be contemporary with the events referred to — but are adopted for this occasion.

National Unit of Coinage.	Government Rating of Gold.	Effective Legal Ratio.	Ratio of obligatory Legal-Tender.	Principal Money in Use.
The Silver Pound.	1663 to ?[1] (the latter date being uncertain.) Guineas at 20s.	1 to 14.[10]	1 to 14.[14] From 1663 to 1717.	SILVER.
	? —to 1694 (September ?) Guineas at 21s. 6d.	1 to 15.[5]	The "Measure" being "lost"—for the mutilation in varying degrees of the Silver-coins, actually in use, worked what I may call a decomposition of the Silver Money—it cannot be said, in the proper sense of the words, that an effective legal ratio existed.	At what precise date the reduction of the stock of Silver-coin and influx of Gold gave the latter a majority in the circulation must remain a matter of surmise. From my present information I should put the date not far from 1710.
	From 1694 (probably September) to June, 1695, the rate of Guineas rose to 30s.			
	June, 1695, to Jan. 1696, Guineas at 30s.			
	March 25, 1696, to April 10, 1696, Guineas at 26s.			
	April 10, 1696, to Feb. 16, 1699, Guineas at 22s.	1 to 15.[13]		
	Feb. 16, 1699, to Dec. 22, 1717, Guineas at 21s. 6d.	1 to 15.[55]		
	From Dec. 22, 1717, Guineas at 21s.	1 to 15.[-9]	1 to 15.[-2]	
				GOLD.

[1] Touching the Government rating, the evidence is quite defective; the statements are in large part matter of inference, and are given subject to revision.

If we seek to characterize by a name the Monetary System of England as the Statesmen of the Recoinage—taking the law as it stood—united to reform its operation, we shall, I think, aptly describe it as the Silver and Gold Standard, with Silver as Unit and Chief-Legal-Tender.

For my part I can frankly say, with no defective consciousness of the part I have borne in monetary discussion, that, barring questions of detail as to the mode of fixing the rating of the guinea, the scheme is precisely what I should advocate under conditions such as those which obtained two centuries ago. It appears to me, in a word, the plain common-sense of what I may call a Local-National Bi-metallic System. The Unit being held by the heavier, the more abundant, and the steadier metal, and full provision made for duly holding the other metal in harness as Money, at par with the Unit, the system was, in my view, arranged with full adaptation to the international elements of the problem as they then stood. I do not hesitate to affirm that it is distinctly the analogue for that day of the Union for Free Coinage of Silver and Gold, the adoption of which was put upon the order of the day before Christendom by the Monetary Conference of 1878.

But, like any other institution of the State, this system required to be properly administered. Its proper administration demanded that the Government should abandon such phenomenal supineness in dealing with the coin as had already wantonly forced a business crisis and heavy losses upon a war-worn state, and should consistently maintain its Monetary System upon the lines of policy clearly marked out for it.

The rating of the guinea must be changed—lowered or raised from time to time, so as to keep the alignment with its Silver-price, as altered from time to time; the alteration arising, in fact, chiefly through action of foreign Mints.

The object of this policy will be easily recognized : it was to keep the English "Standard" securely in its place—a Silver Standard in Meanings Nos. 5 and 7 and 8 of our Introduction, a Silver and Gold Standard in Meanings Nos. 6 and 9. Its effect, as stated in detail, must be, not merely to maintain the local parity of coins of the two metals, or, in other words, to prevent a discount on one or premium on the other at home—for the habit of using both might well avail to secure this result in the earlier stages of a general alteration of the relative value of the metals—but also to foil the speculator in bullion, whose operations may be briefly stated as the bringing in of the metal which was cheaper to him, and getting for it the metal dearer to him, without paying any premium on the latter.

In this way undue alteration of the relative proportions of the two metals in the Money stock of the Kingdom was to be prevented. This, in the case now in view, would mean a draining of the new-made Silver Money from the Kingdom, and so a break-down of the " Standard."

It is further to be observed of the practical outcome of this system—that it tended to secure an abundant circulation, " the plenty of current coins of Gold and Silver," in the words of the Statute of 1666.

It was not a visionary scheme; the iteration to that effect of modern Monetary writers, in their several languages, to the contrary notwithstanding. It was practicable to maintain what later controversy might call a " Double" Standard.

Against this iteration, born not of research, but of the mere imitativeness of fashion, or of the passion of controversy, I maintain that Locke, and Somers, and Montague, and Newton were practical men, and that their country's law had established a good working system. This view can be substantiated in various ways if need be, but the reader can arrive at certainty without a moment's delay, on ascertaining that the alleged impossibility of maintaining such a Double Standard was actually performed at the period in question. France actually enjoyed its Double Standard, in the sense of a concurrent circulation of the two metals, throughout the greater part of the XVIIIth century. The evidence with which I was able to establish this fact is given in the Document of the Conference of 1878, p. 715, and in the Document of the Conference of 1881. (Blue Book, page 280; American edition, page 385.)

It was a good working system, then, which only required proper attention from the Ministry to insure its maintenance.

In order to correct by anticipation a possible—nay, I regret to say, probable—misunderstanding, it will be well for me to state that, in my view, the mere raw elements which go to form this system, were in themselves nothing new; their traces may be met with here and there throughout the centuries of monetary history.

It is a strange fact—and in after times when monetary history shall have been more carefully studied than it is to-day, it will seem even more strange—but, in modern learning, so completely has the "dismal science" of Money been avoided by the historian and the publicist, that among the learned to-day, after a decade which has witnessed more monetary controversy than any series of decades anterior to it, error is quite possible, and is, I fear, common, in dealing with this matter.

In thus saying, that the mere raw elements which go to form the system we are analyzing were in themselves nothing new, I am really confronting what I may be allowed to name a prevalent fallacy of limitation, a distorting narrowness of view, a forgetfulness, or inertia, born, I dare say, of a natural vexation of spirit, and fatigue in threading the labyrinth of Money. One would, in fact, suppose from the tone of late utterances to which I could point—which are, I should add, of most distinguished source—that this matter of parity and disparity between Silver and Gold (coin or bullion) was quite a modern affair. I have to acknowledge that I have myself made the counter-mistake in certain

I

writings (1876-8-9) of taking the obviousness of the opposite view—which is the correct one—too much for granted, and in the course of years of controversy have had occasion to deplore my error.

Hence, it is doubly opportune for me to utilize this occasion, and to justify in detail the view which I once erroneously supposed too obvious to need explanation. I therefore bring to the notice of those whom it may concern, a general statement touching the appearance in history of the phenomena of which we treat. I aver that Money is a genus made up of various species; that no insular isolation of its habitat is demanded by the nature of any of these several species; there is no radical incompatibility between them; their provinces may not only overlap each other, but they are capable, so to speak, of joint tenancy in which the right of survivorship may apply. The use of different kinds of Money is therefore naturally, to some extent, a concurrent as well as a parallel and independent use. Now concurrent use implies valuation of one species in terms of the other, and this valuation may be, in various degrees, official. Such valuation implies parity; and aberration from a once recognized parity implies disparity. The natural plurality of material and unity of Money make probable, therefore, the appearance, not in all times and places, but at least here and there in time and place, of the phenomena of parity and disparity.

Throughout the ages in which man has made general use of Money—however deficient the age may have been in scientific generalizations based upon the facts in view, however limited the recognition may have been of whatever generalizations were actually made, and whatever the default in recording the results of observation, yet the raw material of experience in reference to parity and disparity must have been present in some effective measure. I recall that in my early study of the subject, in exploring the writings of Aristotle with this impression in mind, his observation, or that of one who wrote under his name, that it was *part of the economy of a King to know when to raise or to lower the value of Money*, seemed to me applicable to the matters now in hand, and indeed, a very weighty, very interesting, but at the same time quite a natural observation, and I remember quoting it in print to that effect in 1876. But if it be true, as the tone of much that is said in our time would lead us to suppose, that Sir Thomas Gresham enacted "Gresham's law" in England, in the reign of Elizabeth, and that corresponding events have since occurred, it plainly follows that the Greek—who lived before that day, as well as before the year XI. of the French Republic, or the date of Hamilton's Report on the Mint—in saying those words that I have quoted was but a babbling dreamer, talking to the wind. Now I believe the contrary of this. Indeed, I may go so far as to aver that to the monetary counsellors of Philip of Macedon, or of Alexander, a broad view of parity and disparity could hardly have been as novel as to some otherwise most competent authorities of the present generation in matters monetary. Not that the latter were necessarily unaware of the fact that the use of various kinds of Money is ancient, but that their minds stopped short with this fact; they omitted to proceed very far upon this unattractive path of monetary thought that " wanders through a forest in a mist."

The fault is hardly a rare one, for it is to this unattractiveness that the deficient growth of Monetary Science is to be attributed. By reason of this unattractiveness, there has been little cumulation of the results of experience to hold control of legislation, so that the generations, as they follow each other, seem even more liable to monetary maladies than the swarms of children annually coming within reach of infection are liable to measles. It is under the pressure of some evil which must be speedily remedied that the study of the subject of Money grows general, and that the thinker is supported in his work. Later, when a *modus vivendi* is established in practice, when the crisis is past, and the community breathes freely again, study, and interest in the subject of study, subside; and with the absence of support for the scholar, comes default in the continuity of scientific appreciation. Without seeking further, we may perhaps find in the period just referred to an illustration in point, if we make an apposite supposition of what might have been.

In imagination we can contrast the Monetary Conference of Paris in 1867, as it was, with what it could have been had the monetary lessons of the days of Philip of Macedon, and of Alexander, been available as household words of knowledge to its Delegates.

No material has, in fact, come down to us—indeed, it is not probable that any scientific record ever existed for a thorough general understanding of the monetary events of that time; but it seems to me plain that events occurred which, like those of the period of England's history here under review, must have embodied law and evidence which under easy interpretation could have dispelled the illusions which in fact guided the deliberations of the Conference of 1867.

The action of Philip of Macedon in establishing a Gold Coinage at 12.50 to 1, side by side with Silver—presumably as a preparation for a Persian war—and the changes wrought by Alexander in the monetary relations of the busy world between Carthage and the Tigris, certainly must have afforded ground for fruitful generalization upon the habits of man as a Money-using animal. Surely the lost data for a history of the drachma and the stater, of the Daric and the Median shekel, could have taught a lesson to the franc, and the mark, the Wilhelm and the Napoleon, and to every Sovereign in the field.

But a record can be forgotten or ignored through the *laches* of the present, as well as destroyed by the barbarism of the past; and thus fields of history lie fallow, that only await cultivation in order to serve as nurseries of science.

Coming now from this retrospect to the Monetary System which the statesmen of 1696 in England sought to maintain and to perfect, we can more readily discern it in perspective, and distinguish the originality of its champions. From the point of view of universal history what is really notable and novel in the System I describe, is, as I regard it, merely the determination to maintain in its proper force of supporting numbers of coins, a Unit fixed in the metal better adapted for that function, and with that end to lower, as well as to raise, the rate of currency of coin of the other metal, as occasion should demand.

Here lies its originality.

There had been Monetary Units: but the resolution to maintain them was not a common thing. As we have seen, after standing firm in England ever since the 43rd of Elizabeth, the monetary edifice was trembling to its fall in and after 1690. And coins had been lowered, as well as raised, in various countries. But a definite policy of maintaining a single Unit and dual Money, upon a consistent plan which included lowering as well as raising the rate of currency of the subservient and rated metal, was not that settled practice of government which the authority of the statesmen of the Recoinage might, and should, have made it.

§ 17. THE GUINEA AT 21 SHILLINGS.

After the great Recoinage, the ideas of Locke and of Newton seem to have been as seed sown on stony ground. Montague and Somers, in the changing fortune of politics, were presently driven from power, and, certainly while exposed to the dangers of a partisan impeachment, could have little to say, or to think, of monetary policy. The energies of monetary statesmanship were soon relaxed. The same phenomenal supineness which had allowed recoinage to become a burning necessity; the same heedlessness which had offered the commodities and coin of England, as a prey to a swarm of "Money-mongers" on either side of the Channel, left to the mercy of events the institution which had thus been founded anew at so much cost.

Thus in the end, this act of heroic statesmanship proved, in important measure, an empty sacrifice. The glowing pages of Macaulay's unfinished History have stood unshadowed by the bathos of this finale. He was spared the task of telling the tale of the plundering of England's treasure, and how, in spite of Montague and of Somers, in spite of Newton and of Locke, the heroes of his thrilling story of gallant adventure—freighted with the hopes of a nation, and carried to masterly achievement over the waves of revolution and amid the storms of war—the Standard of England was in the end debased.

Continued default was made in not lowering the rate at which the Government accepted the guinea.

Failing such action, the guinea remained current at 21s. 6d., a rate far above its bullion value, compared with Standard Silver-coin. Evidently so long as the government offices received guineas at 21s. 6d., and so long as the Mints were bound to coin them without limit, and gratis, for all comers, commerce could find its best account in paying guineas in England, and Silver abroad. And so the full-weight standard coin of the Realm—to create a stock of which the State had spent a sum greater than its regular annual revenue, and equal to perhaps a fourth of the country's total stock of cash—was allowed to find its way back to the melting-pot in exchange for cheaper Gold, while speculators on either side of the Channel reaped richly where they had not sown. In the end, the stock of full-weight Silver-coin was brought near to exhaustion, and, the coinage of Silver being unprofitable, since Gold was the "cheaper" metal, slackened and finally ceased.

Finally, came the tardy reduction of the guinea in 1717. The conditions of the market, however, having changed (probably because the effect of England's law had been exhausted) —Gold standing below the high level which it had held at the turn of the century, and which had confused the calculations of that period—the reduction to 21s. proved insufficient; Gold at 15.21, the new ratio, was still over-valued as compared with Silver. It was not, as is usually supposed, an enactment of Parliament that made this fixation, but a Royal Proclamation, upon request of the Commons.

But of the abiding intention to maintain Silver as the Principal Money—in which term the ideas of Unit and of Chief Legal-Tender may be moulded into one—the action of Parliament and Crown in 1717-8, is conclusive evidence.[1] The new fixation of the guinea as a 21-shilling piece was occasioned entirely by the scarcity of Silver, and was expressly intended to remedy it. The over-valuation of Gold is, in fact, expressly stated in the Proclamation of George I. to have "been a great cause of carrying out and lessening the species of the Silver-coins, which is highly prejudicial to the trade of this Kingdom." To reduce the guinea to 20s. was a violent change: 20s. 6d. was inconvenient on account of the fraction, while 21s. probably appeared a sound and conservative halting-place, though it proved, in fact, quite the reverse. With guineas still, after 1717, current at an over-valuing though diminished rate, the transhipment of valuations to the lower standard was inevitable.

Thus by non-action, without apparent intention, England's monetary history of the century was made. The rich Gold-mines of Brazil, and the low ratings of Gold maintained on the

---

[1] Some of the debates in Parliament in 1717-8, the Report of Newton, the Address, and the Proclamation of the King, are reprinted in my "Material for the Study of Monetary Policy," in the Document of the Monetary Conference of 1878.

Continent—kept Gold in the main below 15 throughout the century, and Gold thus remaining, by the failure of English law, the cheaper metal in England, the self-interest of citizens, thus directed, supported a currency several per cent. below the "Standard" in the sense of the established and recognized Unit of Value.

With the impression of this "lame and impotent conclusion" upon us, we can conveniently return to the consideration of the policy applicable to the rating of Gold.

I doubt not the question has quickly taken shape in the reader's mind: "How did it come to pass that a nation of England's force failed to attain an object so plainly within reach of her statesmen as the maintenance of her Monetary Standard in its intended place?"

In the maze of causes or conditions which are responsible for this default, and hence can yield answer to our question, one element of the situation seems to me to detach itself from the mass, and to hold proportions quite commensurate with the occasion. This element is, as I shall state it, the novelty of Gratuitous Free Coinage, and the likelihood that an entirely adequate comprehension of the effect of its working would be lacking.

To-day, in the expanse of the Doctrine of Money, there are so many vast spaces unexplored, that it is by no means strange that mere shortness of vision should have limited the legislator's view at the period of which we write. Who indeed can say that Free and Gratuitous Coinage is so well understood to-day, that even among adepts the applications of that knowledge are commonplaces of thought? A right of the individual to have bullion turned into Money by Government officers with all convenient speed, is given by Free Coinage.[1] The

---

[1] "Free" in the sense in which the word has been used of late years. Lord Liverpool, Mr. Hamilton, and others of the elder writers, use the word "Free" to convey the idea of "Gratuitous Coinage," as well as of what I call "Free Coinage." Believing that it would be a profitable

right to have this work done without expense to the bringer-in, is given by Gratuitous Coinage, and these two rights were, so to speak, created by the statute of 1666.

The Literature of Money is abundant throughout the centuries, but I venture to think that the economic importance of a System of Free Coinage, as compared with what I have called the Seigniorial System, still awaits adequate elucidation. Indeed, I very much fear I shall be presenting a view which has a certain novelty, if I observe that so long as (or wherever) Coinage is treated as a prerogative of a *Münz-herr*, of a Lord of the Mint, whatever his title, rather than an established right of the individual, so long (or there) does Money hold some of the attributes of what we know to-day as a Token-Money, as distinguished from that true Commodity-Money, or, —if I may compound a new word to fit a compound idea— that subdivided-metal-Money, with which England's law has made the world familiar. There is here in my belief a distinction which has not yet gained its meed of general recognition in monetary literature.

Now it is plain that to reduce the guineas meant a certain burden and loss to many holders of them, the number and the burden all the greater as the stock of Gold was now probably greater than the stock of Silver, and it was natural that members of Parliament should be unwilling to impose upon their constituents any greater loss than was obviously necessary. But what was necessary? Here arose the practical difficulty. The precedent of earlier days in England, and the example of contemporary administration of Coinage, all the outgrowth of the Seigniorial System, of charging a heavy percentage for the benefit of the State, in addition to the actual

---

amendment in monetary terminology to distinguish the right to have bullion turned into coin, from the right to have the work of coinage done at the expense, not of the depositor, but of the State. I have used " Free Coinage" to designate the former only, and " Gratuitous Coinage" the latter,—and have used all opportunities to naturalize the distinction.

cost of Coinage united to obscure the path of the legislator.

Had England adopted the policy of a Gold-token currency, which seems to have obtained in the Peninsula, her standard might have been maintained without a greater reduction of the guinea. But to do this, it was necessary to charge Seigniorage on Gold, or limit the coinage of it, or withhold from depositors the privilege of having bullion made Money, or to adopt a combination of these measures. This, however, could only be brought about by inducing Parliament to change the law, to repeal the Act of 1666, or omit to re-enact it in full or in part.

I have no evidence that this plan was ever suggested. But at the same time there is little evidence that the high ratios of the Peninsula were recognized in their true character. If these high ratios served to warrant Calonne in raising the French ratio in 1785 from $14.^{58}$ to $15\frac{1}{2}$ as they did,[1] and to encourage Benton and Calhoun in raising the American ratio in 1834 from 15 to 16, as they did, it is certainly not strange that in earlier days they should have encouraged a similar attempt on the part of England to maintain a high ratio.

This condition of things, to which the fixation of 1717 failed to bring the expected remedy, was naturally a grievance to many right-minded Englishmen. From beginning to end of the century, monetary literature speaks, one might almost say, with one voice of regret, at the practical, not intended so much as permitted, debasement of the Standard. A single quotation may suffice to represent the spirit of many.[2] The following is from Joseph Harris, one of the soundest of writers on Money. It is from the preface of the second volume of his "Essays on Money and Coin" (1757). The volume is,

---

[1] See Document of the Conference of 1878, pp. 257-9, 262. (Ditto, Conf. of 1881, p. 257.) See also Benton's speech, p. 673.

[2] See also Appendix 18.

in effect, a plea for lowering the guinea; 20 shillings being the rate apparently in view.

"My purpose is," says the author, "to defend every man's right and property; to preserve unsullied the national faith, honour, and credit; to preserve a reign hitherto distinguished by equal laws and equal administration of justice, from a blot that would remain to all posterity; to vindicate and defend all these, I say, from an assassination in the dark, by a debasement of the long-established Standard of property."[1]

But the failure to lower the rating of the guinea did not stand alone among the instances of neglect in dealing with the Money of the realm.

Hardly two generations had passed since the Recoinage of the Silver in 1696, before a progressive deterioration of the Gold-coin had declared itself, which slowly forced its way to public recognition. An end was finally put to this disorder by the General Recoinage of the Gold-coin of 1774, a measure, the successful operation of which (see also p. 125) was largely due to the wise counsels of Mr. Jenkinson (afterwards Lord Liverpool).

But this, again, is by no means the only modern instance of monetary evils growing acute through a course of procrastination. Independently of that general Recoinage which

---

[1] A curious instance of that confusion of meanings of the word Standard hereinbefore so fully analyzed, lately struck my eye on looking into the "Dictionnaire de l'Economie Politique" (Guillaumin) to see what notice was accorded to Harris. The article (translated from MacCulloch) notes that the second volume contains a powerful plea against the debasement of the *titre*, that is to say, of the *fineness*. It would be difficult to discover a better illustration of those defects of terminology for which I have endeavoured to promulgate a remedy. The author of the first comprehensive treatise on Money—for I take Chevalier's great work, "La Monnaie," to be no less than this—was one of the editors of the Dictionary. And yet the translator was allowed to take the word "Standard" in Sense No. 2 of the Introduction to this work, and so misses completely a goodly part of the significance of one of the best books, as MacCulloch says, that has ever been published on the subject.

began in 1816, the historian has to relate that to-day, in the full tide of the Gold Standard, England finds herself confronted with an appreciable abrasion of her Gold-coin, to remedy which a Chancellor of the Exchequer has proposed a veiled and partial debasement of the Standard. In the presence of such evidence of the disabilities under which others have laboured, in coping with a deterioration of Money under the insidious inroads of time, the *laches* of the immediate successors of the statesmen of the Great Recoinage is relieved, by comparison, of at least a portion of blame.

On a later page (§ 22) I shall seek to estimate the necessity, or to characterize the causes, of this failure. In the chapter directly following this, I shall show how, at a turning-point of England's history, that fatality of unattractiveness to which I have adverted (pp. 113-116) which haunts the politics of Money, asserted its baleful influence on a weighty scale, in the failure of an accepted guide to apprehend the teachings of the immediate past in his own country.

It is in Lord Liverpool's unconsciousness of truths that were as household words to an earlier generation that an explanation of later history is to be found.

CHAPTER VII.

A LESSON OF HISTORY (*continued*).—THE ABANDONMENT OF THE SILVER POUND.

§ 18. THE ARGUMENTS OF LORD LIVERPOOL.

In spite of the opinion reflected in the writings of Harris and of Stewart, the policy of further reducing the rating of the guinea appears to have received no serious attention from the rulers of the country; and the general condition of the circulation remained, till the close of the XVIIIth century, what it had been in its middle decades, save for the amelioration produced by the General Recoinage of the Gold-coin in 1774.

By this measure, the plan and execution of which are understood to redound to the credit of Mr. Jenkinson, afterward Lord Liverpool (see Appendix 19), regulations were made, not only for coining the nation's stock of Gold anew, but for maintaining the coins in proper condition. This most laudable effort was afterwards described by Lord Liverpool as re-establishing the principle of Legal Tender by weight as well as by tale. In connection with the Recoinage, a statute was passed relating to the Silver-coin which was subsequently revived by other Acts, and which has given rise to general misapprehension; as may be seen in books which contain references to their effect down to the present day.[1]

[1] Lord Liverpool himself, after stating correctly the purport of the law

The occasion of the original Act appears to have been the importation of " considerable quantities of light Silver-coin of the nation, or, coin purporting to be such ; " and, in prohibiting the importation of such coin, the Act withdrew from light coin the privilege of being Legal Tender by tale, for sums above £25.

The effect of the Act is, that a tender of Silver-coins for a debt above £25, in order to be binding in law, must be an offer of coin enough to make up the weight which the proper number of pounds sterling should weigh, at the rate of 5s. 2d. per ounce of standard Silver. It is evident that where the coins were of full weight, the restriction had no application. This law, however, was in force, at first, for only nine years, the statute expiring in 1783.

It will appear, upon evidence presented in later pages, that it was in the years closely following this date, that form was given to the body of argument which subsequently became the " Treatise on the Coins of the Realm." When this work was undertaken, the circulation held little Silver other than coins worn down so that they were hardly more than counters. The monetary question of the day was, how this

(on page 14) says on another page, " The Silver-coins of this realm considered as coins are now Legal Tender only in sums not exceeding £25. . . . Such appears to be the law on this subject." (P. 144.)

" The Act which declared them [the Silver-coins] not to be Legal Tender for any sum exceeding £25 did not pass before 1774." (P. 183.)

In the speech of the second Lord Liverpool in the House of Lords in support of the new Coinage Act, the limitation was stated in the same way, but at £5.

See also Professor Leone Levi's " History of British Commerce," the first edition. In a second edition, lately published, the errors are corrected.

Having had occasion, some time ago, to ascertain the facts, I found it germane to set forth with some fulness the results of my examination (" Silver and Gold," 1876), and, later, to present the evidence in full, by reprinting the statutes, which will be found in the Document of the Conference of 1878, with a title, which conveyed my characterization of them, as " Measures for Maintaining the Coin at Full Weight."

defective state of the Silver-coin was to be remedied. It was hardly advisable for the Government to buy Silver bullion at a premium above the legal ratio and issue Silver-coins at that ratio, for the coins would at once be melted down, and so in the end the Government would have lost the amount of the premium and cost of coinage, and have gained nothing for its pains. This state of affairs had long endured; Silver had been at a small premium over Gold (as compared with the Mint ratio) during the entire course of Lord Liverpool's life. To meet the desideratum of a proper circulation of Silver-coin under these circumstances was, therefore, the practical problem with which he had to deal. The question was, how to make and keep good Silver-coins; and it was in view of this actual situation in the XVIIIth century, when it had proved impracticable under the law as it stood to make and keep good Silver-coins, that his treatise was conceived. The fate reserved for Lord Liverpool's work was peculiar. The adoption of its special suggestions did not become a practical matter till after many years had passed, and till a new order of events, both at home and abroad, had quite altered the terms of the problem to be solved by new legislation. As will be shown in the following section, Lord Liverpool's scheme was not adopted in full; some parts of it seemed to have been swept away, as it were, by the momentum of his general argument in support of its main feature—the reduction of the Legal-Tender of Silver to £2.

That the author's point of view is that of the statesman, the jurist, rather than of the banker, the statistician, the economist, is an observation suggested by the career of his active years, as well as justified by analysis of the work. But how far is this great advantage of position supplemented by appropriate utilization of the results of tributary specialist study? The answer is given by the fact, that the treatise was the product of the leisure hours of a retired Minister, deprived of the advantages which come from the criticism of publicity or of controversy, and from the teaching of practical experience.

The loftiness of its style is not more marked than the involved and tortuous course of its argumentation—peculiarities which are, however, in one sense, really alike elements of strength, as impressing the reader with a dignity and profundity, or rather an impregnable solidity, befitting ideas which have since become institutions. But while the peculiarity first mentioned may be held to have been imposed in a letter from subject to King, the latter seems a natural incident of the peculiar difficulties which attended the composition of the work.

It is but justice to accompany adverse criticism upon his ideas with evidence which relieves the author from the charge of negligence.

"At this period," says Lord Liverpool (namely, in 1798), "I was seized with a violent disease, which has now confined me to my house, and generally to my couch, for more than four years—unable to hold a pen, *or to turn over the leaves of a book, from which I might derive information*. At intervals, however, when I have of late providentially obtained some respite from pain and extreme weakness, I have endeavoured to revise so much as I had before occasionally written :—to arrange other materials previously collected :—and to reduce the whole to a form not unfit for perusal. *A Treatise written on so abstruse and complicated a subject, by one exposed to great infirmities, must contain some repetitions, slight inaccuracies, and other imperfections*. Arrived as I now am on the verge of life, I hasten to present what I have thus written, though not exempt from errors, to Your Majesty, as my last service—if it shall deserve that name—in grateful remembrance of the generous protection which Your Majesty has never ceased to afford me, and of the many and great favours which you have graciously conferred on me." (From page 8, of Lord Liverpool's Treatise. Edition of 1846.)

On another page he observes :—

"I have now completed all I proposed to write on the Coins of the realm, and I have treated shortly of Paper currency, so far as the Coins are affected by it. It is not impossible that a Treatise on a subject so abstruse and intricate, and consequently so difficult to be understood, may be thrown aside by many, and, perhaps, treated with levity; I remember that such was the case when the recoinage of the Gold Coin was undertaken in the year 1774. It is possible that even those who are not without a desire for information may object, that I have consumed too much labour on points that are not worth it—*In tenui labor*. To these my answer is, that they are little aware of how much importance to the commerce of the country is a good monetary system, founded on principles of wisdom and justice; and how much Coins, particularly those of a lower denomination, contribute to the convenience of the inferior orders of society. I am not ashamed, therefore, in my present state of retirement, to have employed my leisure hours on this subject—a subject which occupied the attention and talents of men of no less character than Sir William Petty and Mr. Locke.

"To Your Majesty, if any apology is necessary, I may venture to offer other pleas in my justification. When I was in Your Majesty's service, in the year 1774, I first turned my thoughts to this subject, in discharge of my public duty. It was in obedience to Your Majesty's commands that I resumed the consideration of it, after a long interval, when you appointed me, in 1797, one of the members of the Committee of Privy Council for Coins; *and though a short time afterwards, by the pressure of disease, all thoughts of this nature were blotted from my recollection*, I have experienced, at length, by the favour of Providence, a partial recovery; and awakened, as it were, from the sleep of death, I have been induced a third time to take up the consideration of this subject by the representations that were made to me by Your Majesty's late ministers, of the distressed state of the southern parts of

Ireland, where almost all Coins have disappeared, where a most degraded system of Paper currency has taken the place even of the Silver Coins, and where this Paper currency, from the quantity that has been issued, has fallen in its value, and, consequently, into a state of discredit, very embarrassing to the poorer ranks of Your Majesty's subjects in those parts.

"The subject of which I have treated is of such a nature, that it certainly has no charms to attract the attention of any man; it is, therefore, from a sense of duty alone, *that I have been induced to complete, under all my infirmities, what I had before projected.* Conscious of my own inability at all times to fathom a science, on which men of the most eminent talents have disagreed, I offer with the greatest deference what I have thus written to Your Majesty's consideration. Certain I am, that it will be treated by Your Majesty with every proper degree of candour, and accepted with your accustomed condescension." (Pages 249-251. The italics are mine.)

A notable feature of Lord Liverpool's presentation of his subject is the appeal to precedent in support of his idea of making Gold the Sole Full-Legal-Tender Money of England. His reference to Sir William Petty and to Mr. Locke (in the passage just quoted) is indicative of the general characteristics of the Treatise. He chiefly endeavours to commend his conclusions by precedent and authority—for which he seeks to lay a broad and solid foundation by a review of the history of Monetary Policy and of Monetary Opinion in England—to the learning and acumen of which the recognition of the student of Money is due, but which is infected throughout with a fallacious inequality and incompleteness. It is through this method, involving an apparent remoteness from dogmatic statement, or from abstruse ideas, that he seems to succeed in establishing for the new legislation which he proposes and justifies, a character for a wise conservatism, as being an advance upon lines recommended by a long experience; an impression which has imposed itself upon his own and later generations.

I have endeavoured to describe in Chapter IV. certain regions of thought, some portion of which may have contributed to Lord Liverpool's general ideas of Money, through which he contemplates its history; and I now seek to consider in detail the distinctions upon which he bases his argument, and the conclusions which he seeks to establish.

In presenting my views, I must, if only for brevity's sake, deal with the Treatise upon its merits as a controversial work, which in the controversies of to-day is still a living force; attacking it directly with whatever advantage I may gain from facts newly ascertained, or from truths which are the outgrowth of the present century, and naturally place the critic of to-day at an advantage as compared with the writer of a century ago. But in doing so, I desire also to record my appreciation of the contribution to Monetary Learning embraced in the "Treatise on the Coins of the Realm," and to observe that the default of later times in not emulating Lord Liverpool's diligence in the arid and thankless field of Monetary Study is chiefly chargeable for what is to be regretted in the practical results that followed from his errors.

To one who has read the foregoing pages, Lord Liverpool's argument can be tersely described as the result of confounding together the distinctions which are briefly set forth in the Introduction. Subjected to the analysis which I have there presented—and which, I allow myself to believe, may serve for the anatomy of an institution, as well as for the definition of a term—his reasoning can perhaps be most easily reduced to its ultimate or simplest elements. He ignores Meanings Nos. 5 and 6 for the benefit of Meaning No. 7: the Money Unit is out of sight, while the Principal Legal-Tender occupies the foreground—the distinction between rating, and rated, Money is lost. The result is confusion: a complex of misapprehension of fact, of misapplication of precedent, of misinterpretation of principle.

Should the reader desire, with the minimum of exertion,

to receive the proof which sustains these charges, I suggest that this end can be gained if he refresh his remembrance of the distinctions set forth in the Introduction by the light reflected upon them in Chapter IV.; and that he recall again the relation given in the present and preceding chapters of the actual course of England's later monetary experience.

In the terminology of Monetary Law and of publicistic discussion in the XVIIth and XVIIIth centuries, " current coins," " Money," " Measure of Commerce," " the Standard (or the ancient or true Standard) Money of the Realm" are accepted terms to cover the ideas we are now dealing with. These terms, it must be admitted, fail to convey with precision the distinctions upon which I lay such stress. What, then, is the historical or legal basis for these distinctions? These are the points which it is essential to make clear, and to these we now address ourselves.

Silver was the material of the Pound Sterling; and in the Pound Sterling of twenty Silver shillings, we have Meaning No. 5—the National Unit of Coinage. The current coins and Money were of Gold and Silver; and here we find Meaning No. 6. In the Measure of Commerce, the true or ancient Standard Money, as also in Newton's phrase, " the sole fixed Money of the Realm," we find Meaning No. 7 conjoined with Meaning No. 8; the Principal Legal-Tender and National Unit being either in fact, or *intended to be*, of the same material.

But, as has just been suggested (see also Chapter IV.), this conjunction, though desirable and important, is not inevitable. A desire, an object of policy, a principle to be maintained, are implied in the compound of the two meanings, as well as in each meaning separately.

Here I may perhaps supply links in my chain of argument which otherwise may fail to receive the reader's notice, if I remark that, with this order of considerations, we find ourselves in territory quite foreign to that which ordinarily is held within range of Economic Science, as it is currently defined. The rightful position of law in the doctrine of Money (with which I have dealt elsewhere at some length) [1] is peculiarly exemplified in the events with which we have now to deal. It was possible that this desire, this intent, of which I have spoken, might lack fulfilment, in varying measure; it might come to pass that the material of which the National Unit was made might cease to be the Chief-Legal-Tender, just as it might come to pass that the legitimate National Unit could be dispossessed entirely.

But did it, for that, cease to be a " Standard ?" By no means! We have, then, to do merely with the very familiar case of dispossession, of disseisin, of usurpation. Certainly a legitimate standard which has been ousted from its rightful place, is a different thing from a standard in possession; my contention is only that there is ample place for both of them in that hierarchy of " economic facts " with which Monetary Science has to deal. Of the ideas of ownership or possession, of legitimacy and usurpation, the words I have mentioned as forming the current stock also fail to give any adequate account; and it is this lack—which Lord Liverpool seems to have failed to appreciate and which has never, so far as I know, been well supplied—which I am now seeking to make good.

And it is a vital thing to do this because the defect of nomenclature is not a defect of evidence. The lack of separate words to express these meanings is not due to the absence of experience requiring this classification, and likely to be better apprehended through more convenient names.

So far as the National Unit of Coinage is concerned, my distinction applies plainly enough to the time when the

---

[1] In " Silver and Gold," " Monetary Situation in 1878," &c. See also Documents of the Conferences of 1878 and of 1881, and especially therein in a Paper on " The Position of Law in the Doctrine of Money " (reprinted, London, 1882).

"Measure was lost" in 1695, through the mutilation of the Silver-coins, as well as to the reign of depreciated and inconvertible Paper Pounds Sterling in the opening decade of our century. The Silver Pound Sterling of twenty full-weight shillings had certainly a legal existence in 1695, and so had a Metallic Pound before and after 1816, though government and citizens were dealing in Paper Pounds. The same observation applies to the right of being Principal Legal-Tender. Did Silver cease to be the legitimate Measure of Commerce, the one legitimate ancient Standard Money of the Realm, in the sense of Principal Legal-Tender (while retaining its place as National Unit)—when Gold gained the ascendency over Silver in the circulation? In other words, as soon as they found themselves a majority, did Gold coins *ipso facto* usurp the place of Measure of Commerce in the sense of *legitimate* Principal Legal-Tender? By no means! Such an event occurred both in the earlier half of the XVIIth century as well as at the opening of the XVIIIth. Gold became the Principal Legal-Tender, in fact. In the earlier century the effort to restore to Silver its majority in the circulation was successful; while in the XVIIIth the effort was made, and was long persevered in.

As has been shown on earlier pages, the suggestions of Locke, the repeated recommendations of Newton, all in accord with the spirit of the Monetary System which their generation had inherited, were followed in 1717 by acts of Parliament and of the Crown, which can have no other meaning than to bring Gold into its proper subordination to Silver; and the subsequent agitation in favour of reducing the guinea to 20 shillings, of which a glimpse is given on page 122, is but an echo of this principle which is consecrated by repeated acts of Parliament and of the Crown.

To describe the situation in figures borrowed from the law, the possession, or let us say a present estate, passed to Gold—but it remained liable to be replaced by Silver; and when, in the lapse of time, the possession of Gold (both as Chief Money and as Unit) came to be regarded as a ripening into full title, the return of Silver, like a reversion, still held a place in the popular mind as legitimate. It was the work of the Act of 1816 to cut off this reversion. But, in fact, the Act went further: it also disinherited Silver of its right as Full-Legal-Tender, to which its title had ripened undisturbed through all the centuries of Monetary Law in Britain.

The advice of Lord Liverpool thus established a triple aim, as worthy of effort on the part of lawgivers:—

1. Formally to replace a Silver Unit with a Gold Unit.
2. To secure to Gold the position, not only of *chief*, but of *sole*, Legal-Tender by measures
3. To oust Silver entirely from its position, as Full-Legal-Tender.

I have shown that the real object and reason for this proposition was, that good Silver-coins could not be kept in circulation—a difficulty which had remained, during the greater part of Lord Liverpool's life, a practical hindrance to a proper reformation of the Silver-coins. But the means are obviously out of all proportion to the end in view—a trip-hammer to kill a fly—and the incongruity reaches a far higher degree when it is realized that in fact (as will be shown on a later page) in the last decade of Lord Liverpool's life, the main cause of the difficulty he sought to remedy had disappeared. Waiving the question of the necessity of a reconstruction of the Monetary System of Great Britain, and inquiring merely whether his book can stand as a justification of his scheme upon the ground which he himself had chosen—namely, as a legal argument, an appeal to historical precedent—it is now plain that foundation and superstructure are alike defective.

Both in scientific insight and in practical ability, the author of the Treatise shows himself inferior to his predecessors and authorities with whom he seeks to establish his concurrence.

If we imagine any one of these men—whether it be Sir

William Petty, or Locke, or Joseph Harris—dealing with such questions as arose after the prohibition of Silver Coinage and the suspension of Specie Payments in England, and after the new settlement of the Coinage System in France, we shall recognize the impossibility of their falling into the confusion and contradictions which characterize the Treatise.

In place of the wider considerations which their writings prove to be the natural standpoint which Lord Liverpool's predecessors in the office of monetary adviser of England had occupied, we find a series of pleas of peculiarly narrow range.

Notable among these is the first appearance—and a most modest *début* it is for so great a performer—of the idea of a preference for Gold, which is supposed to have risen to feeble consciousness in the days of the Recoinage of 1696. It is hinted that the high rate at which guineas passed was due to this preference, and stress is laid, in support of the argument, upon the general consent of the people then and after, in using Gold. It is plain that such an anachronistic caprice of the popular affections must tend to support the claims of Gold. This general consent of the people is consistently held in contrast with the authority of the Government;[1] an ascription of infallibility to the *vox populi* which, though it has a most incongruous air as coming from Lord Liverpool, has, I doubt not, done much to generate what has lately been the orthodox opinion touching the relation between Money and the State.

---

[1] The change was "brought about, not by the authority of Government, but by the course of events, with the acquiescence, and, I may say, the general consent of the people." (Treatise, P. 189.)

"This [currency of the guinea] was by general consent, and consequently at the option of the person who received them in payment, and not by the authority of the Government, so that this superior value was not in truth the legal value." (P. 144.)

"After this recoinage the Gold coins passed in payments at a higher value than that at which they were still rated in the Mint indenture, or, than the relative value of Gold to Silver at that time would justify; not, however, by the authority of the Government, but by the general consent of the people." (P. 130.)

How remote these contentions are from the realities of the case, is made apparent in the preceding pages, where the authority of the Government is seen in fact arraying in favour of Gold the perpetual preference, not for a metal but for Money, not for Gold but for gain, for *cheapness*. This was due to a mistake of the Government, for it neither intended to do this, nor apparently knew that it was doing it—the preference, or rather desire, of Ministry, Parliament, and people, being for Silver as Chief Legal-Tender with Gold as its companion. That Lord Liverpool was unaware of the points which I have set forth in the pages devoted in this work to the rating of Gold is, as far as it goes, a justification for his failing to seize the whole truth touching this matter. But that the excuse does not go very far, will be apparent when we consider certain facts which were directly within his knowledge.

These are:

First. That, as he himself testifies,[1] in the days of the Recoinage, guineas were worth as metal forty-four times as much as the average shillings in circulation, and so should have passed at forty-four shillings, and would have passed at that rate, had not the Government refused to take them for more than 30s. The "superior value" and the "legal value" which the author had been contemplating, are therefore shown to have been before his eyes in quite a different position from that he describes in the text.

Secondly. It was from a country then under the rule of depreciated Paper Money, that Lord Liverpool was framing a scheme for metallic coinage. If, therefore, a mere popular preference gives title, and possession is conclusive proof of preference, his argument would serve to justify depreciated paper as the Money for the XIXth century, as well as depreciated Gold for the XVIIIth century.

[1] "The guinea rose only to the value of thirty shillings. It is true that the farther rise of the guinea was prevented by order given to the officers of the Exchequer, and to the receivers of the public revenue, not to receive it in payment at a higher rate." (P. 85.) See also p. 79.

A cognate plea is the now familiar notion, that rich nations should have Gold, while poorer nations content themselves with inferior metals: an appeal to vanity which would be quite appropriate if systems of coinage were matter of personal adornment, and which is at best an *a priori* argument entirely unsupported by facts. That an argument of this sort should have arisen in a Paper-Money country, is a signal instance of the grim humour of fate.

In order to anticipate and prevent a misapprehension, I shall do well to refer here to later pages (Chap. X.), in which the "preference for Gold" of to-day is considered, and which reduce the present importance of such a preference to extremely narrow limits. But for a time when Silver was effectively recognized as the normal currency of the world —to borrow an excellent phrase from Mr. Bagehot—the literal application of the ideas of to-day involves an anachronism. The reader can obtain a glimpse into the subtleties of this matter of "Preference for Gold," if he dwell thoughtfully upon the psychological condition of the plexus of business communities in Europe, which during an entire century, from 1700 to 1800, "preferred" Gold to Silver, but only to the extent of about fifteen to 'one: beyond that rate they "preferred" Silver to Gold.

Lord Liverpool's argument may be epigrammatically stated as follows : " People prefer Gold Money to Silver so much, that they will have it at any rate, and therefore we must make laws to prevent their using Silver Money if they desire to do so."

On another page, the author seriously presents the idea that Gold is to be preferred to Silver, because Gold is less liable to fluctuations of value than Silver : a contention not only erroneous, but obviously improbable when Gold was in some countries a trade coin, in others a rated coin, and generally recognized as the variable portion, while Silver was recognized as the fixed portion of existing Money, and when Silver made an overwhelming majority of it. How little Lord Liverpool apprehended the burden of proof which he undertook to sustain by this contention, is shown by his relying entirely upon evidence showing that *Silver* Bullion fluctuated in *London* more than *Gold* Bullion, *as against Gold Guineas!*

To complete this unique company of arguments, we note here the remark that Gold-coins are superior to Silver-coins, because the former " have a substitute which the Silver-coins have not, at least in an equal degree ; they may be represented by Notes or Paper Currency ; which will answer the purpose of all great commercial transactions, etc." (P. 182.) I cite this remark, in order to exemplify beyond a question the peculiarities of the author's work. At first glance the proposition may seem not merely false, but absurd ; but I do not find it to be so in fact. The point which I believe Lord Liverpool had in mind may be stated thus : People must have small change, so if they have to send money abroad and have not Silver-coins enough to supply the pocket and the till, and yet leave a stock of Silver available for export—which was England's case from beginning to end of Lord Liverpool's life—it is better to send Gold than to send Silver, because the functions of Gold *can* be supplied by paper. The defect of the argument lies in amplifying into a general rule a suggestion of local and temporary convenience ; and the true drift of the argument is in favour, not of Gold, but merely of having an abundance of Silver change.

But the mere form in which the central thesis of the work is presented exposes in the openest manner the hollowness of the argument.[1]

---

[1] This thesis appears in the various categories of what ought to be, should be, can only be, must be, is, and is to be made. An examination and comparison of the following extracts will prove the correctness of the views I have advanced.

" The Money, or coin, which is to be the principal measure of property, *ought to be made of one metal only.* Such is the opinion of Sir William Petty, Mr. Locke, Mr. Harris, and of all the eminent writers on coin." (P. 13.)

" And if the coins, which are the principal measure of property, and instruments of commerce, *can only be made of one* of these Metals." (P. 15.)

His thesis is, that the coins which are to be the principal measure of property, should be made of one metal only. (P. 169.)

Now, so far as I know, no one proposed, nor do I find any evidence that Lord Liverpool had in view, any scheme that coins should be made of *more than one metal*. There was no plan pending in England of coining a compound of two or

"Certain, however, as the principle is—that the Money or coins of any country which are to be the principal measure of property, *can be made of one metal only*." (P. 15.)

"First, I will endeavour to prove that the coins which are to be the principal measure of property, *ought to be made of one Metal only*. . . . . I have observed that Sir William Petty, Mr. Locke, and Mr. Harris, are decidedly of opinion that the coins, which are to be the principal measure of property, *must be made of one metal only*; and it has been assumed that their opinion on this point is too well-founded to be shaken. Lest, however, this assumption should be supposed to be premature, I will here insert the passages themselves which so fully justify it." (P. 124.)

"There is no circumstance that more clearly proves the truth of this principle, 'That coins which are to be the principal measure of property, *can be made of one metal only*'" (than the practice of using 'Bank Money'). (P. 132.)

"From thence results the necessity, in this country, of having coins *made of one metal only*, which should serve as an invariable measure." (P. 135.)

"From the view I have thus given of this part of the argument, it appears, not only from the clearest deduction of reason, and by the concurrent opinion of the most eminent writers, but by the evidence, which long experience in this Kingdom has afforded, to be a certain and incontrovertible principle that coins, which are to have the principal measure of property, *can be made but of one metal only*." (P. 136.)

"As it is clear that the coins, which are to be the principal measure of property, *can only be made of one metal*." (P. 136.) "It will be fortunate if this principal measure of property shall be found within these realms to be in coins *of one metal*." (P. 138.)

"After full consideration of this extensive, abstruse, and intricate subject, I humbly offer to Your Majesty, as the result of my opinion:—

"First, that the coins of this realm which are to be the principal measure of property and instrument of Commerce, *should be made of one metal only*.

"Secondly, that in this Kingdom the Gold-coins only have been for many years past, and are now, in the practice and opinion of the people,

moro metals, an *elektron*, like that of ancient times, or billon, the grossly alloyed metal current on the Continent, or, again, what has lately been suggested in the United States, under the name of a "goloid" coin. In view of this fact, Lord the principal measure of property and instrument of Commerce." (P. 167.)

"If the system now recommended should be adopted, and the Gold-coins *be made* the principal measure of property and Standard coin. . . ." (P. 169.)

"My opinion is, and I hope I shall be excused in repeating it, that the Gold-coins *should continue to be* the principal Measure of Property and instrument of Commerce." (P. 175.)

Such, then, are Lord Liverpool's " principal" statements of law and fact.

A direct and categorical denial and refutation of some of these statements is, however, supplied by no less an authority than Lord Liverpool himself.

He observes, on Page 139 :—" From the 41st Henry III. (1256-7) when Gold-coins began to be coined in the Mints of this Kingdom, and the coins so made of Gold were ordered to be current at a certain nominal value, it must be admitted that these Gold-coins became Legal-Tender no less than the Silver-coins, and consequently that they were from thenceforth *equally with the Silver-coins, the legal measure of property.*"

This, he observes, continued till the date of the coinage of the guinea in 1663, at which date the Gold-coins ceased to be a legal measure of property, a rule which prevailed till 1717, "when Gold and Silver-coins were *equally Legal-Tender or measure of property.*" (P. 140.)

The continued existence of this apportionment of the function of "measure of property" between Silver and Gold at the date of the composition of his Treatise is also recognized in the following passage.

"But if *this measure of property* should now in a certain degree be found to reside and exist *in coins made of different metals.* . . . ." (P. 138.)

Lord Liverpool, therefore, himself shows that law and fact which ought to be, can only be, must be, is, is to continue, and must be made, was disproved by the actual practice of England between the time of Henry III. and 1663, and after 1717. Now, inasmuch as it has been shown in the preceding pages, that between 1663 and 1717, the law and fact are directly in opposition to his first assumption, it is plain that no standing-ground is left in modern England for his doctrine, as he states it.

The limitation of the Legal-Tender of Silver in England is—historically —the product of this phenomenal confusion of thought. "If the coins," says Lord Liverpool, "which are the principal measure of property and instruments, *can* only be made of one of these metals, the inferior coins,

Liverpool's cardinal proposition, that the principal measure of property can be made of *one* metal only, acquires an air of Hibernian simplicity. The subject contains the predicate quite as explicitly, as in the proposition "the larger of two apples can only be one apple." A short cut to final judgment upon the matter in hand will, perhaps, be found in the remark, that if we proceed upon the line marked out by his propositions (see note below) to argue that, because the larger of two apples can only be one apple, therefore it follows the smaller apple is not an apple at all, or, at least, ought not to be so regarded, we shall have sounded the depth and completed the circuit of Lord Liverpool's reasoning.

Before leaving the subject, it is germane to call attention to a curious circumstance, which casts some light on the situation we are considering. I refer to a plea of Lord Liverpool, alleging acquiescence, or waiver, on the part of creditors, as to the debasement of the Standard. When the National Debt was converted, in 1749, from 4 to 3 per cent., an option, he says (page 190), was given to the fundholders to receive their capital. Not availing themselves of this option, they may be held to have waived the point of payment in Silver. But in what "Standard" was payment offered? In Standard

---

made of other metals, *must be* Legal-Tender *only in a limited degree.*" (P. 15.) The reader will note that the *idea of inferiority* is here introduced. For this we may have been prepared by the exercise of the author's prerogative of *defining the sense in which his words are to be taken.*

"The coins which are to be the principal measure of property must, of course, be Legal-Tender without limitation. I shall call this *superior* sort of Money, or coins, the principal measure of property, or *Standard coin*; and having clearly defined my idea, I conceive I *have a right to make use* of these terms *in the sense which I have given to them*." (P. 14.)

And this transition from the fact of a dual Full Legal-Tender, to the doctrine which is the progenitor of the single-metallism of our day, is made in despite of the author's own definition. "The coins of every Kingdom or State *are the measure of property* within every such Kingdom or State, according to the nominal value declared and authorized by the Sovereign, *so far as they are made Legal-Tender.*" (P. 18.) (All the italics are mine.)

Silver-coins of full weight? Hardly. In Gold-coins, which should be equal in market value to such Silver-coins? Lord Liverpool does not say so. Either of these supposed offers would have added a percentage not to be despised to the National Debt, as reckoned in Gold. We are left to infer that payment was offered in guineas, by tale, at 21 shillings,—that is, above their real value. In this case, the option was not an option which touched the question of the Standard at all. Hence there was no waiver, no acquiescence. What more signal evidence than this extravagant error could be found of that lack of precision in monetary thought which seems to belong to the time when he wrote; when the interest of the Public Debt was paid in depreciated Paper, and when a concerted effort of leaders of opinion was needed in order to enlighten the public touching a fact which, to-day, would generally seem self-evident; namely, that tho "high price of bullion" meant that the Paper Money was depreciated?

§ 19. THE ANTI-SILVER STATUTES AND LORD LIVERPOOL'S SCHEME.

In referring the origin of the Anti-Silver policy of England to Lord Liverpool, I have pursued the familiar form of presentation under which an institution is seen as "the lengthened shadow of the man."

That this generalization has narrow limits in certain directions, is an obvious remark. The people and the leaders of England were not, in this matter, mere will-less instruments of a higher power. At the same time, it must be clearly recognized that—perhaps because Monetary Policy is so peculiarly forbidding a region among the sciences of legislation—no salient personality arose in the generation that followed him to dispute with Lord Liverpool the prestige of mastery of it, so that events shaped themselves to relieve the momentum of his influence from friction or resistance.

It will, however, be apparent, as we come to examine carefully the statutes which found place upon the Statute-book, that England proceeded in fact much further in the line of hostility to Silver than the author of the "Treatise on the Coins of the Realm" himself had proposed. Lord Liverpool's scheme of a National System of Coinage is, therefore, entitled to be regarded independently, and in contrast with the Acts of Parliament, and their practical operation, as administered by successive Governments.

The Acts here referred to are, first, the laws of 1798 and 1799, by which the Act mentioned on page 125 was revived, with the addition of clauses which first suspended, and then entirely prohibited, the Coinage of Silver; and second, the Act of 1816, which established Gold as the sole Standard.

The law of 1798-9 seems to have been passed in pursuance to the recommendations of a Committee of the Privy Council, of which Lord Liverpool was a member. In the Statute itself the appearance of Silver Bullion asking to be coined at the Tower Mint is mentioned as the ground of the new clauses; but there is nothing in the Statute affecting the status of existing Silver-coin except as stated on page 126, nor is there any provision formally affecting the Unit of Coinage, or giving a new definition of the Pound Sterling.

With the reign of Paper, 1797-1819, a new element of confusion in the relative position of the metals and coins was introduced. Upon this period I shall make no special comment here, but allow myself to refer the curious reader to other writings bearing on the subject.[1]

In order to form an adequate judgment touching the influence of the Anti-Silver Policy as a whole, it is necessary to distinguish three quite distinct periods, namely: 1st, the

---

[1] See a chapter on the example of England, in a Treatise on "Silver and Gold" (Cincinnati. 1876-7), and certain "Contributions to the Study of Monetary Policy" in the Document of the Conference of 1878.

Restriction of Cash Payment (that is, of the obligation of the Bank of England to pay its notes on demand in Legal Coin); 2nd, Resumption of Cash Payments (replacement of Paper Money by the new Gold sovereigns and convertible notes); and 3rd, The following years down to 1873.

In the publications lately named (page 144), I have set forth, in detail, my grounds for the opinion that the prohibition of Silver Coinage by the Acts of 1798-9, in the first period, and the practical exclusion of Silver by the Law of 1816, in the second, tended materially to augment the monetary evils under which England then suffered, which were of controlling influence upon her economic life, and thus left their mark upon social and political conditions.

As to the latter period—beginning, let us say, in 1830—I waive discussion here. I am quite content it shall be assumed that what is called the "Gold Standard"—meaning thereby the exclusion of Silver from Free Coinage and Full-Legal-Tender, for that is what is peculiar and important in the System—worked well during this period. By this, of course, I do not admit that the Silver and Gold Standard would not have worked better,—a remark which I make independently of the remoter consequences of the Outlawry of Silver in England; namely, the adoption of England's plan by Germany, and the partial extension of that Outlawry over the Occidental World.

But I desire, also, most distinctly to affirm that the Anti-Silver-policy,—the practical adoption of which began, as I have shown,[1] in 1798, rather than in 1816, the date generally referred to in Monetary Literature,—must suffer the ordinary fate of humanity, in that it must be judged upon its own merits. I am, indeed, quite resolute in insisting that the reader shall vivify and clarify his perception, that this policy should not be judged upon merits other than its own. I therefore

---

[1] See Document of the Conference of 1878, pp. 86, 348.

remark, that it is one thing to adopt and establish a system, and quite another thing to inherit it. In speaking of the period of Restriction and of Resumption, when Anti-Silver-policy was peculiarly harmful, I speak of the adopting, not of the inheriting, of the plan of excluding Silver. It was only when it became an inheritance, when it passed into the hands of the second generation, that it became comparatively harmless. But it is quite clear that the failure of a system in twenty-five or thirty years of trial, is a sufficient failure. That is enough for the present purpose. It warrants conclusive judgment of condemnation.

It is not, however, implied by this condemnation of the measures which were actually adopted, that, as opposed to them, the sole alternative was the maintenance, after 1798, of the system which had been in force prior to that date, namely, Silver and Gold Money with Silver Unit and Coinage Free and Gratuitous at 15.[21] to 1. That system could, of course, have been amended, as well as abrogated or abolished. My assertion has only this effect, that the exclusion of Silver from the Mints between 1798 and 1816, and its degradation from the position of Standard Money in 1816, were errors of policy which entailed serious evils.

But, as has been indicated, this order of events, and of considerations bearing upon them, is quite distinct from the task of picturing the situation which was in Lord Liverpool's view as he wrote his Letter to the King. The story of Pandora's box is incomplete, if any trait of the innocence be left out of view, which led to the opening of it.

Lord Liverpool's work was first printed in 1805, but the internal evidence appears to indicate quite clearly that it was substantially written many years before its publication. It is, in fact, this surmise which alone can explain how events of the first importance in relation to Monetary Policy, as, for example, the state of affairs which led to the Restriction of Cash Payments (1797); the Prohibition of the Coinage of Silver (1798-9);

the rise of the Silver-price of Gold in 1798 and after; and the depreciation of the Bank of England notes, are either in the background or entirely ignored in the Treatise. It is the last-mentioned treatment that falls to the lot of the changes just mentioned in the position of Silver; *no mention of them is made in the Treatise.*

This curious fact will assume additional importance, as we come to realize the effect of this rise of Gold, relatively to Silver, upon the practical situation with which the legislator had to deal, and the peculiarly incongruous character of the law of 1798-9 which prohibited Silver Coinage.

In the situation which, as we have seen on an earlier page (127), had claimed Lord Liverpool's undivided attention, while composing the main body of his work, the rise of the Silver-price of Gold, which occurred about the turn of the century, produced a radical transformation. Was he aware of this transformation?

In 1798 Silver was brought to the Mint by private depositors to be coined. Had the Mint remained open, the lack of proper Silver-coin in England would have been, in a measure, supplied. Side by side with the worn-out coin would have appeared a goodly sum of full-weight coin. True the Government must be prepared to bear the expense of coinage, but as the Mint and machinery were there, and the staff and outlay of the Mint would need no inordinate increase, the added expense need not have been great. No doubt, any expense was onerous just at that time. But was not the lack of proper Silver-coin pressing enough to justify it? The affirmative seems abundantly proved by a variety of testimony; as, for instance, by Lord Liverpool himself,[1] who speaks in terms of

---

[1] Referring to the issue of Spanish dollars and of Bank of England Tokens, Lord Liverpool says (page 210), "The justification of this measure rests singly on the absolute necessity there was for these Silver Tokens to pay the seamen of the Royal Navy, and the artificers in the great docks of the kingdom, from the want of Coins of the lower denominations, which

severe reprehension of the failure of the Government to supply proper Silver-coin.

The fact that, with the sanction of the authorities, the Bank of England subsequently issued stamped Spanish Dollars and coined Silver Tokens in large quantities, to supply the need, is another irrefragable proof. But this need, in so far as it was felt after 1798, *was directly caused by the Act of Parliament which prohibited Silver coinage*, and that Act was, as has been stated, passed at the recommendation of the Committee of the Privy Council of which Lord Liverpool himself was a member; and in which, presumably, his influence was paramount. Indeed, the coinage was stopped by command of the Privy Council before the Act was passed.

It will not unnaturally occur to the reader, as justifying this action of the Privy Council, that some apprehension might be felt, lest by keeping the Mint open for coining Silver, an inroad of Silver-coin might come, which would lead to an exportation of Gold, and to an alteration of the Standard. But in this event, would it not have been a simple matter to limit the coinage? The limited capacity of the Mint would in itself have worked as a limitation of coinage, and the field was open for further restriction by Act of Parliament. It was hardly necessary, in order to restrain injurious coinage, to prohibit all beneficial coinage whatsoever.

---

are necessary for that purpose: the blame, therefore, if any such is to be imputed, falls, not on those who permitted these dollars to be issued, *but on those who neglected to supply Your Majesty's subjects with a sufficient quantity of legal Silver Coins, to be employed in those payments*, for which these dollars now pass. But not only Your Majesty's sailors and your own artificers are in want of legal Silver Coins, the labourers in every part of the country, and the manufacturers in the great and populous towns of this kingdom, and *all your good people in every part of it*, particularly the inferior classes, *suffer equally from the want of them*." He also observes of the existing Silver-coins (pp. 187-8), that they are so much in demand that "sometimes when they are wanted for particular purposes, they are exchanged even at a premium above their nominal value."

In this state of affairs, we should naturally look to a work of the scope of Lord Liverpool's Treatise, which became the Great Charter of Monetary Right for the XIXth century—published seven years after the passage of the Act in question—to explain, and to justify, measures of such extraordinary purport as this, which was, perhaps, the first prohibition of Silver-coinage in history, and which interfered so rudely with the normal current of business life, and caused inconveniences so onerous. But there is not a word upon the subject in the Treatise!

Again, it was, as I have indicated, the rise in the Silver-price of Gold which had afforded the motive of the Prohibition of Coinage; and this rise proved permanent. With the turn of the century the rates of the XVIIIth century, which were close to 15 to 1, had made their last appearance. The equation of the Metals fixed by the new Establishment of the Coinage in France in 1803, was $15.^{50}$ between the coins, and $15.^{69}$ if the relative charges at the Mint are taken into account to control the calculations. Now $15.^{50}$ means about 2 per cent. more Silver for Gold than $15.^{21}$, and after 1803 the Market Rates stood, generally, above $15.^{50}$,—that is to say, more than 2 per cent. above the English ratio.

I find in Lord Liverpool's work, no sign of recognition of this general alteration of the rates, although the Recoinage of the Gold-coin at $15.^{50}$ in France in 1785, of which he should have heard, but makes no mention, might have seemed prophetic of it. Of the legislation of 1803 no notice appears in the Treatise, saving, perhaps, the following passage (in a note to page 177): "It is . . . . . asserted that *for some reason or other* the National Institute of France have long had under consideration a new system of coins, particularly with the view of regulating the *relative price* of the two precious metals." The italics are mine. The most notable events of the time are thus completely ignored. Indeed, almost ideal perfection is given to the unconsciousness with which the author of the "Treatise on the Coins of the Realm" treats the practical situation which surrounds him, by the phrase "for some reason or other," which embodies his consideration for his country's great neighbour, the chief metallic power of the world, and for the international side of the monetary question, upon which he was to become so great an authority. The contrast between the range of thought of Mr. Jenkinson, Monetary Counsellor, who became the Earl of Liverpool, and Mr. Newton, who became Sir Isaac, is most brilliantly illustrated as one compares Newton's "France has set us an example," and Liverpool's remark—in a note—that the National Institute of France had long had under consideration a system for regulating the price of the precious metals —"*for some reason or other!*"

How can we account for the lack of attention which these facts reveal—the failure of a Treatise, which aims to establish the principles of England's Monetary Policy, to mention the Acts of 1798-9, the Rise of the Silver-price of Gold, the new monetary law of France?

The explanation comes very naturally, if we conclude that a half-retired functionary who, in 1798, had already passed the boundary of threescore and ten, and who was near to fourscore when his book went through the press, had lost touch and alignment with the busy life of his time; that, at an age when he was entitled to dignified leisure, an invalid, as we have seen him to be, should have retained but the diminishing momentum of the *vis viva* to which direction had been given in earlier years of vigorous manhood.

We now pass to a detailed consideration of Lord Liverpool's plan of a Coinage System.[1]

So far as Gold is concerned, it proposed the formal estab-

---

[1] The following extract from his Treatise, shows the extent to which Lord Liverpool recognized the novelty of his scheme:—

"If it should be objected that the principles of coinage, which I

lishment and investiture, as Pound Sterling, of a new Gold coin, equalling in weight twenty twenty-firsts of a guinea.

For Silver, it proposed (pp. 170-2) that its Legal-Tender should be restricted to £2, and that the cost of coinage should be taken out of the Silver-coin—the cost, the charge for workmanship, *brassage*, *brachiorum labor*, as the author explains it on another page : not the cost of the Mint, or interest on the value of the land and buildings, but the pay for the labour of the arms that manufactured the Silver-coin. "Their intrinsic value, consisting of metal and workmanship," was to be "equal to their nominal value." (P. 188.)

The cost of coinage, then, was to be taken out of the Silver-coin : that is, the coin was to be made lighter by such fraction as would cover the cost of making the coin. But what coin was it that was to be so diminished ? What was the original weight of the coin from which this proposed reduction was to be made ? What was to be the starting-point of the reduction ? The distinguished author is clear on this point.

The weight which he suggests as that from which the reduction was to be made, was not the then legal weight of the English Silver-coin (such full-weight coin weighing then 15.^{21} weights of Silver as against 1 weight of Gold), but an amount equivalent in market-value to the proper amount in

humbly offer for your Majesty's consideration are wholly new. I think they should not be rejected merely on that account, in case they should be found to be reasonable. But what I maintain is, that a system consonant to these principles, *actually exists*, to a certain degree, *at present*, though it has not been formally adopted by Your Majesty's Government." (P. 174.) The italics are mine. But it is now plain that the saving clause, that this new system actually existed " to a certain degree " only, is ineffective to give accuracy to this statement. As a matter of history and of strict law, the Pound Sterling was twenty Silver shillings, until Gold was formally clothed with the functions of a Unit, by the statute of 1816, while the statutory gratuitous coinage of Silver, which was guaranteed by law, and the unlimited Legal-Tender of Silver, can hardly be profitably ignored. The assumed identity of Lord Liverpool's proposed system with that actually in use cannot be admitted, in reality he proposed a radical change.

Gold-coin, and this market-value was to be estimated by the legislator, for the future, through observation of the actual market-rate of the past, or, to use the author's words (p. 172), not "the actual price of such metal at any given time, but according to the average price which such metal has borne for a certain number of years past, or which it is likely to bear in future in the market." (See also page 173.)

Of the Silver thus provided for, however, the reader will carefully note, the coinage was to be free,[1] saving certain eventualities presently to be stated.

---

[1] This statement will excite surprise, and, in fact, if I am rightly advised of the general condition of opinion, these pages can hardly expect to find—at the date of their publication—a single reader learned in monetary affairs to whom they will not give a certain shock. I therefore state fully the evidence on which I base the averment.

1. There is in Lord Liverpool's Treatise, no proposition or suggestion of a proposition for limiting the coinage of Silver, saving the one mentioned in the text above, on page 154.

2. This proposition for limiting the coinage being suggested as a contingent modification of the general plan assumed to have been already set forth, proves the presence of coinage of Silver not so limited as a part of that general plan.

3. The general tenour of the work indicates that freedom of coinage was accepted by the author as an elementary principle, so to speak, or as an established right.

For example, he says on page 6 : "This mischievous practice [traffic in buying Silver with Gold, and Gold with Silver-coin] and the frauds committed in carrying it on, are the more to be apprehended in this country, *where the Mint is free* ; that is, where everyone has a right to bring Gold or Silver to the Mint to be converted into coin ; not at the charge of the person who brings it, but of the public."

Then follows the proposition to establish a "superior" coin of one metal, and a "subservient" coin of the other ; the requirement of which classification is obviously met by the reduction of the Legal-Tender of Silver to two pounds, and by taking the cost of coinage out of the coin.

Again, in a passage on page 174 which follows the lines which are quoted in the preceding page, and to which I also refer the reader, he observes : "The present Silver-coins, such as they are, are subordinate and subservient to the Gold-coins ; and in this quality only are current. In

SECT. 19.] *Lord Liverpool's Scheme.* 153

What would have been the practical operation of this scheme? Its effect can, perhaps, most easily be apprehended to-day, if we imagine it applied in such a country as France, the monetary conditions of which are presumably not unfamiliar to the reader.

Let us suppose, then, that in France the Government had remitted the charge for coining Gold (which, in fact, has been, since 1803, from 9 to 6 francs per kilogram); that Gold had been formally made the Unit of Value; and that the Legal-Tender of the 5-franc piece, etc., had been reduced to 50 francs—the charge for coining it remaining as it has been since 1803.

France would thus have been coining Silver at the same charge as now. The reader will note, however, the difference in the weight of the Silver-coins in France ($15\frac{1}{2}$ to 1) from those actually coined in England; those coined in the latter country, up to 1798, being $15.^{21}$ to 1 of gold; those coined after 1816 being, as we shall presently find, at $14.^{28}$ to 1.

Now, it is a curious fact that Lord Liverpool's scheme, if carried out with literal precision in 1816, when the general rise in the value of Gold had become a long-established fact, would have produced, by reason of the matters set forth in full below,[1] a ratio close to $15.^{50}$, namely, $15.^{40}$, which

---

proposing these principles, it has been my earnest wish that as few alterations as possible should be made in the system of coins which at present exists:" and a few lines later (page 175): "The Silver and Copper-coins should continue to be subservient to, and representative of, these Gold-coins as they are at present."

It will be observed that the statement just quoted from page 6 of Lord Liverpool's Treatise, that "everyone has a right to bring Silver to the Mint," not only fixes and sharpens the meaning of the latter passages, which I have italicized, but serves as additional evidence on the point set forth on page 147, namely, the fact that the Treatise absolutely ignores the existence of the Statutes of 1798 and 1799, which, in fact, prohibited Silver Coinage.

[1] Lord Liverpool's idea was that the probable Market Rate of the future

approaches the French ratio on one side, as the Dutch ratio 15.⁴ approaches it on the other.

Of the practical effect of this scheme, had it been adopted, we shall have occasion to speak hereafter.

It is certainly a novel plan, and one of which it is not easy to judge with confidence, for its operation has never, so far as I know, been tested by practice in any country. Its author so far regarded it as tentative that he adds to it, as I have indicated, certain regulations which are to be put in force if experience should show the necessity of them.

In the event that the quantity of Silver-coin should come to be excessive, either through coinage by unauthorized persons (fradulent coinage, although of the legal weight), or through the regular working of the Mint, Lord Liverpool suggests,[1]

should be deduced from the actual Market Rate of the past. Exactly what the Market Ratio of the metals was between 1816 and, let us say, ten years anterior to that date, does not seem to be known to-day with absolute precision, but I find that such authorities as Dr. Broch (Document of the Conference of 1878, Exhibit A, 1st Session) and Mr. R. H. Inglis Palgrave ('Third Report of Royal Commission on Depression, etc., p. 328), give figures which yield as averages 15.⁶⁹ and 15.⁷⁴, respectively. If we take the mean between these figures—15.⁷¹—and deduct from it 1½ per cent, which was the French coinage-charge (till a reduction to 1 per cent. was made in 1834), we obtain 15.¹⁰ as a fair approximation to the rate to be dictated by the terms of Lord Liverpool's scheme, had it been adopted in full in 1816. If, therefore, we amend this system we have imagined adopted in France, by changing the weight of the Silver-coin from 15.⁹ to 15.¹⁰, we present Lord Liverpool's scheme correctly in detail, as its effect would have been in 1816, subject, however, to the contingent limitations hereinafter set forth.

[1] His language is as follows : "It will be objected in the first place that by the proposed alteration in the Silver-coins those of Gold will occasionally be drawn out of the Kingdom." (P. 179.) To this objection he makes an exhaustive answer, which extends to page 184: "But if it should be thought necessary, for the purpose of preventing this evil [the use of Silver-coins of less intrinsic value to purchase Gold-coins of greater], to employ any farther guard or restriction, I will submit to Your Majesty whether it may not be advisable that the Legislature should vest in Your Majesty, or such others as may be authorized by your royal licence (these will

as a safeguard, that Parliament should vest in the Crown (with power of delegation, presumably, to the Bank of England) the exclusive right to take Silver to the Mint to be coined. At the same time he expresses himself in strong terms in favour of a "great plenty" of Silver.

Such, then, was the Coinage System which, in Lord Liverpool's contemplation, appeared desirable for England.

Upon the probable practical working of the scheme a few brief observations suggest themselves.

If the restrictions of Silver Coinage suggested by Lord Liverpool were applied literally, as he suggested them, namely, when necessary to guard against what I may call a "crowding out" of Gold by Silver-coins, or any discount on Silver-coins (premium on Gold-coin) it is plain—

(1.) That England would have accepted a vastly increased quantity of Silver-coin.

(2.) That the mere facility of coining Silver in England, cumulatively to the effect of the amounts actually absorbed, would have tended both to raise, and to steady, the market-rate of Silver to Gold.

(3.) It is also worth while to remember that Legal-Tender, established by formal statute, is not the sole and exclusive

---

probably always be the Directors of the Bank of England), the sole right of carrying Silver to your Mint to be coined. Your Majesty will thus have it in your power to limit and regulate the quantity of Silver Coins, which may at any time be sent into circulation; but I beg to be understood that I do not mean by this restriction (if it should be thought proper to adopt it), that Silver Coins of every description should not be sent in great plenty into circulation; it is highly important for the convenience of your people, particularly those of the lower classes, that they should at all times be current in great plenty."

Again he observes: "If anyone can entertain the idea, that these coins will be sent into circulation in so great numbers that their value will be depreciated by their plenty. I certainly have no such apprehension. If, however, there should be the least possibility that this consequence would follow, the remedy which I have proposed at the close of my answer to the first objection may be immediately applied to prevent this evil." (P. 188.)

guaranty for the currency of a coin; the practical intervention of the Executive Branch of the Government can establish what may be called a Special or Partial Legal-Tender. If the Treasury, or the Bank of England, chose to support the Silver-coins, by use, they could certainly enjoy a broad field of monetary employment, beyond the statutory two-pound payments.[1]

The following considerations embrace a wider range:—

(4.) The stability thus insured to the ratio of Gold and Silver at a lower figure for Gold than actually obtained in the years preceding 1834-7, would have strengthened the party of Albert Gallatin and the New York Banks in their resistance to the change in the United States from 15 to 16, which was pressed and finally carried by Benton and the Gold-party, then fired by the hope that an Eldorado was latent in the Southern Alleghanies. In place of the half-way change to $15.^{.2}$, close to the French ratio, which was urged by the moderate party in the United States, $15.^{50}$ would have recommended itself, had England been coining at $15.^{10}$ with a seigniorage deducted; and had the United States adopted this ratio in 1837, the modern outbreak of Anti-Silver legislation might never have arisen to disturb the march of progress.

(5.) Independently of the possible action of the United States,

---

[1] It is a curious fact that present experience (1887) supplies evidence of the correctness of these observations. A very large amount of Money not Legal-Tender at all is to-day effectively maintained in circulation by the action of the Treasury. Sovereigns and half-sovereigns to the extent —as I am informed—of not a few million pounds are to-day in existence, although below the weight fixed by statute as the "least current weight." A rigid refusal to take any such coins in any Government office would undoubtedly restrict, if not prevent, their further currency. Of course, the consent of the giver and of the receiver is, so to speak, party to the act of using them as Money; but if "Gresham's law" be true—and I know of no successful attack upon it—the consent to employ a particular kind of Money is not likely to be withheld to-day, when the receiver knows he can use it in payments to be made in Government offices.

it is clear that, had Lord Liverpool's scheme been adopted in full, the example of England could not have operated upon the minds of the monetary reformers of the period 1850-1875, as a convincing precedent for the exclusion of Silver, in a degree approaching the extent to which it has done so in fact; the idea of outlawing Silver could, therefore, never have reached that extreme height of prestige which it has actually enjoyed in the minds of this generation, and thus, in any case, the later history of the century might have been a history of at least comparative peace between Silver and Gold.

We now follow the contrast between the actual course of events and the structure of inference which we have thus based upon the hypothesis of the scheme stated in the "Treatise on the Coins of the Realm" being adopted by Parliament.

Wherein lies the divergence of the Statute of 1816 from Lord Liverpool's plan?

Lord Liverpool's scheme became law in 1816, so far as the following portions of it are concerned:

1. The establishment of Gold as the Unit.
2. Reducing the Legal-Tender-Power of Silver to £2.

The divergence appears in the following features:

1. The Statute ordained that not merely the cost of coinage, as Lord Liverpool advised, but also a heavy seigniorage should be taken out of the Silver-coin. With this change re-appeared under the Regency of George IV. "his Majesty's rate" which had been abolished by the Counsellors of Charles II. Four shillings in the Pound Troy of Standard Silver was the new Mint charge, about six per cent. in all; a figure which includes the cost and the profit.

2. The starting-point for this reduction, the weight which was to be reduced by the Mint charge, was remote from that which Lord Liverpool's plan would have fixed. The old legal ratio, 15.^{21} to 1, was taken as the starting-point, but with this difference between the new shillings and the old, that the new

shilling was coined 66 to the pound.[1] Four shillings, the difference between 66 and 62, were retained by the Mint, and thus the shillings issued were $\frac{4}{66}$ (.0606) lighter than the old, so that weighing 15.[21] they weighed 15.[21] minus $\frac{4}{66}$, or 14.[?]. Of this reduction .[906] might perhaps be taken as a fair charge for cost of coinage, leaving in round numbers 5 per cent. as the seigniorage. The 6 per cent. was, however, but a nominal limit; for, in fact, Silver was not worth 15.[21] to 1 in 1816 or afterward. The average rate of Gold was several per cent. higher than 15.[21]. The controlling factors of the world's demand—England's heavy draft for Resumption purposes upon the world's small stock of Gold being the chief—accounted for that. It followed, that the new Silver coin, if coined on Government account—as a good part of it was certain to be on the occasion of a general Recoinage—gave a net profit of about 8 per cent.

The probable object of these divergences from Lord Liverpool's scheme has, I doubt not, occurred to the reader. It was the profit of the Treasury. The reader has observed that each point of the divergence gives its percentage of profit.

Beside (1), the amount of seigniorage expressly taken, there was (2), the gain arising from the purchase of Silver at a low price, in so far as the coinage was to be done on Government account.

Of the course of discussion among the authorities which led to the adoption of these measures, but meagre records have come to my notice. The proposition made its appearance in public in a Report of that Committee of the Privy Council (Appendix 20), hitherto alluded to, which had been appointed

---

[1] The operation of the change was as follows:—Under the Regulation of 43rd Elizabeth (1604) the Pound Troy of Standard Silver was to be coined into sixty-two shillings, and under the Act of 1666, the coinage being gratuitous, the depositor received sixty-two shillings for every Pound Troy he gave. Under the Act of 1816, for every Pound Troy of Standard Silver, sixty-two shillings were to be issued.

in 1798, and which now, after an interval of eighteen years, " availed themselves," as the Report states, " of the return of General Peace to resume the consideration of the coinage."

The expense of the new Mint, and of the new coinage of Silver, was expressly set forth as the justification for taking seigniorage, although a further argument for it is afforded in the consideration that the proposed rate is "high enough to protect the new coins by a slight increase of their nominal value, from the danger of being melted down and converted into bullion when the market-price of Silver rises," but not to encourage counterfeiting if it falls.

These views were reflected in the debates in Parliament. Indeed, it appears that the idea of an even higher ratio of seigniorage had been entertained in regions of authority, for in the House of Lords the Earl of Liverpool proposed that the coins should be struck at 67, 68, or 69 to the pound Troy, in which case 5, 6, or 7, instead of 4 shillings would have been retained for the Treasury.

The contrast of view between Lord Liverpool and his son is thus shown to be very marked, for in the "Treatise on the Coins of the Realm," the practice of seigniorage theretofore obtaining in France is distinctly characterized as "not very creditable." (P. 179.) But fiscal reasons are proverbially competent to over-ride all others.

It must be distinctly remembered that the Statute of 1816, though known to later times as the Gold-Standard-law, or the Anti-Silver-law, was not precisely so regarded or intended at the time it was framed, but was primarily a measure for the reformation of the Silver coin. The great need for this reformation, however, be it observed, was purely a creation of the forgotten Anti-Silver law of 1798.

The object of the Councillors of the Prince Regent in proposing the Law of 1816 was, as his message states, to remedy "the present defective state and inadequate amount of the Silver Coinage of this Realm." It was most natural, and as we can easily see, laudable, to signalize the return of General Peace, when bayonets were melting into ploughshares, by putting new and shining coins into the pockets of the people in the place of old discs worn bare of inscription, or roughly-coined Spanish dollars, or Bank of England Tokens, all of them badges of the oppression of twenty years of war.

To attain this end without any special expense was certainly a very attractive idea. And why should this attraction fail of its effect? Had science any objection to make: did that far-seeing statesmanship, that can sagely judge of the present by help of the accumulated experience of the past, interpose its veto? In asking this question, we come in sight of the mighty force wielded by those who give direction to the ideas of what ought to be, in higher spheres of civil conduct.

The authority derived from the most important monument of monetary learning then known, the work of a life-long councillor of the aged King of England, and the father of his Regent's Premier, was, in general terms, an authority to elevate Gold, and to subordinate Silver from motives of immediate domestic convenience (as regarded from the point of view of the past, anterior to 1798), and without considering the bearing of such action upon other nations, or upon the relations of the two metals throughout the world, and hence the possible recoil of such action upon England.

Evidently the Treatise had set forces in motion which it was not competent to restrain.

The vice of insularity, in one who was understood to be discussing, from the highest stand-point of State policy, a matter which by its nature was world-embracing—non-insular, anti-insular upon occasion—was a fatal vice; and tended not merely to perpetuate existing distortion of view, but to promote further distortion, and indeed, as the event proved, to inflict upon posterity an accumulating inheritance of obliquity.

If we ask, whence came the impelling suggestion to this peculiar creation of debased Money—for which no precedent that one could suppose valid to English eyes could be found—the solution will recommend itself as at least a probable one, that the profit made in the issue of Bank Tokens had attracted attention to the practicability of an analogous issue on the part of the Government. The total issue of stamped Spanish dollars current at 4s. 6d. (guineas being at 21s.) and of Bank of England crowns and half-crowns coined was several million pounds sterling, and could thus hardly have failed to excite attention.

The wonder is, indeed, that the semblance of a "Real Money," of a true Commodity-Money, was kept up at all; that the new crowns and shillings were not in a greater degree made tokens, counters, or metallic promises to pay; for a larger percentage of seigniorage would have paid not only the expense of the Mint, but might at need have covered other items of outlay; perhaps, indeed, items similar to those which were met by "His Majesty's rate," in earlier days. It is also to be stated, to the credit of the Executive, that no excessive amount of Silver was coined for the benefit of the Treasury.

But the divergence of the Statute of 1816 from Lord Liverpool's plan extends much further. Its provisions touching the Coinage of Silver furnish a remarkable chapter in the history of financial legislation. The Statute was in form and apparent intent a Statute for the Free Coinage of Silver as well as of Gold. Section IX. is as follows :—

"IX. And be it further enacted, That from and after such Day as shall be named and appointed in and by any Proclamation which shall be made and issued for that purpose, by or on behalf of His Majesty, by and with the Advice of His Majesty's Privy Council, it shall and may be lawful for any Person or Persons, Native or Foreigner, to bring any Foreign Coin, or any other coin, or reputed Coin, Plate or Bullion of Silver, in Mass, molten or alloyed, or any Sort of Manufacture of Silver, and to deliver the same at His Majesty's Mint in

London, to be there melted down and coined in Current Silver Coins of this Kingdom ; and such Silver Coin, Plate, Bullion or Manufacture so brought or delivered, Shall be assayed at the said Mint, and melted down and coined with all convenient speed, into Silver Coins of a Standard in Fineness of Eleven Ounces, Two Pennyweights of fine Silver and Eighteen Pennyweights of Alloy in the Pound Troy, and in Weight after the Rate of Sixty-six Shillings to every Pound Troy, whether the same be coined in Crowns, Half-Crowns, Shillings or Sixpences, or Pieces of a lower Denomination; and that as soon as conveniently may be after any such Silver Coin, Plate, Bullion, or Manufacture respectively, so brought to the Mint, shall be melted and assayed, there shall be delivered to the Person bringing in and delivering the same a sum in Silver Coins, of Crowns, Half-Crowns, Shillings or Sixpences, after the Rate of Sixty-two Shillings of the Standard Fineness and Weight hereinbefore mentioned for every Pound Troy of Standard Silver of the Fineness aforesaid, by such Person brought and delivered into the Mint, and so proportionably for a greater or lesser Weight; and that for the Defalcation or Diminution and for the Charge for the Assaying, Coinage and Waste in Coinage of all such Silver so to be brought to the Mint as aforesaid, there shall and may be retained at the said Mint the sum of Four Shillings of the Standard and Weight aforesaid, for every Pound Troy of such Standard Silver so brought in and delivered, and so proportionably for any greater or lesser Weight, making in the whole after the Rate of Sixty-Six Shillings for every Pound Troy of such Standard Silver; anything in any Act or Acts in force in Great Britain or Ireland, immediately before the passing of this Act, to the contrary in anywise notwithstanding.

"X. And be it further enacted, That an Account shall be kept at the Mint of the Amount of all sums of Money arising from the Allowance of Four Shillings for every Pound Troy of Silver to be retained at the said Mint, in manner aforesaid; and that all such Sums so retained shall in the first Place be applied in or towards the Payment of the Expenses of the coining of such Silver; and the Surplus thereof (if any) after the Payment of such Expenses shall be carried to and made Part of the Consolidated Fund."

It will be apparent, that the provisions made for the coinage of Silver in this Statute were conceived with a view to the manufacture of Silver coin for depositors, and the use of the word "seigniorage," referred to on page 159, shows the intent of the authorities to have corresponded with their act. Seigniorage taken out of a coin implies, by its very nature, two weights, so to speak, for that coin,—that is, a nominal weight and an actual weight—a higher weight which has a legal existence or recognition in some form, and a lower weight at which coins are struck, which, as current, are to be made equal by force of law to the former weight which gives their nominal, or "face," value. All this implies Free Coinage. If there is to be no coinage on account of the citizen, if the Government is to do the coining on its own account, putting its own property through the mill and press, and especially if, as in the present instance, their face value is fixed by coin, not of the same, but of another, metal, of what use to talk of a Legal Weight or of seigniorage taken from it? The Legal Weight becomes a pure fiction, and, strictly speaking, the seigniorage a fiction also; the main fact is that the Treasury buys metal, and coins Tokens out of it, and the only actuality in the affair is the weight at which the coins are to be struck.

But notwithstanding this promise of Free Coinage, that is involved in the very structure of the law of 1816, there has been no Free Coinage of Silver under it.

Why? Because the Proclamation mentioned on page 161 has never been made. Through the omission of such Proclamation the contingent limitation which Lord Liverpool suggested for use in case of need has become the constant and rigid rule. The result is, of course, a practical nullification of the scheme of Lord Liverpool; a departure from his plan really more serious than the imposition of "seigniorage" in the place of "brassage." Now it is this anonymous provision of the law which established the most aggressively Anti-

Silver feature of the English system, the complete degradation of Silver to a Token-Money, with its coinage carried on on Government account for the purpose of gaining profit by the issue of under-weight coin.

Who is responsible for this system? Surely not Lord Liverpool, except indirectly, as we have shown him to be in the matter of seigniorage. And yet it is certainly understood —universally understood—that the exclusion of Silver from Free Coinage has existed since 1816 under his sanction as that of a competent and responsible scientific authority. We now, therefore, ascertain that another of the guarantees for the militant error of the day is spurious.

In exposing what I find to be the defects of Lord Liverpool's argument, I have specially analyzed only his errors of commission. But there is an error of omission in the Treatise to which our study of England's history enables us to attach peculiar weight. It is an omission which affords a certain explanation of whatever there may be in the Treatise of the doctrinaire's crudeness—a lesson not lacking in suggestiveness for the future. I refer to the failure to discuss what had been during the greater part of the XVIIIth century the question touching the relative position of Silver and Gold in England, which, of all others, was chiefly present in the thoughts of those active in monetary discussion—namely, the question of *lowering the guinea*.

It is quite easy for us now to see, after the fact, that as the general rates of Gold and Silver actually remained so steady during the XVIIIth century, a reduction of the guinea to 20s. 6d. or 20s. would have provided England with the Silver Money she desired to have. How does it happen that, with those rates in full view, a Treatise which came into existence because of the necessity of providing *good Silver Money*, failed to consider what would have been the effect of a change which must have prevented any lack of Silver-coins, and which had been so abundantly proposed and discussed?

The reader will clearly understand that I have not intended by this to present the idea that Lord Liverpool ought himself to have proposed to cut down the guinea to 20s. 6d. or 20s. either in 1774 or in 1798, or in 1805. That is a matter quite apart, which I do not propose to discuss. I am merely pointing out a most notable proof of the unpractical character of Lord Liverpool's work. No matter what his own practical plan, when he undertook to establish by argument the principles of monetary policy for his country, upon its relation to which that plan must stand or fall, it was incumbent upon him to make a full and fair statement of alternative schemes, and of general opinion on the whole subject.

Should this be regarded as an exaggerated demand upon a "Treatise on the Coins of the Realm," it will be found germane to observe that some statement on this head is what most readers would naturally expect to find in such a Treatise. Something of this kind is called for under the ordinary canons of construction of the duty incumbent upon an author who undertakes to discuss a subject; there is an implied promise to that effect in the very title of the book. To the absence of fulfilment of this implied promise is in large measure due the darkness that followed the book: it became an impassable barrier which cut off the XIXth from knowledge of the learning of the XVIIIth century.

§ 20. THE MONETARY THEORIES OF SIR WILLIAM PETTY, OF JOSEPH HARRIS, AND OF SIR ROBERT PEEL.

In the roll of honour upon which Lord Liverpool inscribed the names of those who in his view represented the wisdom of the past touching the nicer questions of the Standard, Sir William Petty stands first in the order of time, and first likewise in distinction.

It was he who in Lord Liverpool's belief first propounded the solution of the great, the chief, difficulty which for centuries of her history had oppressed the statesmen of England, and which—all relief failing—had remained to his day (1631-1685) a burden to the Commonwealth.

What was this difficulty?

It was a difficulty which hardly can be regarded as peculiar to England, or one which had lost its force when Lord Liverpool wrote. On the contrary, it has pervaded the XIXth century as with a congenital malady, and if the XXth century is to escape from suffering by the same cause, it will only be by dint of prudent regimen. We are speaking of nothing less than the unstable equilibrium of the metals, the variability of their relative value, the danger of local alternation from one to the other; in a word, that difficulty of maintaining a steady circulation of the two, or a fixed ratio between them, which is the staple source and aliment of the Battle of the Standards.

So ancient withal is this difficulty, that, if I may venture to direct a ray of thought toward such remoteness, I suggest that its story is better known to the totality of men who have lived on the earth than that of Adam and Eve in Paradise; for the Silver Adam and the Golden Eve, each the source of the other's woes, wherever known, appeared not merely as tradition, but withal as a fact of the day, appealing to present pecuniary interest. We have, in fact, to deal with a product of that alleged primal curse of duality with which fate has afflicted man, a natural result of that act of Creation or provision of Nature in making two *precious* metals, two metals, instead of only one, fit to be Money, which in our day a school of economists have discovered to be a gross blunder on the part of its responsible author. This, then, is the difficulty for which Petty found the solution—in doing which he was but an avant-courrier, announcing for a remote future the coming of a great reform.

For the XIXth century, the name of Petty is obscured in the dusk of time. It can boast no such lustre as those of Locke and of Newton. But, certainly, if the opinion of the chief promoter of a policy which has mastered our century is to count as authority, Petty is one of the great path-finders in the realm of monetary thought, to whom a generation that has gone far toward outlawing Silver should, at least, pay devoutest homage.

"It is proper to observe," says Lord Liverpool, "that James I. consulted Sir Francis Bacon, Sir Edward Coke, and many other eminent men who lived in those times; but they all appear to have been at a loss for a remedy to the evil to which the country was then exposed. The Treatise of Sir William Petty, entitled, 'The Political Anatomy of Ireland,' in which he delivered his opinion, that the coins, which were to be the principal measure of property, could be made of one metal only, was among his posthumous works, published in the year 1691; and as far as I am informed *this extraordinary man was one of the first who fully asserted and maintained this opinion, suggesting thereby the remedy so long sought for in vain.* Mr. Locke and others followed him in supporting the same opinion, but this true principle, which solved the difficulty, *has never yet been carried effectually into practice.*" (P. 131.) The latter statement is also referred to Petty, for he is quoted to the effect "that one metal of the two precious metals is only fit matter for Money; and as matters now stand, Silver is the matter of Money." But he (Petty) "expresses a doubt *whether in that sense there is any such Money or rule* [*measure*] *in the world.* So that he confirms the principle, but *doubts whether the governments of the world have ever conformed to it.* Sir William Petty judged rightly. It is certain that the governments of Europe have not in general paid attention to this rule; nor is it surprising, that persons wholly occupied in official business, should not have had leisure to study or understand a subject, which is in its nature so abstruse and complicated." (P. 137.)

He also spoke of Sir William Petty as one who "had certainly great abilities, and was *more of a man of business and*

of the world than either Mr. Locke or Mr. Harris, etc. etc."
(P. 137.)

It is by no means Lord Liverpool alone who treats Sir William as a well-spring of thought—*fons et origo doctrinæ*. In such important utterances as the great speeches of Mr. Wellesley Pole in the Commons, and of the second Lord Liverpool in the Lords, in support of the Coinage Bill of 1816, and in the great speech[1] of Sir Robert Peel on the Bank Charter Bill in 1844, the name of Petty still stands as the eldest in the line of supposed authorities for the Outlawry of Silver.

In addition to the extract above mentioned, Lord Liverpool cites him as follows:—

"Sir William Petty observes *that Money is understood to be the uniform measure of the value of all commodities;* and then adds that *the proportion of value between fine Gold and fine Silver alters as the earth and industry of men produce more of one than the other. That Gold has been worth but twelve times its own weight of Silver, but that of late it has been worth fourteen; so there can be but one of the two metals of Gold and Silver to be a fit matter for Money.*" (Pp. 124-5.)

But on an earlier page of the Treatise (p. 14) the doctrine is stated with the directness and force of a commandment.

"*Sir William Petty says that one of the metals is the only fit matter for Money.*" All the italics are mine.

What was, in fact, Sir William Petty's idea as to the true "matter for Money?" After an examination of his writings, I am unable to find anything which commits Petty to the opinions which Lord Liverpool imputes to him. So far as I can see, his idea was simply the idea which Locke, and Newton, and later, Harris, held so firmly, namely—to use the terms which I have sought to justify in this work—that the

[1] See references in "Currency and Standard of Value in England," by Mr. R. H. Inglis Palgrave, in the third Report of the Commission on the Depression of Trade and Industry, 1886. See also Appendix 26.

Unit must be maintained in one metal, and that coins of other metal must be rated in reference to the Unit. And that is all!

To prove that this is the case is, obviously—from my standpoint—to exonerate Sir William Petty from the charge of grave error. But justice to his memory is not satisfied with so brief an allusion. I desire, therefore, to add that while I cannot concur in Lord Liverpool's effort to exalt that ingenious Doctor at the expense of Locke, yet the former's path-finding insight in economic thought commands my hearty homage.

A consideration of the circumstances under which Petty wrote supplies, as in the case of Locke, a context which of itself adequately explains the peculiar use of words which has given rise to so complete a misunderstanding of his position. Living under the régime of Free Coinage of Silver and Gold, with Silver the Chief Money, a century and a half before any serious effort was made to outlaw one of the metals, it would require strong evidence to show that, because he preferred to give the name Money to Silver, he wished to do what it was inevitable he must do if he was a single-metallist, namely, deprive Gold of its monetary use. Such evidence does not exist. The whole matter seems thus to resolve itself into a point of style, or use of words.

If it be inquired, how Lord Liverpool could so far err, I can perhaps justify my evading the question by quoting Sir William Petty himself, and saying, "To explain this fully, one might launch out into the deep ocean of all the mysteries concerning Money." It may, however, be observed that it did not comport well with Lord Liverpool's argument clearly to recognize that Silver was then, by law, all that he thought Petty meant it should be, actually a very true "principal Money, made of one metal only." Symptoms appear in the Treatise of an effort to question that this was a fact[1] in Petty's

---

[1] "Mr. Locke, who *thought* that Silver-coins were the only Money of Account or measure of property." (P. 16.)

"It is probable that he was not well informed of the history of our coins,

time. It occurs to me that it might perhaps be said the title of Silver to that place was not as firm in Petty's time as after the Recoinage of 1696, which operated, one might say, as a guarantee of that title, signed by Crown and Parliament and people. But the fact remains, the title was good, and was not seriously questioned. The pound Sterling was 20 shillings of Silver, and made a majority in value of the circulation. But at the same time Gold was coinable without stint, and Legal Tender without limit, *at a rate.*

Now, under these circumstances, the language used by Petty touching Gold and Silver is as harmless and innocent of evil intent against the use of Gold Money as the similar language used by Locke. Indeed, it is quite as justifiable to charge Newton with a desire to demonetize Gold because he said (see page 89) that Silver was the only true Money in England, as to make a like charge against Petty because of the expression that only one metal can be fit "matter for Money." With the distinction between what I shall call "rating Money" and "rated Money," a matter of their daily observation and experience, either phrase was a natural and harmless form of statement.

Lord Liverpool quotes from Petty's posthumous work "The Political Anatomy of Ireland;" and does not appear in the course of his wide reading among the monetary writings of that century to have happened upon other productions of Petty. Had he done so, he would have found that the expressions of his "Treatise on Taxes and Contributions" (1662) and of his "Quantulumcumque Concerning Money" (1685) are quite innocent of any indication of opposition to the rated currency of Gold. As for the passage before quoted, which would have pointed out these circumstances (of a practical nature) to him. *He asserted as a certain fact* that Silver Coins made the Money of Account or Measure of Commerce in England and the neighbouring countries. How far this assertion is *well-founded* we shall have occasion to show hereafter." (P. 83.) The italics are mine.

that Governments had failed to carry out his idea, this may explain itself as referring to the failure to maintain the complete subordination of Gold to Silver by a consistent policy of rating and of coinage; and if this be correct, the interesting fact is brought to light that Petty's mind had passed along the way which Locke and Newton were to follow in action as well as thought.

The views of Joseph Harris, the author of that "Essay on Money and Coins," which was pronounced by MacCulloch one of the best works ever published on the subject, have already been quoted in another Chapter (see page 123), and the substantial identity of his idea of what I have called a Unit of one metal and rated Money of the other, with the view of Petty, of Locke, and of Newton, dispenses us from a detailed examination of Harris's work. One reference, however, which Lord Liverpool makes to it deserves a special examination. In citing Harris for the third time in his Treatise, Lord Liverpool observes:—

"In another part of his Essay he asserts, *that all other metals, Gold as well as lead, are but commodities rateable by Silver.* He supports this opinion by the authority of many great and eminent men, whose writings and speeches on this subject he quotes in his Essay." (P. 137.)

Now the object of Lord Liverpool in citing this, as other passages, from the acknowledged masters of monetary thought, was to justify a policy the ultimate effect of which was, as later generations have clearly seen, to make one metal Money in England, and the other metal a "commodity." The analysis already presented (page 80), in explaining a similar expression of Locke's, has shown that the distinction between the secondary Money-metal and other commodities, is not readily, and at first glance, recognizable in its true character.

Through this citation, unexplained, as it stands, by reference to other utterances of Harris, it appears that the author of the "Treatise on the Coins of the Realm," may himself have quite misunderstood, and in any case ran great risk of leading his readers to misunderstand, the cardinal point of Harris's doctrine, in precisely the manner already set forth on page 80, to which I refer the reader.

To a man like Harris, who wrote so excellent a book in order to induce England to reduce the rate of currency of the guinea, this distortion of his views would, perhaps, have aroused as holy a horror as that which incited him to speak of the *laches* of England's rulers in not reforming the coinage, as "an assassination in the dark." [1]

The Monetary Theory of Sir Robert Peel has been glanced at in earlier pages (pp. 75, 86, 92, 93), and it has been made apparent that his ideas were in part drawn from a tissue of

[1] A curious proof of the persevering force of Lord Liverpool's Treatise, in setting the fashion for modern thought, is afforded by the following lines, which came under my eye long after the above pages were penned. They are from an interesting article on "the Queen's Assay-Master," in "Murray's Magazine" for May, 1887, by Professor Roberts-Austen, the present incumbent of that honourable office. Referring to Joseph Harris, who held the same office in its elder form from 1748 to 1764, the writer speaks of Harris as the author of "a careful and *singularly advanced* Essay on Money and Coins, which proves him to have been a *rigid mono-metallist*, as it contains the expression of an opinion that only one metal can be Money, a standard measure of property and commerce in any country. This essay is specially referred to by Charles, Earl of Liverpool, in his celebrated letter to King George the Third, dated May 7th, 1805, in which the advantages of a single measure of value, and Gold as that measure, are set forth with great vigour and clearness. This letter has since its publication remained the authority on the subject to which it relates." (P. 604-5.)

The italics are mine. The reader will readily note how complete the insulation has been. Thanks to the influence of Lord Liverpool, the excellent work of the older Assay-Master in the field of Monetary Statesmanship is *terra incognita* to his successor of to-day, who apart from his well-tried excellence, in his chosen field of science, has made interesting researches in monetary history; to-day, in 1887, the work of the Monetary Counsellor of 1774 is still operating directly as a non-conductor, to destroy communication upon the most important monetary issue of the day, from an elder and better teacher in the politics of Money.

spurious evidence. It seems quite probable that, both in 1819 and in 1844, he not only accepted Lord Liverpool as his master, without much inquiry into detail, and with still less criticism, but also took the Act of 1816 on trust, as the last word of science; thus even ignoring the divergences between Lord Liverpool's ideas, and the outcome of the Act, which are set forth in the preceding pages (Sect. 19). It was, therefore, inevitable that his ideas should fall into confusion, and that, being in this field the controlling individuality of his time, he should lead his people into captivity, at least so far as the range of his own error extended. That the error was very natural is, perhaps, sufficiently admitted in what has been said elsewhere; certainly, if the truth were all obvious and easily found, so that he who runs may read, there would hardly be need of a work like this to explain it.

Here, again, the word "Standard" may serve as a safe guide to the situation. Peel was the champion of the Gold Standard: and as such it is plain he was the champion of Metallic Money against paper, of Commodity-Money against credit; the champion of unity, of conservatism, of persistence in maintaining ancient right. All this is involved in the advocacy of the English Gold Standard: this I myself can state to-day as my own conviction, *provided that the definition of the word Standard be limited either to Meaning No. 5, or to Meanings Nos. 5 and 7* of the Introduction. In that case there is nothing to exclude from English law the Free Coinage, or the Full-Legal-Tender of Silver: nothing in English law which ignores the elementary fact that Silver possessed the advantages of Metallic-Money over paper, of Commodity-Money over credit, or that unity, conservatism, and ancient right were better served by retaining Silver than by excluding it; and it remains open to me to maintain further, that however well the demands of unity, of conservatism, and of ancient right would be fulfilled by Gold, they would be even better fulfilled by Silver, as Unit and chief Money, than by Gold, in which case Gold would remain a Standard, but not *the* Standard.

But vital monetary truth is swept away if the word "Standard" in Meaning No. 7, be applied to Gold alone, for in this case Meanings 5 and 6 are, as it were, absorbed and lost, and the door is shut to Silver. Now it was in this sense, *without notice taken of the distinctions I have drawn*,—that, as the champion of ancient right, Peel gave the law which rules English thought to-day.

It was a glory of Confucius that (as his words are given in English) he was "a transmitter and not a maker": and the same admirable trait reveals itself in the words of Peel which are quoted in these pages. Inasmuch as it lies with the present generation to be a transmitter as well as a maker, I allow myself to observe that the contentions I present in this work go no further than to say that it is the duty of the present generation to practise a fidelity to ancient right, which according to the modern current use of words shall be counted rather English than Chinese.

The following are important passages from Peel's speech in 1819 (Hansard's Debates, vol. xl., p. 679) :—

"Upon the necessity of establishing such a [metallic] Standard he could appeal to the opinion of all writers upon political economy, and to the practice of every civilized country, as well as that of our own, antecedent to the year 1797. All the witnesses, indeed, examined before the Committee [of 1810] strongly recommended the establishment of this Standard, one witness alone excepted (Mr. Smith, a very respectable man), who was an advocate for the indefinite suspension of cash payments. But when this witness was asked whether the suspension of cash payments was to exist without any standard of value, he answered, 'No; the pound should be the Standard.' He was required to define what he meant by the pound. His answer was, 'I find it difficult to explain it, but every gentleman in England knows it.' The

Committee repeated the question and Mr. Smith answered, 'It is something that has existed in this country for eight hundred years—three hundred years before the introduction of Gold.' This was, indeed, the only definition he could give. But turning from this attempt at definition, and the theory of Adam Smith, it would be recollected that Mr. Locke, after elucidating the subject of identity, dispelling all the erroneous views with reference to innate ideas, and endeavouring to penetrate even the properties of eternity, could not, with all his power of reasoning, and subtlety of disquisition, succeed in defining what he meant by an abstract pound. On that point, indeed, this distinguished man was evidently misled himself, and, of course, misled his readers."

Here follows the passage heretofore quoted concerning Sir Isaac Newton.

"Sir Isaac Newton," he says, "retiring from the sublime studies in which he chiefly passed his life—from the contemplation of the heavenly bodies—from an investigation of the laws by which their motions were guided—entered on the examination of this subject [the definition of an "abstract pound"]; but that great man came back, at last, to the old, the vulgar doctrine, as it was called by some, that the true standard of value consisted in a definite quantity of gold bullion. Every sound writer on the subject came to the same conclusion . . . ."

In the Appendix (No. 26) I give a fuller statement of Sir Robert Peel's doctrine, gathered from the speech of May 6, 1844, on the Bank Charter Bill; and I there mark by italics the passages to which the reader's attention seems to me specially due.

If I read these lines aright, the "True Standard of Value" and the "Abstract Pound," in Sir Robert Peel's classification, were the same; and the concrete substratum of the idea—the body, so to speak, of this soul—was an amount of Gold equal to twenty twenty-firsts of a guinea (or to the sovereign authorized to be coined by the statute of 1816).

It was in this unity that the "old, the vulgar notion" was supposed to coincide with the conclusions of Newton; and it is Locke's failure to grasp the golden idea that drew upon him Peel's rebuke: it being plainly a case of gross negligence: for certainly Locke ought to have been able to compass this idea, when, as explained to Parliament, he had been coping with eternity. I shall not enter upon this order of questions, for I hope that Locke and Newton now need no defence. Indeed, I pray that the spirit of these gentle sages may descend upon minds that are still in bondage to the errors which spurious evidence engendered in the mind of Peel.

My desire is merely to test and verify the distinctions set forth in the Introduction by applying them to the facts which were in view of the legislators of 1819 and 1844.

Upon careful examination of the plexus of ideas set forth in the extract given in the text, it will be seen to embrace what *was*, what *is*, what (in Mr. Peel's opinion) *ought to have been*, and what *ought to be*. So far as the later history of English Money is concerned, I shall touch upon its salient points in the coming pages, and shall gain, perhaps, some material for judging what *ought*, at various periods, to have been done. We now have to do with realities in the sense of true explanations of the nature of an existing monetary system.

So far as the "True Standard of Value" is concerned, that has been considered in the first Chapter. It would be an anachronism to demand that the requirements therein established should have been realized in 1819.

But the Abstract Pound, what can be said of it—this pound which, it was said, every gentleman in England knew, which had existed for eight hundred years, and yet which, to say the least, it was not easy to define? In order to ascertain what it was, I shall once more refer the reader to the Introduction of this work, and to the considerations touching the Money Unit in Chapter IV. Upon utilizing those pages as a preface, it will plainly appear that my doctrine and words are expressly designed to analyze and distinguish the phenomena here named "Pound" and "Abstract Pound." As I know of no adequate treatment of this subject in monetary literature to which I can refer, I must here give some extended exposition to Meaning No. 4 of the Introduction.

A National Unit of Account is a legal entity, a creature of law; that is to say, a product of those cumulative and continuously active forces of human will which create and maintain institutions. The Pound Sterling of twenty shillings of twelve pence each was present in the consciousness of the English people as a matter of language, of law, of history, of experience. Unique as an institution, it is to be apprehended by a side glance, so to speak, through analogies. It had existed, in continuity, throughout the centuries, as, one might say, the English Church or the English Parliament existed; or, to enter a less ambitious field of comparison, as a lord of the manor, Black Rod, the head of a clan, or tenant-in-tail, or, again, as a Royal Forest or the Speaker's Mace, existed. In order that I may throw a broad net, and thus, perhaps, catch some meaning which will naturalize itself in the reader's mind, I add to this list already given of concrete analogies more or less remote, the following, which are nearer the region of abstractions—namely, an incorporeal hereditament, an office, a dignity, a right, a franchise—and I also suggest the notion of an official but impersonal corporation.

The right of succession inhered in the National Unit, so that (as in the case of the various entities I have enumerated) its material substance could undergo change without interrupting its physical existence or the exercise of its functions; and in the case of a conflict of laws, or untoward conjunction of events defeating the intention of the law, it might be in abeyance, or have its being *de jure*, so to speak, and not *de facto*; or, again, different objects could claim the office with varied justification, while, so far as the mere power is concerned, it lay within the jurisdiction of the State to give to various substances, at the same time, the character of the Pound Sterling. In earlier sections of this Chapter some historical instances are presented which are here peculiarly in point (see p. 134), although the bare facts to which the words " Pound Sterling" would themselves directly lead the inquirer, are a sufficient exemplification. Originally a real pound of pure white Silver, the " Pound in weight" descended to be a "Pound in tale" of coin, and eventually reached, with the 43rd Elizabeth (1604), a weight in coin only thirty-two-ninetieths of what it had been at the outset of its career. Whether, at any time in later centuries, Gold was temporarily clothed in its own right with the character of Pound Sterling, is a question which admits of discussion. It is not, however, questionable that a weight of Silver—coined under the authority of the Crown—had always the legitimate and paramount title till the happening of the events hereinbefore set forth. Through the *laches* of Government and consequent practice of the people, habit had been attaching itself to Gold as Chief Money, when panic brought on the Restriction of Cash Payments (1797). This Restriction was continued by repeated Acts of Parliament, and thus led to a general transhipment of valuations from Gold to Paper.

Now that the general facts here stated, in the mass or in outline, were within the view of Peel, and of the witness whom he quoted, is an inference fairly to be drawn from what is known of their competence, or of their opinions. We have merely to inquire into the adequacy of their scientific analysis; its depth and its precision, or, in other words, how far they saw below the surface. The times were evidently not propitious for the dispassionate labour of science. The controlling feature of the situation, with which, as a member of the House of Commons, the speaker of 1819 had to deal, was that, though peace had long since blessed the world, and Napoleon, its great disturber, was safely caged in St. Helena, yet England remained under the régime of depreciated Paper-Money. It will be observed that in this discourse, although delivered three years after the Anti-Silver Act, Peel treated the question of the Standard as an open one. It was, in effect, an open question in spite of the settlement of 1816, from which the Gold Standard dates itself, for that settlement was in large measure inoperative in practice.

How general this feeling was, is well shown by the following extract from a communication addressed to Lord Liverpool, the Premier, by Mr. Huskisson, in February, 1819:[1]—

"If Gold is to be our only standard, and only Legal-Tender to any amount, I should adhere to my suggestion of paying in bullion all sums above £25 at the present standard price; of taking a brassage upon the Gold coinage which would raise its value in currency to £4 the ounce, and to a reduction of the amount at which Silver should be a Legal-Tender to 20s. If Silver is to be our only standard (we cannot have two) and unlimited tender to any amount (leaving Gold to fluctuate according to the relative value of the two metals in the market), I should retain the present seigniorage upon the Silver coin, making all sums of £5 and upwards (the lowest denomination of Bank note) payable in demand in Silver Bullion, at the old standard of 5s. 2d. per ounce. Of these two plans I should prefer the former, but either would be consistent with good faith."

The vital question of the day was, whether in time of peace England should continue indefinitely to relieve the Bank of England from the obligation to pay its notes on demand in "cash," and whether, in daily life, the calculations of business should be chiefly expressed in terms of a Paper Standard. What Money-metal, or whether both metals, should be treated as

---

[1] From the life of the second Earl Liverpool, by C. D. Jonge. I am indebted to Mr. Paul F. Tidman for bringing this passage to my notice.

"cash" was a secondary matter. It was, then, in view of this situation, that the speaker sought to rally support for the restoration of a true Standard of Value, and so entered upon the definition of the Pound Sterling.

He asked "what is the Pound?" and, seemingly unconscious of the facts here pointed out, maintained that there was only one thing entitled to the name.

From the considerations hereinbefore set forth it follows that the real question at issue is to be stated by the inquiry, "What substance was best entitled, upon grounds of justice and of sound policy, to be securely established by law as the Pound Sterling?" But the theorist of 1819 was quite superior to such considerations. Standing before Parliament with the "Treatise on the Coins of the Realm," the Bullion Report of 1810, and the Act of 1816, behind him, he was, perhaps, hardly called upon to "go behind the record," and, indeed, had he applied himself to reconstruct the learning of his time from his seat in Parliament, he certainly would have merited unique fame. But no addition is needed to the picture of Peel, criticizing John Locke before the English Parliament for not being, so to speak, sound on the Gold Standard, and praising Newton to the skies for supposed anachronistic opinions from which Newton would probably have recoiled, not merely as an imputation upon his judgment, but upon his honour. The entire statement, so far as it attempts to justify the Exclusion of Silver, is baseless; and yet it is through the intervention of Peel that the Exclusion of Silver was transmitted to the present generation, and it is by favour of his mistake that people in England to-day believe that the Gold Standard necessarily implies the exclusion of Silver as Full Money.

The situation, as set forth in accordance with our former analysis, was, briefly, as follows: As matter of ancient law and right twenty Silver shillings were entitled to the office of Pound Sterling, and the Silver Pound was, in this sense, the *legitimate*

National Unit of Coinage. But the Silver Pound had, in fact, been long since in part dispossessed by the Gold Pound, $\frac{20}{21}$ of a guinea; and, later still, Gold had been, to a large extent, ousted from possession by a Paper Pound,[1] which was, however, so far as mere form was concerned, a promise to pay a Metallic Pound.

As for the practical question at issue in 1816 and 1819, it may be worth while to say that, from the point of view of to-day, it is natural to assert, and difficult to deny, that to have established the Silver Pound in its former place with its golden satellite by its side, (but with the ratio of weight changed to conform the English to the now firmly established French ratio,) would have assured the replacement of paper by metal under conditions the most favourable to all great interests involved. This conclusion relates exclusively to the interests

---

[1] It is, perhaps, difficult for the modern reader to realize that this form of a promise to pay was, for the time, nothing but form—that the English "Standard," in Meaning No. 7 of the Introduction, was Paper—and hence it may be useful to present the following piece of documentary evidence, which shows how such competent authorities as the Treasury and the Bank regarded the matter:—

At a Committee of Treasury, 28th March, 1804.
" Resolved.
" That, in the Opinion of this Committee, it will be advisable to attempt an Encouragement to the Importation of Gold, by offering a higher Price than the Coinage Price; and that it will be right for the Bank to offer £4 An Ounce, and to let it be known that it will continue to give this price for three months to come.
" That the Governor be desired to mention this to the Court."

At a Court of Directors, 7th June, 1804.
" Resolved.
" That the Bank do continue to purchase Gold at £4 per Ounce until the 30th of September next."

From Appendix to Reports of Committee on Resumption of Cash Payment, 1819.

present at that day. For the generation which now, seventy years later, inhabits England, it is plain that greater interests than those of that day were hanging upon the choice of measures. Had the course just suggested been taken, Parliament, instead of giving legal sanction to a vendetta or feud between Silver and Gold, would have blessed posterity with the invaluable heritage of inter-metallic or inter-monetary peace.

I venture to believe it is also shown that such action would have been entirely in keeping with the views of Locke, of Newton, and of Harris—the acknowledged teachers of English policy—and the conjecture is well warranted that Peel would have known what their teachings were, had not the "Treatise on the Coins of the Realm" proved so complete a non-conductor between the XIXth century and the remoter and wiser past. That he might consistently have made their views the rule of action for his country, is obvious, from the historical facts herein set forth, and from the justified confidence of his country in his statesmanship. But beside this we have evidence in his own utterances which will be referred to on a later page.[1]

[1] See page 190 and Appendix 26.

CHAPTER VIII.

Silver before English Public Opinion.

§ 21. The status of silver in England since 1816.

The provision of the Law of 1816, which made the opening of the Mints to Free Coinage of Silver contingent upon a Royal Proclamation, finds a simple and obvious explanation in the peculiar conditions of the time. The primary object of the law was to provide a new Silver Coinage, and the first and chief work to be done was to withdraw or to replace the existing Silver-coin, a measure involving great effort and great expense. That the work should be done by the Government itself, and that the Government should desire to reduce the expense as much as possible, was most natural.

In the end the difference between the rate of issue and the cost of the Silver coined from 1816 to 1821, proved to be about half-a-million pounds sterling.[1] But, in order to enjoy these benefits, it was necessary that the right of coining Silver should remain in the hands of the Government; and this result was easily attainable by making a Proclamation a condition precedent for Free Coinage, a proceeding quite in accordance with custom—as will clearly be seen on reference to other provisions of the Statute, and to the Proclamations (see Appendix 21) which were needed to make crowns and

[1] Against this was chargeable the loss which was liquidated upon the withdrawal of the old abraded coin.

"Sovereigns, or twenty-shilling pieces" current and lawful Money.

When, however, the withdrawal of the old coin had taken place, the idea of issuing a Proclamation for Free Coinage naturally came within practical range, and the records of the time show that the question excited attention, but I know of nothing to show that it excited any very deep interest. This was of course quite natural—not that Free Coinage and Seigniorage are entirely incompatible, or that Section IX. of the Act of 1816 necessarily would not " work." To modern ideas, indeed, it seems an anomaly—Free Coinage of tokens—and, no doubt, to calculate its probable operation is to unravel a very tangled skein. But at that time, when " Silver was Silver," when it was Specie and Bullion just as Gold was, the main object of one interested on the Silver side, must naturally be the restoration of Silver to its former position as Full-Legal-Tender, and undiminished in weight: and the Silver-coins provided for by the Act of 1816 were naturally regarded chiefly in relation to that object: the first question seeming to be whether or no these Silver-tokens should be retained side by side with a full-weight Silver-coin to be issued under an amended law.

Upon this greater issue there were expressions of opinion from time to time, to which we shall recur after following to the end the story of this statutory right of Free Coinage of Silver conditional upon a Proclamation.

It is one of the curiosities of monetary history that this contingent right has existed down to our time,[1] although quite

---

Whether this older rule survived the new code established by the Coinage Act of 1870, is a question for the curious. The original Bill brought in by the Chancellor of the Exchequer and Mr. Stansfeld contains the following proposed re-enactment of the Act of 1816:—

(56 Geo. III. c. 68.) "Where, after the date in that behalf fixed by a proclamation under this Act, any person or body brings to the Mint any silver bullion, such bullion shall be assayed and coined, and delivered out

forgotten by the busy world; for I do not recall any reference to the point in later controversy, or indeed any sign of knowledge to-day that the ratio of 1717, and the Standard of Elizabeth, still lurk in shadowy form in the monetary field. Perhaps in the future, when such insensibility shall have become impossible, and when monetary science shall have won its proper place in the academic curriculum, it may become a standing exercise for the advanced monetary student to deal with the knotty problem, " what would have been the effect had Free Coinage of Silver under the Statute of 1816 been put in force after 1871 ? "

Chief among the expressions of opinion bearing upon Silver in the period preceding the Gold discoveries are those which appear as expert evidence, namely, before a Committee for Coin (Privy Council) at the Board of Trade in 1828, and before the Parliamentary Committees appointed to deliberate in preparation for the renewals of the Charter of the Bank of England, in 1833 and 1844, and upon the Mint in 1837. Of

to such person, at the rate of sixty-two shillings for every 5,760 grains imperial weight, or 373·24195 grams metric weight, of silver bullion of standard fineness so brought, in whatever denomination the same is coined."

To this the following lines also have reference :—

" No undue preference shall be shown to any person or body under this section, and every person or body shall have priority according to the time at which he or they brought such bullion to the Mint."

The Act, as finally passed, omits the foregoing, retaining only the other Free Coinage clauses which refer to Gold only; but it also contains the following :—

" 11. It shall be lawful for Her Majesty, with the advice of Her Privy Council, from time to time by proclamation to do all or any of the following things, namely,

*   *   *   *

(10.) To regulate any matters relative to the coinage and the Mint within the present prerogative of the Crown which are not provided for by this Act."

If the Free Coinage of Silver provided by the Act of 1816 was within " the present prerogative of the Crown," and was not " provided for by this Act," it would seem to have remained intact.

these the most important is the clear and strong utterance of Mr. Alexander Baring, M.P. (afterwards Lord Ashburton), whose position can here be tersely indicated by his reply to the question, "whether it was possible and desirable to maintain a Silver Legal-Tender at or near the French ratio," namely, "I have always thought so, and certainly think so still. I have no doubt about it." (Appendix No. 23.)

The following piece of evidence (which it was my fortune to discover in a Parliamentary Paper), coming from Mr. Drew, the Governor, and Mr. Palmer, the Deputy-Governor, of the Bank of England in 1828,—against Silver, but giving the reason why,—is also of interest as indicating the gulf that separates the opinion of the earlier day from that later doctrine of Metrical Unity with Gold as the Unit, to which full reference has been made in Chapter IV.

Question:

"1st. Whether, in the opinion of the Bank, it be desirable that there should be established and maintained in this country, at the same time that we maintain the existing Silver currency, a Silver currency as a Legal-Tender, the value of which should bear to Gold nearly that proportion which is established in France, say about 15½ to 1. . . . .

("In replying to the three preceding queries, the Bank will bear in mind that the object is to retain Gold as the bulk of the currency, and to have Silver as an aid to it.")

Answer:

"1. Provided there be sufficient Silver currency in the country for the small payments, there does not appear to the Bank to be any advantage in the proposed addition of Silver, as a general Legal-Tender, *from the great difficulty of retaining Gold as the bulk of the currency under such an arrangement.*" (Appendix 24.)

(The italics are mine.)

The reader will observe that the difficulty of keeping Gold as the bulk of the currency was the point: not the difficulty of keeping Silver at par with Gold, nor the idea that to have Silver as Legal-Tender was *per se* an infraction of, or a derogation from, the " Standard" established by the Act of 1816. Evidently, the dream of Metrology had not yet set the fashion of thought. Indeed, so little was the current opinion distorted by false theory, that I find in the minutes of evidence before the Committee on the Royal Mint of 1837 an adumbration of the most advanced thought of to-day.

The mere faint suggestion of a fixed price to be paid by Bank or Mint for Gold and Silver Bullion, and that Bullion can remain at par in different states "as we get more civilized," are certainly worthy of commemoration, and the credit of these seems to lie in part with the Chairman of the Committee, Mr. Joseph Hume, and the witness Mr. Haggard, Chief Clerk of the Bullion Office of the Bank of England. (See Appendix 25.)

Mr. Haggard published in 1847 a pamphlet,[1] entitled "Observations on the Standard of Value and the Circulating Medium of this Country," in which he sets forth a plan for the reformation of the English Monetary System, which is of peculiar interest, and I therefore present it here in brief, stating it entirely in my own words:—

> The Standard of Value to be Silver Bullion; four ounces ($\frac{37}{40}$ fine), being the substratum of a Paper Pound Sterling.
>
> The Full-Legal-Tender circulation to consist of paper representing that Bullion; the Paper (Bank notes, so-called) being Legal-Tender from the Bank, as well as between individuals.
>
> The Coin to consist of Gold and Silver at $15\frac{1}{5}$ to 1, Gold Legal-Tender for £200, Silver Legal-Tender for £2, both kinds charged with "seigniorage."

In speaking of the ratio, $15\frac{1}{5}$ to 1, Mr. Haggard adds the

---
[1] I am indebted for knowledge of this pamphlet to Mr. S. O. Gray, the Chief Accountant of the Bank of England.

words "the same as France," which contain a reason equally in accord with the views of Sir James Houblon and Mr. Michael Godfrey, and of Mr. Gibbs and Mr. Grenfell.

That the tradition of Silver Money in England maintained itself among learned men, in despite of the course of events, is nowhere better shown than in the words of Sir John Herschel, who, though Master of the Mint, was not afraid to say, in 1853, of the Single Gold Standard: "I do not mean to say a Silver Standard would not be better; I believe it would, and I believe a binary Standard, half Silver, half Gold, at the option of either party to insist on, would be better than either." (Rep. Dec. Coinage, 1853, p. 46.)

We now come to consider the views of Mr. S. J. Loyd, afterwards Lord Overstone. Without attempting to review those endless campaigns of controversy as to Currency and Banking, for which the theory of the Bank Act of 1844 serves as an ever-ripening apple of discord, it is germane and practical to ascertain at head-quarters, so to speak, what was then the General Order on the subject of Silver.

In the various markets, and in most of the currencies of the world, Silver and Gold stood side by side—with little fluctuation of relative value—and no one seems to have thought of inquiring why they stood by each other so steadily, or how this comfortable Balance of Power was maintained. At the same time England had excluded Silver-coin from being Full-Legal-Tender, and there was no present probability that this settlement would be disturbed. The practical dangers and difficulties at that time in England with which a monetary reformer had to deal, were naturally connected with the issue of Bank-notes, and lessons of reform were to be drawn from England's experience in the period of Restriction, and of Resumption, from the panic of 1825, and from the depression of 1837 and 1839.

Such was the genesis of the novel features of the Bank Charter Act: it purported to deal with the superstructure,—

with the parts of the monetary edifice where repair was needed, with the attics and balconies, and lighter apparatus connected with it, rather than with its main body, or its foundation, that is to say, with Silver and Gold, with Money and the State. It was natural that, as in elder times the phenomena of the solar system seemed to the learned world to find their centre in the earth, so now a certain order of things should be equally well taken for granted. To Lord Overstone, whose ideas were embodied in that Act, Money, Coin, Bullion, used generally, included Silver as well as Gold, and it was only when the relation of English Coin to English Paper came into play that the yellow colours were displayed and Gold alone was spoken of.

Overstone's great principle, "That a metallic currency, by virtue of its own intrinsic value, will regulate itself," was evidently constructed upon an unconscious assumption of the permanence of existing conditions, an assumption which was very natural, while England's Money was enjoying so comfortable a lateral support from the laws of other countries, that in a statement of the metallic reserves of English Banks the experienced theorist did not feel called upon to distinguish Silver from Gold. What better evidence could be asked of the success of the then existing "Bimetallic Union" than this confidence of Lord Overstone in Silver as Standard Bullion, if not as Standard Money?

In 1832, when he urged the publication of a statement of the assets and liabilities of the Bank of England, he gave no suggestion that a distinction be made between the Metals, and in the returns provided for in the Bank Charter Act of 1833, the Bank regularly published its statements of "Bullion," while it regularly held a goodly proportion of Silver. The effect of the Bank Charter Act of 1844 upon the status of Silver was to limit, and yet at the same time to legalize, the function of Silver, as what I may call Lawful-Money-metal, or Standard Bullion, as distinguished from Standard Coin.

In completing the list of restrictions upon the issue of Bank-notes and of Paper-Money in England, the effort was made to have assurance trebly if not quadruply sure that the notes which remained should be ever convertible, and inasmuch as the law made them convertible into Gold it was found necessary, as the Statute declares, to limit the amount of Silver which the new Issue Department of the Bank could hold. Henceforth, one part of Silver to four parts of Gold became the limit for Silver. That the new law was regarded as touching the question of the Standard, or that the Standard had not passed beyond Parliamentary action in the sense of being a compact or Act of Settlement, or other law by which the faith of the nation is pledged—is amply recognized by Sir Robert Peel in the speech reprinted in the Appendix (26). The principle of principles, in his view, is that there must be Standard Metal, Standard Coin, or Standard Bullion, and it was consistent with this principle that it should be either Gold, or Silver, *or both*; but he invited Parliament, as we have seen, in the name of all the great writers on this subject—Petty, Locke, Harris, Liverpool—to declare for the Single Standard, and that Standard, Gold.

It was, of course, very natural that in fixing the limit to the amount of Silver Bullion which could serve as a deposit for Bank of England notes, it was ordered that the statement of assets should note the character of the Bullion—and the returns down to a late date show an ample use of Silver. But the regulation of the Statute, so rigid in everything else, shows, on the one vital point, the Gold-value of Silver, a quite phenomenal laxity.

Under the Act of 1844 Silver Bullion is still " Bullion "—and so it remains to-day. Nothing is said in the Law of the *amount* of Silver, except that it shall not be " an Amount of Silver Bullion not exceeding one Fourth Part of the Gold Coin and Bullion."

From the standpoint of to-day, the *naïveté* of this Section is monumental. We recall unlimited pages of Utopian economy and Saturnian statistics, which are wisdom if Silver and Gold are "commodities and nothing more," but are no better than the crackling of thorns under a pot if Silver and Gold are something more than mere commodities: we recall, on the other hand, the inner light and holy fire that inspired the crusade for Golden Metrical Money whose banners were blessed at all the shrines of learning in Christendom, and then we turn to Section III. of the Bank Charter Act, and see that "*Silver Bullion not exceeding one fourth part of the Gold Bullion*" is a part of the Base of England's Money! What does it mean? In the vaults of the Issue Department of the Great Bank two primordial elements, one "the fourth" of the other! But how "the fourth?" That implies quantity. Is it the fourth part in effective bulk, as if one were comparing a gallon of oats and a quart of wheat, or is it weight that is spoken of—four pounds of Gold to one pound of Silver? By no means! On the contrary: in bulk, the Statute provides for nearly seven times as much Silver as Gold; in weight, nearly four times as much. "But how is this?" the reader well may say; "the Statute says nothing of this." Not explicitly; and yet everybody has so understood it. For Silver and Gold are something other than elements, or commodities; they are Money, generally exchangeable for each other by the *fiat* of Christendom; and everyone knew it, and thought no evil of it; and it was under the advice of Lord Overstone and of Sir Robert Peel that the British Parliament rightly took Gold and Silver and their relations to each other for granted. It was the new-fangled notion of astrological Money, based on Utopian economy and Saturnian statistics, which came into fashion long after 1844, that sought to repudiate these truths, and which set one emperor after another trying to crown the edifice of his reign by turning the monetary foundations of it upside down.

After meditation upon these lines, those most prosaic words

" Silver Bullion not exceeding one-fourth part of the Gold," looked at fixedly, may come out before the eyes in flames, a writing on the wall for these Utopias ; a prophetic inscription, which the waves of time cannot deface—" Woe be unto thee, thy days are numbered : thou art weighed in the balance, and found wanting."

An early instalment of retribution was visited upon these Utopias when the following communication was sent to the Monetary Conference of 1881 :—

" Subject to these considerations [viz., the return of the Mints of other countries to such rules as would ensure the conversion of Gold into Silver, and Silver into Gold], the Bank Court are satisfied that the issue of their notes against Silver, within the letter of the Act, would not involve the risk of infringing that principle of it which imposes a positive obligation on the Bank to receive Gold in exchange for notes, and to pay notes in Gold on demand.

" The Bank Court see no reason why an assurance should not be conveyed to the Monetary Conference at Paris, if their Lordships think it desirable, that the Bank of England, agreeably with the Act of 1844, would be always open to the purchase of Silver under the conditions above described."

§ 22. INTERNATIONAL CONCURRENCE IN THE PAST AND IN THE PRESENT.

This action of the Bank of England in 1881 affords a convenient vantage-ground from which we can look back upon the expanse of monetary experience that lies between the present time and the days when that Bank was founded. The point which seems to me to appeal to us for attention is— the simplicity of the task of insuring order in the relations of the Money-metals for England's use, the practicability of it, or, to express the idea in another form, the absence of great interests, or of natural obstacles to work against the fulfilment of the task.

Let us, for a moment, imagine the guinea reduced at the beginning of the XVIIIth century below 21 shillings—that is, to a figure which would have offered near accord with the then French ratio, and have firmly established the precedent of diligence in observing the principle of international concurrence. The reader will mark well, the supposition cannot be regarded as extreme or improbable. It merely supposes a more scrupulous observance of a plain, business-like, common-sense principle, to which, as I have shown, at the date mentioned, the officers of the Bank of England, the Warden of the Mint, and the chief economic adviser of the Government, had respectively proved their adhesion. Science and business experience thus united at the time in recommending this harmony of ratio between neighbouring states. Moreover, England, in fact, tried to do the thing recommended. Now, although England did it ill, instead of doing it well, it is entirely practical to consider what would have been the result, if she had done this thing well, instead of doing it ill.

We ask, then, Supposing England's Money brought into unison with the " par of her neighbours," or the " example of France" accepted in full, what would have happened—what might have happened ?

Obviously, we can contemplate as one result, a concurrent Silver and Gold Standard (with Silver Unit in each country) in France and England, at ratios close to $14\frac{1}{2}$ to 1. From such a state of affairs, other events might well have proceeded in time. As it was, great changes came. France abandoned Seigniorage (once 7 and 8 per cent.) ; England abandoned that statutory inhibition upon the exportation of coin which makes so wide a difference between the position of the metals in the present, and in the past. But with the ratio of $14\frac{1}{2}$ so securely in possession, it seems at the least safe to say that the change in France to $15\frac{1}{2}$ would not have occurred in 1785, nor would it have been adopted in 1803. The effective reason for that change ¹ was the scarcity of Gold in French circulation. But our supposition implies that England would have parted with much Gold, certainly enough to give France what she needed; so that, really, our supposition may be held to remove the reason for the change of 1785, and, therefore, for the readoption of $15\frac{1}{2}$ in 1803.

Inferring thus from history as it is, to history as it might have been, it is legitimate to think that concurrence of ratio between England and France, in 1700, would have maintained concurrence through the century then beginning.

But concurrence in the XVIIIth century would have made concurrence natural in the XIXth. Had the Monetary System which I have called the Silver and Gold Standard with a Silver Unit, which was, in fact, suffered to go to pieces in the shallows of debasement, been maintained, it would not only in the XVIIIth century have served every purpose of England better than the halting system with which she was forced, through the default of statesmanship, to content herself, but it might well have reduced both the evils attendant upon the issue of Paper-Money during the Napoleonic wars, and upon the Restoration of Cash Payments; and its presence later, would have spared civilization the spectacle of the Battle of the Standards, in the midst of which we stand to-day, the aimless Thirty Years' War of Money against Money, which coming times will look back upon as a reproach to our century, and which still awaits that new settlement of peace which in after times may well be compared in its importance to the Treaty of Westphalia.

If England, the original instigator of this War of Coinages, is still to hold the place of an obstacle to concord, certainly Englishmen owe it to themselves amply to justify this course.

---

[1] This entire matter is set forth in a paper on "The ratio of $15\frac{1}{2}$ in France," in the Documents of the Conferences of 1878 and of 1881.

If the principle of international concurrence in dealing with the Money-metals is to be rejected by England to-day, it must be for reasons whose roots lie deep among the forces that have made her history. I challenge the search for such reasons.

What are the generating forces that produced the Anti-Silver sections of England's later monetary laws, which exclude that ancient Standard of the Realm in vindication of which Somers and Montague and Locke and Newton won their monetary fame? An answer is to be found in the preceding pages.

Undoubtedly in the line of the earlier years, some Money-mongers (as they were well named), whether of high or of low degree, have profited by the disorder of Money, but beyond this where are the obstacles to order? Evidently, the heedlessness of rulers, slight errors of opinion in their advisers, inertia of governments, were the obstacles to realization of the demands of an actual harmony of all great interests which made entirely for order.

But all these obstacles are of subordinate quality; they belong neither to the rank of instincts, nor of habits, nor of passions, nor of interests, which are the great irresistible forces that make history; they are all, in fact, resolvable into a slight failure of illumination on the part of men in control of a nation—an obstacle, therefore, which was removable by turning on a little more of the light of learning and of business sense, which are the rightful heritage of a great commercial Power.

So far as the present century is concerned, the Anti-Silver laws are shown to be, historically, the outcome of heedlessness, of confusion of thought, of cheese-paring finance, of fables agreed upon, of visionary system-building, and of mythical science—of error, which, in order to be well forgiven, must soon be well replaced.

Turning now from considering these lessons of the past to the task of present action, we note at once that the terms of the monetary problem have suffered change in the centuries.

Like feudal robber-knights and war-levying bishops, the seigniorial system of coinage has passed away; more orderly conditions prevail, and it is now not only possible, but common, that nations should act together effectively in matters of such common interest as the regulation of Money. In earlier times, the task of establishing a more closely concurrent monetary policy between nations than then obtained, would have found no obstacle in difference of metal of which the Unit was made: but the idea of such a task, while not unknown, as I am able to prove by English testimony, which I recommend to the reader's attention,[1] could have but feeble life in an age when shiftless debasement was a common exercise of prerogative,

[1] "Of CONTRACTING WITH FOREIGN NATIONS BY AMBASSADORS TO KEEP THEIR MONEYS AT A CERTAIN STANDARD.—Amongst all the Remedies propounded against the Alterations of Moneys, there is none more specious than this, nor more frequent in mention, both in provisional Edicts, which are made for the Reformation of Moneys, and in Considerations held for the purpose, for it is said to advance it: That if we contract with other Nations for a certain and stable standard of Moneys which may be equal, then we shall avoid all the Inconveniences that do grow by the raising of Moneys, because we shall never raise them, and we shall avoid all the Inconveniences that do grow by the not raising of Moneys, because other nations shall not raise theirs. Besides for this Remedy there is alledged the example of former Ages, wherein it appears that in many Treaties with forein Nations our Kings did contract for the mutual standard of their Money. But however the Proposition be specious and frequent, yet, of all other Remedies, if it be thoroughly examined, it will appear the most difficult, or rather impossible, to be effected; and if it were effected, it would turn to no use, for thus stands the state of this business, almost all the Silver which is now drawn out of the Earth, cometh from the West-Indies, all which intirely aboordeth first in Spain, whence it is dispersed into other Countries Eastward; which do draw it unto them by setting an higher price upon it; for, as if there were no Cloth in all the World but in England, no other Country could have Cloth except they did pay dearer for it than in England; and by so much dearer by how much it were more remote from England, because to the original price, there must of necessity be added an increase in regard of the time, the charge, and hazard of transporting it; so fares it with Silver, that all Countries which will draw from Spain, do necessarily set a greater price upon it, by how much they are more remote from thence, and this is the Reason why

and tampering with the coins a favourite means of filling the purses of a favoured few.

The earlier events set forth in the preceding pages are the story of England's efforts in emerging from these conditions. The statute of 1666 was the assumption by Representative Government of the task of regulating the work of the Mint upon a new principle, and upon lines of stability and publicity consonant with the needs of a nation, rather than responsive to the exigencies of a Court. The Statutes of the Recoinage, dealing with evils assailing the very life of the nation, sought to give a new solidity to the time-honoured establishment of the Silver Measure of Commerce, with Gold as Current coin. Had the work thus begun been continued upon the lines which I have shown to have been well traced by the architects of this political edifice, the dual Money of the world would have found its regulation in this form.

To-day, the question of this regulation has entered a distinctly different phase through the change of the relative quantity of the metals in the hands of man.

For the Monetary legislator of to-day, the appearance of Gold

the sphear of Silver seemeth to roll from the East to the West, until it come unto him, where it seemeth to fall into a Gulph. But of Gold it is not so, because that comes in so great abundance from the East as from the West.

" Now then it were a great Prejudice for England and France to contract with Spain for a certain standard of Silver, except they could likewise contract for the same standard with the Low-Countries, and Italy, who draw part of their Silver from them, as they draw theirs from Spain: for others, they should give a stop to the coming in of their Silver, and should leave the issue of it open. Nor would Turkey contract, unless they could also contract with Persia for the same, where Silver is yet higher than in Turkey, and so forward into China ; neither would the Low-Countrie men contract, except they could contract for the same with the Hanse-Towns, where Silver is higher than in the Low-Countries: neither would the Hanse-Towns contract, except they could contract for the same with Prussia and Poland; neither would they of Poland contract, except they could contract with Muscovie ; neither would Muscovie contract, except they could contract with Persia ; and so forward in all such places Silver is still at an higher and higher rate.

" But suppose it was possible to draw all those Countries to a certain contract, what would be the use of it ?

here and there in the place of Silver as the formal and statutory Unit of Coinage, has tended to complicate the problem ; but this effect has been largely neutralized by the counter-increase of the relative stock of Gold through the rich outpourings of the mines. The actual diversity of material adopted for the Unit in different countries is unlikely to form an obstacle to a concurrent policy of the nations,—which must of necessity embrace both metals,—because such diversity can produce no serious embarrassment except in an event which may be excluded from consideration because nature excludes it from probability : that is to say, in the case of a future breaking-up of the Union, or dislocation of the parity between the metals which it shall have established.

Admitting either metal as Money at an identical ratio, certain to have a fair supply of either metal relatively to the other, it is a matter of subordinate importance to the nations which are so to unite, whether one or the other metal bears the Unit in this nation or in that. In 1873 the United States made Gold the official standard of value: it would mean no derogation from this position if, under proper guarantees of international concert, they should give the same rights to Silver which Gold had under the Silver Standard of William III. Similar privileges given to Silver in England would leave the Gold sovereign in the future still, as it is now, the corner-stone of the English system ; in other words, in the free enjoyment of all the rights it has beneficially pos-

"I did in a former Chapter observe that most Countries, and particularly France and Low-Countries do seldome or never raise their Moneys, but when people by Custom and general Use have raised the money before hand, beyond the Publick Declaration and the State is forced to follow the People whom in this case they do not master.

"To what end is it to contract with those Nations for that which is not in their power to observe ? And that which is alledged for the course of contracting, with forein Nations, out of the example of former times, doth clearly convince the vanity of this Proposition, for it is manifest, as I have shewed in the former Chapters that notwithstanding these Contracts the Money was continually from time to time raised."—Chap. XVII. of Rice Vaughan, on "Coins and Coinage" (London, 1657).

sessed. England would have her Gold Standard and her Silver and Gold Money in 1886, just as she had her Silver Standard and her Gold and Silver Money in 1696, but under guarantees of permanence hitherto unknown.

These observations are put forth merely with a view of assigning its rank to the question of the Single Monetary Unit under the conditions that obtain to-day. I do not intend thereby to express an opinion as to the question whether a change of the Unit, or whether the simultaneous formal adoption of a Silver Unit and a Gold Unit—in Jefferson's phrase, "putting the Unit in the two metals"—is advisable in any particular country or group of countries; a matter which it is not necessary to discuss at this time.

Recurring, then, to the scruples which support the inviolability of the present Standard of England, in the sense of National Unit of Coinage, the Pound Sterling of Gold which in 1816 became the lawful successor of the Pound Sterling of Silver, whose story begins with the misty dawn of history, it has, I hope, become clear that no rightful jurisdiction of it need be invaded by any use of Silver as Full-Legal-Tender in England, however abundant, which should proceed under the conditions of international or foreign action that stand ready for fulfilment. No one thinks that the English Standard is debased to-day by the circulation of Bank of England notes as Legal-Tender, although part of them have behind them only credit, and many might have Silver Bullion, if the Bank used the privilege accorded by the law of 1844. Why should Silver always at par with Gold have any more serious effect upon the integrity of the Gold "Standard?" It is generally understood in other departments of thought that "things which are equal to the same thing are equal to each other."

CHAPTER IX.

NOTABLE ARGUMENTS AGAINST INTER-METALLIC PEACE.

§ 23. CERTAIN THESES OF PROFESSOR ERWIN NASSE.

Many of the arguments current among monetary writers have been met, directly or indirectly, in what has gone before; and the task remains to me of presenting a brief summary of the remaining armament of opposition to Joint Restoration of Silver.

Professor Erwin Nasse stands in the front rank of monetary writers of his time, and has lately[1] put forth a work on the Monetary Question in Germany ("Die Wachrungsfrage in Deutschland") which appears to me the most important publication which the defence of Demonetization has produced, and therefore well entitled to be openly confronted. Admitting as fact the cardinal doctrine of Unionists that Anti-Silver-law and practice have broken the par which the Dual-Standard-law established; admitting also the duty of the State to interfere in order to protect against an alteration of the Purchasing Power of Money, and thence advancing to the concession that international concert may, under conceivable circumstances, become a necessity, Nasse still seeks to bar all passage for progress by the theses—

1st, not only that a Silver-and-Gold Union without England is not safe under any circumstances: but also, 2nd, that the evils now existing are not sufficient to warrant Germany in com-

[1] February, 1885.

mitting herself to the establishment of international concert in the matter of Money.

Upon the first thesis I shall say nothing; and, after all that has gone before, I need enter but partially upon the second thesis. To Nasse's view, however, of the nature and character of the question involved, as a whole, I must take exception. He regards Germany's accession to a Silver-and-Gold Union as an infraction of the independence of Germany. He objects to what he calls " our sacrificing the right of independent regulation of our Money in so essential a point as the use of Gold and Silver, and betaking ourselves to a contractual dependence in relation to foreign states."

To my mind this appears to be in essence the expression of a certain restiveness; of an unwillingness that a certain nation should bear the ordinary burdens of civil intercourse. That these are, in certain circumstances, burdens, is true; but they must be borne: the only option is between bearing them well or ill. In the course of ages our race has gained an ample experience of analogous purport in those regions of conduct, for example, which are regulated by the Law of Father and Child, the Law of Husband and Wife, the Law of Landlord and Tenant. But surely if these bodies of law are of man's contriving it was not men, but the nature of man, that made the necessity for them: if there were no burdens to be borne there need be no laws. The wise regulation is born of a necessity, and not of an unrestricted, unconditioned will.

So of the relation of the State to the matter before us, concurrent regulation of Money. Man is a trading being, in spite of Professor Nasse: he may regret it, but such is the fact. And with the fact comes, for each nation, an interest in the action of other nations, and a need for concurrent action in the interest of all. If it were a question whether the German nation should transfer its fair domain from the planet Luna, where there is no conflict of monetary systems, to the planet Terra, where there is such conflict, we must, I think, concede that Professor Nasse's position has its strength, but not till then!

In discussing the question of degree of existing evils, Professor Nasse, to my surprise, allows himself to indulge in a variety of pleas which seek to defend the demonetization movement from responsibility for the contraction and depression, which in England are admitted, by the highest authorities, to be in fair measure due to this cause.

But beside this, he denies the fact of an important general rise in the value of Gold. This subject has been discussed in the preceding pages, and it is needless now to recur to it. Professor Nasse's error on this point is beyond question. But he also undertakes to make light of the drag upon international trade arising from the fracture of the par formerly maintained by alternative coinage in the Silver-and-Gold nations. Here again he has all England, so to speak, against him. Now, if Professor Nasse is really measuring interests, measuring the foreign trade of Germany with the foreign trade of England, of course it may well appear that Germany's interest is numerically quite small. But is it not customary to weigh interests rather than count them? If England has five children, while Germany has but one, an alarm of scarlet fever need not produce perturbation in the exact ratio of 5 to 1.

The facts upon which Professor Nasse lays great stress are the expansion of Indian exports and imports of late years.

In his reasoning on this head he neglects what appears to me the gist of the matter. The notable effect of Indian exports does not arise from the mere provisioning of Europe with these articles, but from their low price: a price made artificially low by the effect of Anti-Silver-laws, which have thus had the effect of disorganizing home valuations[1] in the States which adopted these laws. Their price is the obvious

---

[1] See Section 6.

result of the rise of the Silver-price of Gold. But this rise, a specific product of European Outlawry of Silver, is capable of being considered apart from the continuance of fluctuations and uncertainty in the Silver-price of Gold, which, cumulatively to the great upheavals by which (Silver-Gold) investments are seriously deranged, add a constant force to make business aleatory, and injuriously affect international trade.

In the following sections we shall confront some of Professor Nasse's minor positions in detail.

§ 24. SILVER OUTLAWRY AND THE MANUAL-LABOUR CLASSES.

It appears that the apology for demonetization contains one aggressive argument which wears the uniform of Humanitarianism. A social transformation is said to be in progress, by which the manual-labour classes are winning a greater share of the profits of work. Hence it follows—What follows? From the use which is sometimes made of this argument, however ingeniously it is brought forward, the unwary would really infer that it was desirable to demonetize Money, contract prices, and produce a general depression of business, in order to improve the condition of the manual-labour classes!

Compared with this the *naïveté* of Charles Lamb's Chinamen who burned their houses down in order to enjoy roast-pig, is sagacity itself. What a satisfaction it must be to a simple-minded member of the rank and file of Silver Outlawry who, in his heart, is troubled at the condition of things, and

> "Back recoils, he knows not why,
> E'en at the sound himself has made,"

to find that, after all, he has been a friend of the working-man all the time, a philanthropist without knowing it!

But it will be said, it is impossible that responsible writers can have maintained such an absurdity—and I must frankly admit this: but must observe also, that it is one thing to use an absurdity oneself, and another to allow others to use it.

Responsible writers seem to use this argument to prove that the employers of labour are mistaken in thinking that prices are low; it is not that at all: it is that wages are higher than they once were, and profits are smaller; thus employers feel depressed and discouraged: but the country ought to rejoice, not to mourn.

But the same general argument which Mr. Pirmez and Professor Nasse desire to make effective for Belgium and Germany, has been tried in England on the most effective scale and has been "found wanting." The Belgian and German arguments are likely to prove equally transitory with the English.

Before leaving this important subject we may conveniently set forth certain theses which will be found germane: affirming, namely:—

1st. That like Causes B and C and Counter-cause D, set forth in Chapter III., this growing command of the manual-labour classes over the comforts of life is a tendency of the time, and must have been in existence while prices were rising after 1850, as well as while they have been falling since 1873. (See page 19.)

2nd. That accounts of the condition of hand-workers are incomplete and utterly misleading when they depend upon the *daily* rate of wages merely: for then the main point is omitted, namely, the *annual* rate, the amount of wages, steady employment, regular and constant work.

3rd. That accounts of the industrial activity of peoples in late years, are merely a comparison of bad years with bad years; not of years of full prosperity, when the brain of the man of enterprise and the arms of the labourer were working "full time," each "rejoicing as a giant to run his course."

4th. That for many years certain strong influences have been at work to obscure the perception of what real prosperity means, and what a nation or a community can do, when its men of enterprise are working "full time." These influences grow out of the facts

(A.) That the great school of whilom orthodox doctors, who obtained control of the patient world, and prescribed demonetization are, unfortunately, bound by powerful motives to maintain that the patient is doing well—in spite of appearances:

(B.) That hopefulness and cheerfulness in adverse times are a duty.

There have been for years, therefore, good reasons why men of influence should be unconsciously led, not only to ignore the quality of general prosperity, but also with after-wisdom to disable the benefits of former prosperous years: for the collapse of 1873, relating back, imputed a degree of lightheadedness to investments of the preceding years, which, but for a State policy of contraction, need not have seemed a justified charge. We can picture to ourselves the effect of enforced idleness as compared with working full time, by the query how far the brains and hands that have been idle or unprofitably engaged in England since 1873, would have gone toward putting Asia in harness by a railroad from the Mediterranean to the Indus, or bridling Africa with a curb of steel from the Congo-mouth to Zanzibar.

5th. That the question of moment is, therefore, not whether a nation can exist and pay its way, in spite of a certain monetary policy, but whether such a policy tends, as compared with another policy, to infuse that blood in the veins of people which impels them to work "full time," and makes them happy in doing so.

6th. That to re-integrate the foundation of the world's business by settling the Silver Question would have this tendency is so plain as to need no argument here.

§ 25. LIONS IN THE PATH OF THE REINSTATEMENT OF SILVER.

Many others beside Professor Nasse have discovered among the lions in the path of a Silver and Gold Union the dangers,

1. That Treaties will not be faithfully carried out :
2. That some nation will issue Paper Money :
3. That too much Silver will be produced from the mines :
4. That some terrible unloading of Silver, and buying up of Gold, will take place.

Upon analysis these objections resolve themselves into an indictment against modern governments, that they are not competent to manage their common interests intelligently.

I submit that while it is true that, if there be no common interest in the stability of the world's Standard of Value, then, of course, there is no ground for, nor safety in, united action; yet if there be ground for such action the world does not lack mental capacity to act intelligently in the matter. So if it be for the interest of the nations to shirk carrying letters and to steal postage-dues from each other, then there is no ground for a Postal Union. Undoubtedly war, for example, interrupts the Postal Service and may cause the issue of Paper Money: but whatever harm is so done, would it not be done if there were no Postal Union at all, or if there were no Monetary Union at all? Where, then, is the validity of this order of objection? It does not exist. So,

> "In the night, imagining some fear,
> How easy is a bush supposed a bear!"

The gentlemen do "protest too much!" If, for example, Nasse is right in denying the evils of the lack of a common measure between nations, he should go on and deny the evils of the lack of a common measure between provinces; he thus denies the advantage of the unification of German Money; and, beyond, the path is open before him to oppose the entire institution of Money as a common measure between men;

and thus, in logical sequence, he should seek to subvert the history of civilization on that line. So if this alleged incapacity of nations to bear the ordinary responsibilities of social life exists, then seclusion behind a Chinese wall, well guarded with flying torpedoes, must be the statesman's dream. But this new analogue of Gulliver's Laputa is not the statesman's dream; in spite of Tariffs and of Armies it is a trading age we live in, and its glory is that all the Chinese walls are riddled with lines of rapid transit and transport, and, accordingly, the possibilities of business management, whose strategic lines cross the borders of nations, are greatly enlarged in comparison with earlier times.

So long, then, as plain matter-of-fact common-sense trading human creatures possess the surface of the earth, we may be allowed to hope that the Treasuries and the Banks may be able to protect national interests under a rational system of Monetary Union consonant with the spirit of the age, quite as well as the Post Office Departments manage a Postal Union. It is a great task, and the responsibility of it is great; but it is not to be met by ignoring it.

As for the prophecy of an inundation of Silver from the mines, those who give weight to it should take to heart certain facts, among which I will only mention here the following : The advocates of Silver Outlawry are not novices in prophecy : and for many years an increased output of Gold was the object of prediction. Meantime, the once infallible recipe of the schools for an increase of product, namely, a decrease of the cost of production, has been at work. Prices have been falling since 1873, and so the cost of producing Gold has been diminishing. And yet both the prophecy and the science of other days have been set at naught; for the annual product of Gold has been waning,—dogma and prophecy are alike foiled. Evidently the metals are too "precious" to be amenable to reason.

But even if we waive the point, and suppose the output of

Silver should increase, how much is the increase likely to be? Nothing per cent., a little per mille, upon the stock of Money in the hands of man!

Evidently no experience of the past, no probabilities of the future, on this head, can be united to construct data upon which the action of nations can be based. Indeed, I venture to say that the mere idea of such a thing as an inundation of Silver, is an artificial product of error, that it is really an outcome of the refusal of economists to recognize in their true relation the conditions of Silver supply and demand in the years following 1870. The fall of Silver relatively to Gold was originally attributed by the partisans of Gold, not to an increased demand for Gold coupled with an enormously reduced demand for Silver—for to admit that would be to admit that monetary law can affect the value of Money—but to a slightly increased annual supply of new Silver. Thus it came to pass that the few millions of the bonanzas, a minute fraction of the existing stock of Precious Metal, were expanded by learned fancy into an "inundation," in order to meet the emergencies of erroneous theory.

As far as the stock of Silver now in sight is concerned, the great mass of it is in Asia, and chiefly in China. One who dreads that the Chinese People are about to change their second nature, and reject Silver for Gold will, I fear, turn deaf ears to any considerations which I can present. But for this, I should endeavour to make clear my view that the chief reason why there should be a desire to replace Silver with Gold is that Silver is not now as good Money as Gold in England, which is at present the world's clearing-house, and so close the matter by observing that it rests with England to remove that disability.

This remark serves also as an antidote to fears of a violent sequestration of Gold, which, it is alleged, will follow the Reinstatement of Silver. Can anyone suppose that a continuation of the present scramble for Gold promises relief from that danger, especially when such a signal is raised as the enormous absorption of European Gold in India?

Passing to other objections, I select the following from the evidences of misapprehension current in learned circles:—"The essence of all such schemes (inconvertible paper and Bi-metallism) is to prevent, or mitigate, a fall of prices, or to create a rise of prices by an immediate abundance of money. But the effect is necessarily transitory . . . The annual product of the two bears the same relation to the total stock of both, that the product of one does to the stock of one metal. Hence the permanent causes of scarcity remain."

In the latter sentences, the facts as to the past and the doctrine of chances as to the future are quite ignored. The annual product of the two metals has been, and the chances are it always will be, in steadier relation to the total stock, than the product of either alone to the stock of either respectively. The statement is also quite inconsistent with that threat of a coming inundation, or over-production of Silver, which plays so large a part in maintaining the prejudice against its reinstatement; for if the permanent elements of scarcity remain, there can be no inundation in sight. The reader will also note the strange rigidity of the quantity-theory which ignores confidence as an element in the volume of business, and assumes that a world at war with itself will act in quite the same way as a world at peace.

But these matters are unimportant here, as compared with the point that there is a radical difference between "inconvertible paper" and "bi-metallism": that it takes more than a printing-press and paper to create Metallic Money, and it is not the same thing as Paper-Money when it is created.

If the possibility which Jevons[1] suggested, and of which a hint was given long ago by Mr. Thorold Rogers[2] and by Mr.

---

[1] "Investigations in Currency," etc., 1884, p. 328.
[2] "Princeton Review," Jan. 1879.

Giffen,[1] were to become fact, and one-pound notes should come into vogue south of the Tweed, then, at their issue, there would be the "immediate supply" of Money which has been spoken of, for the notes would set free so and so many millions of Gold; 20 millions was the figure which Jevons spoke of. Now these notes are created out of nothing: but how is the immediate abundance of Money to be produced with Silver? Where is the reservoir which is to swell the tide so suddenly? It does not exist. Truly it may be said of such arguments,

> "The earth hath bubbles as the water has,
> And these are of them."

Considerable importance has been given in late discussion to the question how far can the law of alternative Coinage and of Dual Legal-Tender in a given country, affect the relative price of the metals, when one metal has been entirely exported from that country, because of its higher value elsewhere.

The answer seems naturally to be that the law remains as it was, the trade of that country—domestic and foreign—and all the valuations of that country stand as they did; and hence to the extent of the relation which the monetary operations of that country bear to the total of operations affecting the metals, the country exerts a constant pressure to maintain its legal ratio, as the market-ratio throughout the world. In other words, the laws in question are effective in attracting the would-be rising metal to the legal ratio:

1. Negatively: in that they are excluded from operating to maintain the exported metal in its supposed elevation.
2. Positively: so far as an open field for the monetary use of the exported metal, at the given ratio to the metal retained, and not above, affects the action of individuals or of governments.

[1] "Journal Statist. Soc.," March, 1879.

France is the favourite field of illustration and of argument upon the influence of Alternative Coinage and Legal-Tender, and the lines of attack against the Reinstatement of Silver, which seem to be most in vogue, bear upon the premium on Gold in Paris between 1820 and 1850.

Now, the utmost that is alleged to-day about that premium on Gold is, that it frequently rose to over 1 per cent., and on more than one occasion was about 2 per cent. (once being $2.\frac{1}{10}$.) The general average is below 1 per cent.

As the bulk of the Money in use is admitted to have been Silver, it is quite plain that the "price" of Gold must have been subject to any special demand caused by sudden, peculiar, local need, such for example as led in Paris in 1878—so I was informed at the time, in the office of MM. Hottinguer & Cie.—to a premium on 100 franc notes over gold.

But, independently of such special circumstances, it is plain that beside the question of the exchanges, the state of the coinage, the *quality* of the bullion for sale, the nature of the transactions and their extent, are all necessary to be known if the Anti-Silver contentions based upon this premium are to be made good. Moreover, the matter of what I have called the Mint-ratio[1] must come into play, and as the Mint-

---

[1] "The ratio of 15½ to 1 is a ratio between the Coins. The Silver in the Silver 5-franc piece weighs 15½ times as much as the Gold in the Gold 5-franc piece. This ratio has been maintained without alteration since 1803. The mint price, however, has undergone various changes. It was fixed in the law of 1803 at 9 francs per kilogram of standard Gold, 3 francs per kilogram of standard Silver. The kilogram of standard Silver containing 200 francs, and that of Gold 15½ times as much, or 3100 francs, the mint ratio stood as 3091 : 197, or 15.69 + : 1. In 1835 the mint charge on Silver was reduced to 2 francs to the kilogram, that on Gold to 6 francs. The mint ratio became, therefore, 3094 : 198, or 15.626 : 1, and so remained till 1850. In 1850 the mint charge on Silver was reduced to 1 franc 50 centimes the kilogram. The mint ratio became, therefore, 3094 : 198.50, or 15.586 : 1, and so remained until 1854. In 1854 the mint charge on Gold was raised to 6 francs 70 centimes the kilogram. The mint ratio became, therefore, 3093.30 : 198.50, or 15.583 : 1."—*Extract from the Document of the Conference of* 1878.

ratio till 1835 was 15.⁰ to 1—giving a figure corresponding to a premium on Gold of near 1¼ per cent.—and was 15.⁰ after 1835, it is plain that it is well worth considering.

But the facts hereinbefore stated (page 59), and which there, so far as I know, appear for the first time in the battle-field of the Standards, are themselves competent to give a quietus to the whole argument.

If Gold in England, the home of the Gold Standard, moved within a range of ¾ per cent. as measured in Gold itself, the wonder is that it remained in France, measured in Silver, as near 15½ as it did; and the premium in Paris between 1820 and 1850 is thus transformed into an argument for Silver and for laws that keep Gold and Silver in harness. Of like effect is the subsequent steadiness of Standard Bullion at the Bank of England; which shows how the steady market, the purse always open for purchase of bullion, insures its complete parity with the Legal Unit: and thus, as the market can be kept steady, the purse always open, for the two metals as well as for one alone, a similar parity of coin and bullion of two metals is shown to be easily attainable.

§ 26. A DILATORY PLEA.

There is one order of dilatory plea which is wont to assert its place, one may say, in almost every train of argument which makes defence of something that ought to be reformed. It is that the evils complained of are merely transitory.

In past years, when we laid down a well-grounded forecast of the evils which everybody has since been forced to admit, our friends the enemy stoutly ignored the facts. As the years go on, and our forecast is justified by the event, as year after year the same order of facts to which we were wont to point, extorts unwilling admission, we observe, not repentance, nor sufficient works of repentance, but the plea that these same evils, which our adversaries or their friends with such light hearts precipitated upon the world against all protest, are merely transitory.

Transitory! Even Professor Nasse thinks that the dragging down of the prices of agricultural products in Europe, due to this artificial change of level between Indian prices in Silver and European prices in Gold, is transitory.

Transitory, unquestionably! But so is cholera transitory; so are battle, murder, and sudden death. Whoever prays to be delivered from these, may also pray to be delivered from such reasoning.

It will be noticed, too, that the word is quite vague; no one is committed by it to anything serious; if the plague lasts ten years, or twenty, or thirty, still, from a high point of view, it is transitory.

Who, indeed, can measure the helplessness, if not the criminal negligence—I speak here not of persons, but of a tendency which I may for the moment personify—of one whose rightful province is limited to local diagnosis, and who allows himself to deal with cure? I have read sober words, written by men, no doubt, morally worthy as well as mentally gifted, but of which an Adam Smith would have said, they should have been written in blood. "Your child is dying, madam; but never mind; there will always be children in the world."

Observe, I pray you, that our imagined statistician is quite right; it is perfectly true. Generations may suffer untold evil, but absolute depopulation and deprivation of wealth are not likely to occur: while, to the observer of economic phenomena, such a pageant of morbidity would be of the profoundest interest, a continual field-day; like a clinic of rarities in disease to a medical enthusiast, or, to a hunter an unlimited succession of game of every clime. But of course, meantime, the prosaic millions of to-day, who have their one life to live, and who are provided with nerves of pain for the ills of life, even if they be merely such as rob youth of its promise and age of its peace, serve as the raw material of experiment, and fill with their hearts' blood the stream on which the doctrinaire sails his little boat of theory. The well-known caricature of a century ago recurs to mind: the Minister at Versailles and the fowls called together, as they discover, merely in order to decide the question how they would prefer to be cooked—and told, when they objected to being killed at all, that they were wandering from the question.

To demand of monetary legislation that it should advance the material welfare of the people, has now for many years been treated in certain quarters as a wandering from the question— as if the populations of States existed in order to maintain dogmas, or the reputation of dogmatists. Surely to the XXth century all this will seem very strange: popular government and yet a "Continental corner" on Gold values, liberty the watchword and the iron-handed tyranny of a Gold-monomania the fact. How soon will the world of plain citizens who are not interested in the plenary inspiration of any economic dogma, nor in maintaining the reputations of any special class of practitioners, come to make up their minds that they object, so to speak, to being killed, or, in fact, to anything that points in that direction?

I am aware that tender consciences have been troubled by the fear of consequences which may in some remote future arise from the Reinstatement of Silver, and I have elsewhere indicated a reply to certain specified objections. But in general I have also to say that the statesman, by virtue of his office, acts rather as a physician than as a priest. Certainly it is well, if it be practicable, to prescribe for ten years hence, but surely it is not well to omit to cure the patient in the meantime, under any circumstances. A business lifetime, the average duration of an investment, how long are they?

Whatever the answer, the first years will come first—first for the economic subject, first for the statesman whose business it is to promote his well-being.

These self-evident observations may seem uncalled-for, until one is made aware of consolation being administered by those whose dogmas are responsible for many of the calamities of the last decade, on the ground that the value of money was even greater a few decades or a few centuries ago!

When such things as these pass current—arguments from which one would suppose that the sense of humour, that instinctive modesty of the intellect, would recoil of itself—one begins to suspect that there are unknown callous spots in the mind, a survival of some former state of barbarism, or that, by reason of some unexplained retardation or eddy in the current of our development, the elementary truth reflected in Longfellow's simple phrase,

> "Act in the living present,
> Heart within, and God o'erhead,"

is excluded from the political dictionaries now in use.

CHAPTER X.

A Monetary Balance of Power.

In a detailed statement of objections to the working of a Bimetallic Union when founded, Professor Nasse lays stress upon two facts, and he rightly insists upon them, enforcing his appeal with the excellent phrase from the French, " there is nothing so brutal as a fact."

These facts to which he accords such favour are—

1. The modern preference for Gold over Silver;

2. The actual depreciation of Silver so far below $15\frac{1}{2}$, the ratio ordinarily held in view as the one to be restored in a Monetary Union.

Truly there is nothing more brutal than a fact, unless it be two facts. But there are facts and facts. There is, for example, the prepotent fact, that the modern preference for Gold over Silver was *nil* until it succeeded in getting laws passed to bolster up Gold, and to outlaw Silver. Now, what the Monetary Unionist has been speaking about all these years is the law, not the preference: surrender the law, and the preference which was *nil* before, will it not be *nil* again, or sufficiently near a nullity?

Does Professor Nasse believe that if Germany, knowing what she does now, had the work to do over again, she would ever pass such laws? Impossible! How much, then, is this "preference" worth? Preference for preference, Germany's preference for Gold is the greatest monetary preference of which history can boast. Let us assume, then, that it was Germany's preference for Gold that led her to pass Anti-Silver-laws, and so set the world in flames of controversy and calamity. And yet this was but a passing whim. Germany has recovered herself: that is to say, the majority of Germans who think of these things have come to understand the general situation : they find things done that are very hard to undo; but if they were to be done again they would not do them. Where, then, is the preference? Has it not ceased to exist? Or is the word "preference" a seine that draws in all states of mind, akin, however remotely, to desire for one alternative rather than another; and is the mere existence of a thing proof of the "preference" for it in the community? By this reasoning the community can be charged with a preference for any and all abuses that may exist in its borders; which is absurd.

But behind this range of ideas I find others, which it will be well to meet on their own ground.

Let us assume that there *is* a preference for Gold; not in the sense of a conscious and frivolous intention in ruling classes of rejecting Silver, but of a constant though slight pressure in favour of Gold in the minds of all men, even of men who live happily in Double Standard countries, and have voted for the reinstatement of Silver. Such a pressure would be the analogue for the XIXth and XXth centuries of a demand for treasure in which a Prince's ransom could be carried on the person, which is believed to have appeared as a factor of the monetary situations in past times. I have myself surmised that the great rise of Gold in the XVIth century was in part traceable to such a disposition, arising in the long period of war which in a measure reached its close with the Treaty of Westphalia; a disposition, however, which would be followed by important results, not merely because it animated the individual citizens, but rather because it would afford an opportunity for the political action of the community, through the wills of the various Lords of the Mint. Whatever the historic rate of equation between the two metals, Gold is always the "better," that is to say, the less perishable, less "heavy" metal. Must there not be, then, an ever-present, ever-active element of perturbation, working against any ratio of equilibrium which man may attempt to establish?

To give the argument I oppose its maximum of advantage, I will call it a natural and ineradicable tendency to deflection. I will also contribute to the armament of the doctrine I oppose, an observation which occurred to me as important, and which I do not remember to have seen or heard. The attractions of Gold may be divided into relative or quantitative, and intrinsic or metallic. In the first come portability and rarity, in the latter colour, untarnishability, specific gravity, etc. Now the former attractions must increase with every upward movement of the ratio; Gold becoming ever more rare, more portable, as compared with Silver. Hence this pressure for Gold tends not only to perpetuate itself, but to increase its intensity.

Assuming, then, that the fact exists, we seek reply to the question how it is to be dealt with.

I shall observe, in the first place, that this alleged natural force and tendency with which we have here to do is a domestic affair, so to speak, for mankind. The preference for Gold is not, as we might suppose from the tone taken by some of the trumpets of learning, an event built upon a cosmic scale. This point is more important than to some readers it may appear, for there are really minds in which this preference enjoys the prestige, one might say, of the persistence of force, or of the precession of the equinoxes, or of the perseverance of the saints.

Secondly: I wish to repeat my former inquiry, how much is the preference worth? At this my adversary will, perhaps, be surprised; and I can conceive that he may be inclined to charge me with levity, especially when I follow this inquiry by asking him: Whether he has abandoned "Gresham's law?" But I venture to hope the novelty of this transition from one idea to another will disappear, for a most vital tie between the ideas exists, whether it has been perceived or no. The working of human self-interest, under the domain of a law which allows two kinds of Money, one inferior, the other superior, to do the same office, produces certain results, and the statement of the process is called "Gresham's law." But wherein lies this superiority or inferiority?

The answer is that the "inferior" Money is the "cheaper" Money. Wonder of wonders!

More *prefer* the inferior Money! But how is this? Where is that happy valley we were lately wandering through, where men *preferred* imperishability, rarity, divisibility, portability, in their Money? To all this Gresham's law turns a deaf ear—cheapness, sordid cheapness rules the day. If Gresham's law be true, an ounce of cheapness is worth a ton of preference. And who is there to deny that Gresham's law is true? Alas! alas! how brutal a fact may be!

Another fact of the first order is—the modern preference for paper over both Silver and Gold. This preference neutralizes to a decisive extent the advantage of lightness, and while robbing Gold of its great advantage enables the two metals to act equally well by an attorney, paper, and so relegates them to the untrammelled exercise of their highest function, that of a combined monetary mass more nearly constant in quantity, as used in its relation to population and business, than any mass within the ken of the economist. I say "as used," and seek to support an amendment to the older doctrine of the schools applicable to the point before us by stating that, in my view, a legal ratio between the metals, created and maintained *jure gentium*, is an element or factor in this quantity and constancy.

As to the difficulties involved in the question of the ratio, a solvent is applied to a goodly portion of them by recalling the fact, that there is in the world no large stock of Silver for sale. All but a trivial amount is in use as money, ornament, or treasure, and not "in the market;" in the sense that a Gold-price can be predicated of it without due reservations; and as for "cheapness," this cheapness must disappear when the Mint-rate of the assumed Monetary Union shall become effective and Silver shall become generally coinable into Money. Of the probable effect of the establishment of a ratio, which should bring the metals more closely together than they stand as bullion to-day, while detailed prediction can at best move within but narrow limits, yet in general it can safely be affirmed that (assuming the currency of existing Silver coin to remain undisturbed), this change would directly operate chiefly upon trade between Silver-using and Gold-using countries, and upon the great stocks of Money only in so far as their purchasing power is affected by the state of this trade. So far as such trade is concerned it is also to be noted that no injurious effect can be safely predicated, in the estimate of which the following points shall have been ignored: namely:

First: That the change in question is, as far as it goes, a restoration of the *status quo ante*.

Second: That its impact is reduced by being distributed between the two metals.

Third: That in so far as the change is regarded as a settlement, and firm establishment of the foundations of business, there is some credit entry against every debit.

As for the permanence of the ratio which shall be adopted, I have to observe that once a ratio is adopted by a majority of nations a new order of affairs supervenes, and any change of that ratio is beyond the ken of present statesmanship. In so far as the question exists, it is a question distinctly belonging to the future; and to the future I am content to leave it.

I here approach a subject which, shortly before his lamented and untimely death, occupied the attention of Professor

Jevons (see "Investigations in Currency and Finance," London, Macmillan and Co., 1884, p. 352); and the existence in print of specific comments of a mind like his upon my position on this subject may warrant some words of explanation on my part. It does not seem to me probable that, if England were to join the Chief Powers in forming a Silver and Gold Union, there would come in the future any necessity for a change of the ratio it should adopt. But this forecast of mine is not a tenet, nor are those who hold it justly chargeable with the responsibilities of foreknowledge absolute. Some great revolution, either in the use, or in the stock-on-hand, of one or the other, or of both, of the metals, must take place in order to make such an alteration necessary. It must, however, be a revolution the parallel of which has never occurred, and hence can hardly be treated as within the domain of probability. Who, indeed, is there left to-day to deny with argument and proof that if England wills its maintenance at the ratio of $15\frac{1}{2}$ to 1, the Union can stand any shock of altered circumstances of which history affords a precedent? Now, if coming decades or ages have such a surprise in store as that we have described, it will evidently be necessary for the world to meet the emergency as best it may; and it is also true that it is impossible to cross the stream until it shall be reached.

There is a lesson of which we come in sight in thus anxiously scanning the horizon of the future from the headlands of thought, which I would gladly commend to certain thinkers of the European Continent who are disposed to indulge in tremors for the security of the Monetary Union of the future, the establishment of which they seem to dread, and to wield extraordinary gifts of prophecy of a coming cataclysm, in order to alarm public opinion as to the danger of a nation's linking its monetary fortunes with those of the rest of mankind. This lesson is: That the fortunes of each nation are already so linked—although very unskilfully—that it is not the linking but the unskilfulness which troubles the monetary peace of the world; that the cataclysm, if it comes, will at any rate affect all nations in their due proportion; that, whatever may happen, the emergency will best be met by an unbroken front of nations, united, with England at their head, to confront a common danger; and that, withal, if time and use shall have enlarged the power of legislatures and of cabinets to guard the interests of their constituents by acting in concert promptly, wisely, on business principles, the alleged future attack of fate may be foiled entirely, and so lose the name of danger—if it comes.

Turning back, then, from the future to the present, we see that this Union of Nations which it is, in my belief, the interest of these nations to form, is not necessarily engaged to a variable ratio, nor is it bound to a ratio explicitly fixed to-day by contract for all eternity; but, if the words be used subject to the limitations usually applied to political action, the Union can safely accept a "fixed ratio."

I should, perhaps, further explain that I have no intention of seeking to repel any considerations bearing upon the ratio to be adopted by a Monetary Union; that is, to my mind, distinctly a point of detail, however important, which it is the interest of each nation to submit to the free decision of the members of the projected Monetary Union itself. The true objective point of argument is that the Union ought to be formed.

When that question shall be brought into the way of settlement by the adhesion of England, then the question of the ratio will be in order, and will, it is to be hoped, be amicably determined by the nations concerned.

Recurring after this introduction to the mustering and review of facts in which I have asked my reader to accompany Professor Nasse and myself, I now challenge attention to a fact of all-transcending rank—a fact of facts: and that is nothing less than the hypothesis of fact upon which Professor Nasse's argument proceeds. Professor Nasse was assuming a Silver and Gold Union to have been formed; and founded, of course, upon a ratio which the nations shall have chosen. He is offering predictions touching what will happen in that event. Now, I aver that in this supposed action of nations we have before us a national, a continental, a world-wide fact, a fact which is competent to neutralize facts as well as dreams and dogmas that may come in its way.

What, then, is the nature of the event in question? It is necessary to have a clear idea of that, in order to test the sagacity of any forecast relating to it.

Here lies the difficulty: it is no light task to calculate the effects of the displacement of an existing order, and hence it is very natural that among those who cling to the old order, there should be default in fully accepting the hypothesis they are bound to enter upon. And yet there is nothing strained or unpractical in the hypothesis before us, of concurrent action of nations to make a new settlement of the relations of the Money-metals. Germany and England are the only Powers whose assent is still denied, and in principle, the object whose attainment waits for that assent is admitted to be desirable by both Powers; so far at least as their Declarations to the Nations in the Conference of 1881 can be said to bind them. The question is, therefore, rather a matter of amount, than of principle: a question, how large a contribution Englishmen shall advise England, and Germans shall advise Germany, to make in order to attain a desired end? But it is generally understood, and fairly to be believed, that Germany's full assent awaits the concurrence of England, and in England the cause is before the Court, and upon the calendar for hearing. The hypothesis, therefore, is quite a practical one, within short reach of realization.

Now I affirm of this hypothesis that it implies not merely in vague terms that this new settlement of the Money-metals is undertaken, but that it is undertaken in earnest, that the forces of civilization are marshalled in support of this new settlement.

The leading nations have wisely come to recognize that the paramount interest of each nation is to attain stability in the greater Standard of Value, by an harmonious adjustment of that duality of material of the world's Money, which is, so to speak, an ultimate fact of nature; and upon that basis they have entered into bonds of intermonetary peace. But this consensus of nations is a solemn judgment of nations. Upon what? Upon the past, whose crowning misdemeanour is that its laws became the plaything of a whim,—of a petty preference for shadow, as against substance.

Such judgment, then, being interpreted, is found to signify that to enact laws in order to foster the alleged preference of the individual for one of these materials over another, is to institute discord injurious to the State. I affirm that such a fact is not only competent to make an epoch, but to insure that the epoch will be taken care of after it is made.

Apologists of discord in the world's Standard of Value may rest assured that, if this great deed of mercy and of peace is worth doing, it will be worth sustaining. To my view, to say it is not worth doing is to derogate from civilization by maintaining that chaos is better than order.

Si quis igitur, amore veritatis inveniendae, his dictis voluerit contradicere vel contra scribere, bene faciet; et si male locutus sum, perhibeat testimonium de malo, sed cum ratione, ne ipsa videatur gratis et voluntarie condemnare, quod non potest efficaciter impugnare.

Se aucun donecques, pour amour de bérité enquerre, vouldroit contredire à icelles ou escripre contre, bien sera, mais se j'ay mal parlé porteige tesmongage du mal avec raison, affin qu'il ne soit veu pour néant et de sa singulière voulenté temerairement condamner ce que bonnement ne se peult impugner ne contredire.

Finis tractatus de mutationibus monetarum a magistro Nycholao Oresme (✠ 1382).

APPENDIX.

HISTORICAL MATERIAL FOR THE STUDY OF MONETARY POLICY.

THE HISTORY OF THE GUINEA

ILLUSTRATED
BY
CONTEMPORARY DOCUMENTS.

HISTORICAL MATERIAL FOR THE STUDY OF MONETARY POLICY, SUPPLEMENTARY TO PAPERS PRINTED IN THE DOCUMENT OF THE INTERNATIONAL MONETARY CONFERENCE OF 1878.

THE HISTORY OF THE GUINEA,

ILLUSTRATED BY CONTEMPORARY DOCUMENTS.

CONTENTS.

NO.		PAGE
1.	The Original Order for the Coinage of Guineas, December 24, 1663	229
2.	The Statute of Free and Gratuitous Coinage, 1666 (Extract)	230
3.	The Mint Indenture of Thomas Neale, 1686 (Extract)	233
4.	Silver before the House of Commons, April, 1690	234
5.	Report of a Committee in Favour of Debasing the Coin, March 12, 1694-5	236
6.	Petitions concerning Guineas at 30 Shillings, February, 1695-6	238
7.	The Bank of England and the Guinea in Camp before Namur, July, 1695	240
8.	Statutes relating to Coinage and Currency of Guineas (1696):—	
	A. The Guinea at 26 Shillings	243
	B. Suspension of Obligation to Coin Guineas	244
	C. The Guinea at 22 Shillings	246
	D. Repeal of Statute Suspending Obligation to Coin	247
9.	Action of the Treasury touching the Currency of the Guinea, October, 1697	248
10.	Letter of the Commissioners of Excise Touching the Rating of the Guinea in 1694-6, July 22, 1698	249
11.	John Locke and the Ratio of 15·58 to 1:—	
	A. Order of Reference to the Council of Trade, Sept., 1698	250
	B. Report on Lowering the Guinea	250
	C. Orders to the Government Officers not to take Guineas for more than 21s. 6d.	253

NO.		PAGE
12.	Instances of Contradiction between Statements of Doctrine in Locke's Writings on Money, 1690-1698	255
13.	A Private Letter of Locke touching the Recoinage, March 30, 1696	257
14.	"Memoirs of the Great Recoinage," MS. by Hopton Haynes .	258
15.	Reports Relating to the Coinage, MS. signed by Sir Isaac Newton, 1700-1702:—	
	A. Report Touching the Currency of the French and Spanish Pistoles in England, January 20, 1700-1 . . .	261
	B. Report concerning the cutting of Counterfeit Money . .	262
	C. Report Touching the late Change of Ratio in France, September 28, 1701	263
	D. Report Touching the Rating of the Guinea, etc., 7 July, 1702	264
	E. The Value of Gold in Proportion to Silver in Several Parts of Europe	267
	F. Proposals for Preserving and Increasing the Silver Coin of this Kingdom, July 7, 1702	270
16.	Order in Council, Lowering the Currency of Louis d'ors and Pistoles to 17s., Feb. 5, 1700-1	272
17.	Minute of Orders to the Mint Officers, Feb. 12, 1701 . . .	273
18.	Sir James Steuart and Adam Smith on the English Standard, 1759	273
19.	Biographical Notice of Lord Liverpool	275
20.	Report of the Committee of the Privy Council on Coins, May 21, 1816	278
21.	The Proclamations of the New Currency, 1817	281

HISTORICAL MATERIAL—MISCELLANEOUS.

22.	Contraction in 1818-1822	287
23.	Alexander Baring (Lord Ashburton) on the Silver and Gold Standard in England	288
24.	The Restoration of Silver before the Bank of England in 1828 .	291
25.	A Silver Discussion in 1837	294
26.	Sir Robert Peel on the Standard of Value, May 6, 1844 . .	297
27.	Monetary Treaties in the Past	302
28.	State Papers relating to the Policy of Monetary Union, 1878, 1881, 1882	306

THE HISTORY OF THE GUINEA,

ILLUSTRATED BY CONTEMPORARY DOCUMENTS.

No. 1.

AN ORDER FOR THE COINAGE OF GUINEAS.

[*MS. Mint Records, vol. vii. p. 52.*]

CHARLES R.

Our Will and Pleasure is and Wee Doo hereby require and authorise you to cause to be Coyned all such Gold and silver as hereafter shal be brought into our Mint and delivered unto you in the name and for the use of the Company of Royall Adventurers of England trading into Affrica with a little Elephant in such convenient place upon our gold and silver coynes respectively as you shall judge fitting which Wee intend as a marke of distinction from the rest of our gold and silver moneys and an Incouragement unto the said Company in the Importing of Gold and Silver to be coyned. And that our Twenty shillings peece of Crowne gold to be coyned by the Mill and Presse may be even Twenty shillings in value after the rate commanded and allowed in our late Proclamation for the raiseing the price of gold in this Our Kingdome of England, or as neere as conveniently may bee. Our further will and pleasure is, and wee doe hereby likewise command and authorise you to cause the pound Troy of our Crowne gold hereafter to be cutt into forty and fower peeces and an halfe the whole peece being to passe for Twenty shillings and the halfe for Tenn and soe the rest of our gold coynes accordingly in proportion. And this shalbe your sufficient warrant for soe doeing. And the Warden Comptroller and Assaymaster of Our Mint and the rest of Our Officers there are to take notice of Our Will and pleasure herein that our said moneys may passe accordingly. Given at our Courte at Whitehall the 24th day of December 1663.

By his Ma^{tes} command

HENRY BENNETT.

To Our Trusty and Welbeloved Sr Ralph Freman Kn^t and Henry Slingesby Esqr Masters and Workers of Our Mint or either of them.

No. 2.

THE STATUTE ESTABLISHING FREE AND GRATUITOUS COINAGE OF SILVER AND GOLD IN ENGLAND.

18 *Caroli II. C.* 5 (1666).

AN ACT for encouraging of coinage.

Whereas it is obvious, that the plenty of current coins of gold and silver of this kingdom is of great advantage to trade and commerce ; for the increase whereof, your Majesty in your princely wisdom and care hath been graciously pleased to bear out of your revenue half the charge of the coinage of silver money ; (2) for the preventing of which charge to your Majesty, and the encouragement of the bringing gold and silver into the realm, to be converted into the current money of this your Majesty's kingdom, we your Majesty's dutiful and loyal subjects do give and grant unto your Majesty the rates, duties or impositions following, and do beseech your Majesty that it may be enacted ; (3) and be it enacted by the King's most excellent majesty, by and with the advice and consent of the lords spiritual and temporal, and commons, in this present Parliament assembled, and by the authority of the same, that whatsoever person or persons, native or foreigner, alien or stranger, shall from and after the twentieth day of December one thousand six hundred and sixty and six, bring any foreign coin, plate or bullion of gold or silver, in mass, molten or allayed, or any sort of manufacture of gold or silver, into his Majesty's mint or mints within the kingdom of England, to be there melted down and coined into the current coins of this kingdom, shall have the same there assayed, melted down and coined with all convenient speed, without any defalcation, diminution or charge for the assaying, coinage, or waste in coinage ; (4) so as that for every pound troy of crown or standard gold that shall be brought in and delivered by him or them to be assayed, melted down and coined, as aforesaid, there shall be delivered out to him or them respectively a pound troy of the current coins of this kingdom, of crown or standard gold ; (5) and for every pound troy of sterling or standard silver that shall be brought in and delivered by him or them to be assayed, melted down and coined, as aforesaid, there shall be delivered out to him or them respectively, a pound troy of the current coins of this kingdom, of sterling or standard silver, and so proportionably for a greater or lesser weight ; (6) and for every pound troy of gold or silver that shall be brought in and delivered to be assayed, melted down and coined, as aforesaid, that shall be finer upon assay than crown gold or standard silver, there shall be delivered for the same so much more than a pound troy as the same doth in proportion amount unto in fineness and value ; (7) and for every pound troy of gold or silver that shall be brought in and delivered to be assayed, melted down and coined, as aforesaid, that shall be coarser or baser upon assay, or worse in value than crown gold or standard silver, there shall be delivered for the same so much less than a pound troy as the same doth fall short in fineness or value ; and so for a greater or lesser quantity.

II. And it is hereby further enacted by the authority aforesaid, That there shall be no preference in point of assaying or coinage ; but that all gold and silver brought in and delivered into the mint, to be assayed and coined, shall be assayed, coined and delivered out to the respective importers, according to the order and times of bringing in and delivering the same into the mint or mints, and not otherwise ; so as he that shall first bring in and deliver any gold or silver to be coined, shall be taken and accounted the first person to have the same assayed, coined and delivered ; and he or they that shall bring in and deliver any gold or silver next, to be accounted the second to have the same assayed, coined and delivered, and so successively in course : (2) and that the gold and silver brought in and coined, as aforesaid, shall be in the same order delivered to the respective bringers in thereof, their executors, administrators or assigns successively, without preference of one before the other, and not otherwise: (3) and if any undue preference be made in entering of any gold or silver, or delivering out of any money coined, contrary to the true intent and meaning of this act, by any officer or officers of the mint or mints; then the party or parties offending shall be liable by action of debt, or on the case, to pay the value of the gold or silver brought in, and not entered and delivered according to the true intent, meaning and direction of this act, as aforesaid, with damages and costs to the party or parties grieved, and shall be forejudged from his or their place or office: (4) and if such preference be unduly made by any his or their deputy or deputies, clerk or clerks, without direction or privity of his or their master or masters, then such deputy or deputies, clerk or clerks only shall be liable to such action, damage and costs, as aforesaid, and be forever after incapable of serving or bearing office in any mint in the Kingdom of England.

III. Provided always, That it shall not be interpreted any undue preference, to incur any penalty, in point of delivery of monies coined, if the officer or officers, or their deputies or clerks, shall deliver out or pay any monies coined to any person or persons that do come and demand the same upon subsequent entries, before others that did not come to demand their monies in their order and course, so as there be so much money reserved as will satisfy them, which shall not be otherwise disposed of, but kept for them.

IV. And for the more orderly and clear performance thereof, be it enacted, and it is hereby enacted by the authority aforesaid, That the master-worker of his Majesty's mint or mints for the time being, shall at the time of the delivery and entry of any gold or silver in the said mint or mints, give unto the bringer or bringers in thereof to be coined, a bill under his hand denoting the weight, fineness and value thereof, together with the day and order of its delivery into the said mint or mints.

V. And for the further encouragement and assurance of such as shall bring any gold or silver into his Majesty's said mint or mints to be coined; (2) be it enacted, and it is hereby enacted by the authority aforesaid, That no confiscation, forfeiture, seizure, attachment, stop or restraint whatsoever shall be made in the said mint or mints, of any gold or silver brought in to be coined, for or by reason of any imbargo, breach of the peace, letters of mart or reprisal, or war within any foreign nation, or upon any other account or pretence whatsoever; (3)

but that any gold and silver brought into any of his Majesty's mint or mints within the Kingdom of England to be coined, shall truly and with all convenient speed be coined and delivered out to the respective bringer or bringers in thereof, their respective executors, administrators or assigns, according to the rules and directions of this act.

[The remaining Sections provide for an import duty on liquors to maintain the Mint, and making good a grant, made six years before, to Dame Barbara Villiers, widow, of the sum of two-pence by tale out of every pound weight troy of Silver moneys thereafter to be coined.

This statute was kept permanently in force by 25 Car. II., c. 8; 1 Jac. II., c. 7; 4 and 5 W. and M., c. 24; 12 and 13 W. III., c. 41; 7 Annae. c. 24; 1 Geo. I., c. 18; 9 Geo. I., c. 19; 4 Geo. II., c. 12; 12 Geo. II., c. 5; 19 Geo. II., c. 14; 27 Geo. II., c. 11, and by 1 Geo. III., c. 16. The next re-enactment is that of 8 Geo. III., c. 1, which continues the act until the statute of 9 Geo. III., chap. 2, re-enacts it in perpetuity. Although practically abrogated, so far as Silver was concerned, by the clauses for prohibition of Silver Coinage in 38 Geo. III., c. 59, (1798,) this statute remained in force till 1816; when, by 56 Geo. III., c. 68, so much of it as guaranteed gratuitous Coinage (see also *supra*, p. 161) of Silver was repealed, and the coinage was ordained of Silver Coins which should contain about 6 per cent. less Silver than Coins under the former standard, while the Mint price remained the same and payable in Silver, and the Legal Tender of the Silver was reduced to 40 shillings. The statutes 1 Geo. III., c. 16, 9 Geo. III., c. 2, 38 Geo. III., c. 59, 56 Geo. III., c. 68, are reprinted in the Document of the Monetary Conference of 1878.]

No. 3.

EXTRACT FROM THE MINT INDENTURE OF THOMAS NEALE, 1686.

[*MS. Treasury Papers, vol. ii. No. 21.*]

"And the said Thomas Neale doth by these presents covenant etc. . . . . . to make four sorts of Money of Crown Gold one piece that be called the Ten Shilling piece rüng for ten shillings sterling and there shall be four score and nine of those in the Pound weight Troy, one other piece which shall be called the twenty shilling piece running for twenty shillings sterling and there shall be 44 of those and one ten shilling piece or the weight of a ten shilling piece in the Pound weight Troy."

[Then follow similar provisions for the 40s. piece and £5 piece.]

No. 4.

SILVER BEFORE THE HOUSE OF COMMONS IN 1690.

[*From the Journal of the House. A. 1690. Mercurii, 9° die Aprilis.*]

* * * * * *

A Petition of divers working Goldsmiths in and about the City of *London* was read ; setting forth, That the Petitioners, in the Course of their Trade, observing the great Scarcity of Silver, have upon their Search, found, at the Custom house, That, since the First of *October* last past, Entries have been made of Two hundred Eighty-Six thousand One hundred and Twelve Ounces of Silver or Bullion, and Eighty-nine thousand Nine hundred Forty-and-nine Dollars, and Pieces of Eight, by divers private Persons, for Exportation ; and doubt not but that it will appear, That not only the *East India* Company for many Years, but also divers *Jews* and Merchants, have of late bought up great Quantities of Silver to carry out of this Kingdom ; and given Three-half-pence *per* Ounce above the Value : Which hath encouraged the Melting down of much Plate, and milled Monies ; whereby, for these Six Months past, not only the Petitioners in their Trade, but the Mint itself, hath been stop from coining : And praying the Consideration of the House in the Premises.

Resolved, That the said Petition be referred to a Committee : viz. Mr. *Foley*, Mr. *Machell*, Sir *John Knight*, Sir *Rich. Reynolds*, Sir *Sam. Bernadiston*, Sir *Levin Bennet*, Mr. *Thornhaugh*, Sir *Wm. Ellis*, Mr. *Slater*, Colonel *Birch*, Lord *Falkland*, Mr. *Palmes*, Mr. *Perry*, Mr. *Hutchinson*, Mr. *Buscawen*, Mr. *Kenyon*, Mr. *Wilmot*, Mr. *Fuller*, Sir *Cha. Windham*, Sir *Edw. Philipps*, Mr. *Francklyn*, Mr. *Glemham*, Mr. *Burdet*, Mr. *Arnold*, Sir *Walter Young*, Sir *Jonath. Jennings*, Mr.

Gray, Mr. *Pelham*, Sir *Ralph Dutton*, Mr. *England*, Sir *Tho. Fowles*, Mr. *Ryder*: Who are to consider of the said Petition ; And report their Opinion thereupon to the House : And they are to meet this Afternoon at Three of the Clock, in the Speaker's Chamber.

*　　　*　　　*　　　*　　　*　　　*

Mercurii, 7° die Maii.

Sir *Rich. Reynell* reports from the Committee to whom the Petition of divers working Goldsmiths in and about the City of *London* was referred, That they had considered the Matters to them referred ; and had directed a Special Report to be made of the whole Matter to the House : The which he read in his Place ; and afterwards, delivered the same in at the Clerk's Table : Where the same was read ; and is as followeth ; viz. :—

"That it appears, by a Certificate from the Custom-house, dated Seventeenth *April* last, That great Quantities of Silver have been of late exported ; whereof we had a particular Account for the last Five Years: That above Seven Parts of Eight had been shipped off by the *Jews*, who do any thing for their Profit : The Reason was plain ; that the *French* King, of late, finding his Money very scarce, had raised his Coin Ten Pounds *per Cent.* : Which was an Encouragement to send Silver to fill his Coffers : Which the Jews, for their Profit, exported daily in very great Quantities ; That, on *Monday* last, they had shipped off about Sixty thousand Ounces by the Name of Foreign Silver ; and great Parcels more were ready to be shipped : which did make it scarce and dear, to the utter Ruin of the working Goldsmiths.

That there were also *English*, as well as *Jews*, who, for their Advantages, would doubtless melt down our Crown Pieces, &c. and sell for Foreign Silver, to the Undoing of the whole Nation for want of Money, unless a present Remedy were found to prevent Exportation of any Silver or Gold.

"That the Committee hold also Certificates from the Officers of the *Mint*, for divers Years ; and do find, that, of late, very small Quantities have been coined.

"That it was offered, that the Profit of melting down One thousand Pound of milled Money for Exportation, was Twenty-five Pounds ready Money, and upwards.

"That Silver was coined at the *Mint* at Five Shillings and Two-pence *per* Ounce ; but, at the Time of Exportation, was generally sold at Five Shillings and Three-pence Halfpeny *per* Ounce : which gave Occasion of its being melted down, and transported as Foreign Silver.

"That divers Proposals were suggested :

"1. A total Prohibition :

"2. A qualified Prohibition for certain Times, or an Imposition for Exportation for Silver :

"3. The enhansing our own Money.

"So that, though the Committee found the Complaint of the Petitioners very just, and the Inconveniences to the Kingdom very great, they could not agree of a Way for the preventing the same ; but were humbly of Opinion, That it was worthy of the Consideration of the House."

Resolved, That the said Report be re-committed to the same Committee, upon the Debate of the House : And that they do thereupon prepare a Bill or Bills, as they shall see cause ; and present the same to the House : And that, in order thereunto, the Committee do sit *de die in diem* ; and have Power to send for Persons, Papers, and Records : And that the Officers of the *Mint* do attend the said Committee : And that Mr. *Neale*, Mr. *Norreis*, Sir *John Bancks*, Mr. *Thornhaugh*, Sir *Christopher Musgrave*, Mr. *Coquisby*, Colonel *Birch*, Mr. *Christy*, Sir *Peter Coryton*, Sir *Jerv. Elwes*, Sir *Jos. Tredenham*, Mr. *Evans*, Mr. *Slater*, Mr. *Tho. Foley*, Mr. *Hen. Herbert*, and all the Members of the House that are Merchants . . . . . And they are to meet this Afternoon at Three of the Clock.

* * * * * *

No. 5.

REPORT OF A COMMITTEE IN FAVOUR OF DEBASING THE COIN, March 12, 1694-5.

[From the Journal of the House of Commons.]

Mr. *Scobell* reported from the Committee appointed to receive proposals, how to prevent clipping of the coin of this Kingdom for the future ; and the Exportation of Silver ; and to report the same to the House ; That the committee had received several proposals accordingly ;

and had agreed upon several resolutions, which they had directed him to report to the House; and he read the same in his Place; and afterwards delivered the same in at the Clerk's Table; Where the same was read; and are as follows: viz.:—

"1. *Resolved*, That it is the opinion of this Committee, That the best way to prevent clipping the Silver Coin of this Kingdom for the future is, to new-coin the same into milled money.

"2. *Resolved*, That it is the opinion of this Committee, That ten hundred thousand pounds is a sufficient Sum to make good the Deficiency of the present clipped coin of this Kingdom.

"3. *Resolved*, That it is the opinion of this Committee, That the Crown and Half-crown, hereafter to be coined, shall be of the present weight and fineness.

"4. *Resolved*, That it is the opinion of this Committee, That the Crown piece shall go at five Shillings Sixpence; and the Half-crown shall go at Two Shillings Nine-pence.

"5. *Resolved*, That it is the opinion of this Committee, that the present milled crown Piece go for 5s. 6d., and the half-crown for Two shillings Nine Pence.

"6. *Resolved*, That it is the Opinion of this Committee, That all money to be coined under the denomination of the Half-crown, shall have a remedy of six-pence in the Ounce.

"7. *Resolved*, That it is the opinion of this Committee, That for as much of the present coin, as any Person brings into the mint, he shall have weight for weight, and the overplus by a Bill or Ticket, at per cent., on a Fund, to be appropriated for that purpose.

"8. *Resolved*, That it is the opinion of this Committee, that the present laws, against clipping be enforced by some Additions.

"9. *Resolved*, That it is the opinion of this Committee, That all persons whose professions require such like Tools or Engines, as may be made use of for coining or clipping, be obliged to register their names, and places of abode; and that it be penal on such as neglect to do the same.

"10. *Resolved*, That it is the opinion of this Committee, that it be penal on all such persons on whom clippings are found.

"11. *Resolved*, That it is the opinion of this Committee, that it be penal on all such persons as give more for any silver Coin than it ought to go for by law.

"12. *Resolved*, That it is the opinion of this Committee, That no presses such as are used for coining, be in any other place than his Majesty's Mint.

"13. *Resolved*, That it is the opinion of this Committee, that it be penal on all such persons as shall import any clipped or counterfeit money.

"14. *Resolved*, That it is the opinion of this Committee, that it be penal on any person to export English Bullion; and the Proof to lie upon the Exporter.

"*Resolved*, That it is the opinion of this Committee, that it be Penal on any person to counterfeit any foreign Mark upon Bullion.

"*Resolved*, That this House, will, upon Saturday Morning next, take the said Report into Consideration."

No. 6.

PETITIONS CONCERNING THE GUINEA AT THIRTY SHILLINGS, Feb. 13, 1695-6.

[*From the Journal of the House of Commons.*]

"Jovis 13° die Februarii, 8° Gulielmi Tertii.

*   *   *   *   *   *

A Petition of several Graziers, and others; traders in Cattle in the Market of West Smithfield, London, and also of many Butchers that use the said market; and of several others receiving and paying Monies, for Cattle bought and sold in the said Market; was presented to the House, and read; setting forth, That about £40,000 per week is returned in the said Market for Cattle; which, for almost 12 months past, for want of current silver had been paid in Guineas at 30s. a piece; great Part whereof they are forced to keep by them for stock to trade with, and are now in their Hands: That a sudden Fall of the Price of Guineas will disable them from supplying the City of London, and Parts adjacent; and will tend to the Ruin of the Petitioners; And praying the consideration of the House in the Premises.

Ordered, That the consideration of the said Petition be referred to the Committee of the whole House, to whom the consideration of the Price of Guineas is referred.

A Petition of divers Merchants, Woolendrapers, and other Traders, in and about the City of London, was presented to the House, and read; setting forth, That the commerce of this Nation is at present brought to a stand, by the uncertain value of our Gold, and our Silver being drawn to a low ebb, it may prove of ill consequence to the publick good, unless speedy means be taken. That the Petitioners think, a gradual sinking the Value of our Gold, from one period of time to another, will be the only effectual means to prevent the designs of unfair Traders, and to make the loss fall more easy, and less surprising, than by reducing them at once, which will also prevent the Exportation; And praying, That the Gold Coins may be settled, and made current in all payments, in such manner as the House shall think fit.

Ordered, That the consideration of the said Petition be referred to the committee of the whole House, to whom the consideration of the Price of Guineas is referred.

A Petition of divers Merchants and Traders in and about the City of London, was presented to the House, and read; setting forth, That by reason of the Badness of our Silver Coins, some Men have taken occasion to raise Guineas to 30s. a-piece; which being about 40 per cent. Value here, above the proportion of Gold to Silver in any other part of Europe, hath caused the bringing over to us vast quantities of Gold; causing the Exchange to fall; and consequently, the carrying out of our Silver, in that disadvantageous proportion; to the impoverishing the Kingdom; That notwithstanding the care taken to reform the Silver Coins, yet certain Persons continue buying and selling Guineas, being employed therein, as they believe, by persons promoting their Private Gain; whereby, they are still kept up to 29s. and 30s., at which Rate, the Petitioners are forced to receive them for Debts; but cannot pay them so to the King's receipts, or upon Bills of Exchange, so that they are necessitated to buy Silver Money with their Guineas at 3, 4, and 5 per cent. Loss; and thereby contribute to the Gain of those Persons who keep up that trade: That at this time, great quantities of Gold is bought up in, and imported hither from Holland, where four of our milled crowns, and Two weighty Shillings will purchase a Guinea; the Profit whereby is so great, that, if some speedy stop be not put to this pernicious Trade, our milled money will be melted down, and carried away as fast as it can be coined: And praying the House to take the said Inconveniences, and Loss of Commerce, into Consideration, and to find some speedy and effectual way to prevent the said abuse.

Ordered, That the consideration of the said Petition be referred to the Committee of the whole House, to whom the consideration of the Price of Guineas is referred.

* * * * * *

A Petition of several Merchants and Tradesmen of the City of London, on behalf of themselves and others, was presented to the House, and read; setting forth, That the Petitioners have of late, through the unsettled Price of Guineas, been imposed upon by Bankers and Goldsmiths, to whom the Petitioners have been compelled to pay Guineas at under 29s. a-piece, or what Rate they please to take them at; though the Petitioners have, and must if they continue trading, receive them at 30s. a-piece of their Customers and Country Chapmen, or else they must receive no money by reason of the Scarcity and Badness of our Silver Coins: And praying, That the Price of Guineas may fall gradually, as the House shall think fit.

Ordered, That the consideration of the said Petition be referred to the Committee of the whole House, to whom the consideration of the Price of Guineas is referred.

No. 7.

THE BANK OF ENGLAND AND THE GUINEA IN CAMP BEFORE NAMUR IN 1695.

In presenting the following document, I suggest the question whether it does not supply the key to a problem which has slumbered unsolved for many a year—namely, Why the Bank sent three of its directors, Sir James Houblon (the Governor), Sir William Scawen, and Michael Godfrey (the Deputy-Governor), to the King's headquarters before Namur?

When these papers were first presented to the British Association in September, 1885, the account given by Macaulay of this famous visit was the only one within range of the general reader. Lately, however, in April, 1887, has appeared a work on the "First Nine Years of the Bank of England," from no less a hand than that of Professor Thorold

Rogers. On looking over its pages for allusions to this visit, I find that after speaking of a decline of Bank Stock from 100 or 99 in March to 90 or 92 in succeeding months, followed by a rise from June 14 to June 28, to 99, the author says that he " finds nothing to account for this decline, beyond the uncertainties of the war, excepting, perhaps, a rumour that the Bank was about to establish a branch at Antwerp, and coin money there for the army in Flanders." He then observes, " For this or for some other purpose the Bank sent three of their directors to the King's headquarters."

In Francis's " History of the Bank of England " the incident is mentioned in the following terms : "The funds supplied by the new Corporation changed the scene ; but the transmission of specie was difficult and full of hazard, and Mr. Godfrey left his peaceful avocations to visit Namur, then vigorously besieged by the English monarch." (I. p. 72.) Now it seems that the original of this letter was written at Antwerp many days before Godfrey's death in the trenches, and the circumstances as we know them, as well as the very explicit language of the letter, point to the rating of Gold in the Government Offices of Account in England as the motive for the visit.

The contrast shown by this letter as between current opinion to-day touching the interposition of the Government in the regulation of money, and that which was entertained in 1695 by those who were on the ground in the midst of the crisis, and who were responsible to the country, to the King, and to their stockholders, is also brought into the strongest light by the important work of Professor Rogers.

The omission to take note of matters which were certainly not buried in oblivion, as this letter has been, is quite phenomenal. The following extract from " The First Nine Years of the Bank of England," which is not in the text, being merely a note (page 35), seems to be the main suggestion in its pages touching the principles of monetary policy affecting the money-metals. "Silver was virtually the currency of the country, and throughout this crisis the Government was able, as Governments are able, to regulate the price of the bullion which is the material of the popular and nearly universal currency, by the coin which they produce. It is quite another thing to try the regulation of two kinds of bullion and two currencies, both equally universal."

In contravention to these dicta, it appears that the Government was induced to regulate two kinds of bullion, and thereby saved the State.

[*MS. Treasury Papers, Vol.* 34, *No.* 4.]

Camp before Namur $\frac{1}{11}$ July, 1695.

Sir,

Herewith I return you the inclosed Warrant with the Signification of His Majesty's Pleasure that the Lords Commissioners of the Treasury do countersign the Same.

Having received a letter from the Comm^{rs} of the Bank of England whereof the enclosed is an extract, concerning the excessive price of Guineas, I am commanded by His Majesty to send the same to their Lo^{ps} for their consideration and opinion thereupon; which is all from

Your most humble Servant,

W<small>M</small>. B<small>LATHWAYT</small>.

His Majesty just now commanded me to send you the enclosed Reference.

Mr. L<small>OWNDES</small>.

(Indorsed)

$\frac{1}{11}$ July 1695.

From Mr. Blathwayt July 1695 concerning a complaint by y^e Bank at y^e great price of Guineas &c.

Extract of a Letter from the Commissioners of the Bank to Mr. Blathwayt Dated att Antwerp 7th July, 1695. N.S.

We cannot forbeare sending you a duplicate of what we wrote you the 2nd of this month, nor repeating of Our Instances by your hands to the King that a stop may be putt to this mischeevous high price of Gold and Guinees in England, which, as we have said, if not speedily done, will have most fatal and certain evill consequences, besides the utter disabling us or any one else from paying the army, this is a most perplexing matter to us, not so much for the loss we sustain by the contract made wth my Lords of the Treasury, but for that (if this pernitious Trade of sending Gold from all parts of Europe to England continue) it will be impossible to comply with it, but we will hope that his Majesty will speedily direct my Lords the Justices by Proclamation to give remidy hereunto by reducing the price of Guinees to the Par of our neighbours before this extravagant rise.

(Indorsed)
Commissioners of the Bank about the rise of Gold.

No. 8.

STATUTES RELATING TO THE COINAGE AND CURRENCY OF GUINEAS PASSED 1696.

A.

The Guinea at 26 Shillings.

7 & 8 Gul. III., c. 10, s. 18.

And for preventing the further increase of the Rate of coined Gold and the mischiefe which may thence befall this Realme Be it enacted by the Authority aforesaid that from and after the Five and twentieth day of March One thousand six hundred ninety six noe Person shall receive take or pay any of the pieces of Gold Coine of this Kingdom commonly called Guineas att any greater or higher rate than Twenty six shillings for each Guinea and not to exceed the same in proportion for the Pieces of Gold called Halfe-Guineas Double-Guineas and five Pound Pieces. And in case any Person shall offend herein he shall forfeit for every such Offence double the Value of the Gold soe received or paid and alsoe the Sum of twenty Pounds the one Moiety to His Majestie and the other Moiety to the Person or Persons who shall sue or informe for the same to be recovered with Costs of Suit in any of His Majesties Courts of Record by Action of Debt, Bill, Plaint, or Information, wherein no Privilege, Protection, or Wager of Law, shall bee allowed, nor any more than one Imparlance.

And be it declared, that nothing in this Act contained shal. extend or be construed to compel any person or persons to receive any Guinea or Guineas at the said Rate of Twenty-six Shillings.

B.
SUSPENSION OF THE OBLIGATION TO COIN GUINEAS.
7 & 8 Gul. III., c. 13 (1695-6).

An Act for taking off the Obligation and Incouragement for coining Guineas for a certain time therein mentioned.

WHEREAS by an Act in the Eighteenth Yeare (of the Reigne) of King Charles the Second intituled An Act for incouraging of Coinage and continued by an other Act made in Five and twentieth yeare of the (Reign of the) said King Charles intituled An Act for continuing a former Act concerning Coinage both which said Acts were revived by an Act made in the First yeare of the Reign of the late King James and are continued by an Act made in the Fourth Session of the last Parliament intituled An Act for reviving continuing and explaining several Laws therein mentioned which are expired and neare expiring Itt is provided that whatsoever Person or Persons Native or Forreigner Alien or Stranger shall from and after the Twentieth day of December One thousand six hundred sixty six bring any Forreigne Coin Plate or Bullion of Gold or Silver in Masse molten or allayed or any sort of Manufacture of Gold or Silver into his Majesty's Mint or Mints within the Kingdom of England to bee there melted down and coined into the current coine of this Kingdome shall have the same there assayed melted downe and coined with all convenient speed without any defalcation Diminution or charge for the Assaying Coinage or Waste in Coinage so as that for every Pound Troy of Crown or Standard Gold that shall bee brought in or delivered by him or them to bee assayed melted down and coined as aforesaid there shall bee delivered out to him or them respectively a Pound Troy of the Current Coins of this Kingdom of Crowne or Standard Gold. And whereas great Quantities of Gold have been lately imported from Foreign Parts which being coined here as aforesaid into Guineas have been (on occasion of the present ill State of the Silver Coins) taken and accepted by the Subjects of this Realm at very high and unusual Rates and Prices tending to the great Damage and Loss of the Publick. The continuance of which Practice (unlesse speedily prevented) will run the Nation vastly in debt to Foreigners for the repayment whereof the Silver Moneys of this Kingdom must inevitably be exhausted on Terms of great Disadvantage therefore to prevent the further Growth of soe great an evil Bee it enacted by the King's most Excellent Majesty by and with the Advice and Consent of the Lords Spiritual and Temporal and Commons in this present Parliament assembled and by the Authority of the same that from and after the Second Day of March in the year of our Lord One thousand six hundred ninety five till the First Day of January then next following there shall not be any Obligation of receiving into His Majesty's Mint or Mints to be coined any gold whatsoever nor shall any of the Officers of His Majesty's Mints be obliged to coin any gold within the time aforesaid for any Person whatsoever anything in the said recited Acts or any other Law to the contrary notwithstanding.

And be it farther enacted by the Authority aforesaid that the several Impositions upon Wine, Vinegar, Cider, Beer, Brandy and Strong Waters imported levyable and payable by the Acts before recited shall be applied entirely toward the Encouragement of the Silver Mint according(ly) as is therein expressed without any relation to the Coinage of Gold during the Continuance of this present Act. Anything in the said former Acts to the contrary in any wise notwithstanding.

Provided nevertheless that it shall and may be lawful for the Royal African Company of England to bring to His Majesty's Tower of London to be coined during the continuance of this Act such gold as shall bee imported by them the Husband of said Company first making oath before the Warden Comptroller or Master Worker of the Mint for the time being (which Oath any of the said officers of the Mint are hereby authorized to administer) that all the Gold so brought to the Mint to be coined for the use of the African Company was imported on the Account of the said Company in return of their Goods sent to Africa and on no other account which Gold shall bee received by the Officers of the Mint and coined into Halfe-Guineas and delivered back in the same manner and with like Encouragement as it ought to have been before the making of this Act Anything herein to the contrary notwithstanding.

And whereas the Importation of Guineas from beyond sea may prove very prejudicial to this Kingdom in the present Conjuncture if not prevented Be it therefore enacted by the Authority aforesaid That from and after the said Second day of March until the said First day of January it shall not be lawful for any person or Persons to import Guineas or Halfe-Guineas into this Kingdom on any pretense whatsoever (upon Forfeiture of all such Guineas or Halfe-Guineas as shall bee so imported one Moiety thereof to His Majesty and the other to such Person or Persons who shall seize or prosecute for the same to bee recovered by Bill Plaint or Information in any of His Majesty's Courts of Record at Westminster wherein noe Essoigne Protection Priviledge or wager of Law shall bee allowed nor any more than one Imparlance).

C.

THE GUINEA AT 22 SHILLINGS.

7 & 8 Gul. III., c. 19, s. 12.

And whereas the uncertaine Value of coined gold has been highly prejudiciall to Trade and an encouragement to certain evill disposed persons to raise and fall the same to the great Prejudice of the Landed Men of this Kingdome Be it therefore enacted by the authority aforesaid that from and after the Tenth day of April One thousand six hundred ninety six no person shall utter or receive any of the pieces of gold coin commonly called Guineas at any higher or greater Rate or value than two and twenty shillings for each guinea and so proportionably for every greater or lesser piece of coined gold and whoever shall offend herein shall incur the penalties and forfeiture provided in an Act made in this present Parliament for those that shall receive or pay Guineas and other pieces of coined gold at a greater or higher rate than in that Act is directed to bee recovered by the same ways and means that the Penalties and Forfeitures of that Act are to bee or may bee recovered.

D.

REPEAL OF THE ACT SUSPENDING THE OBLIGATION TO COIN GUINEAS.

8 & 9 Gul. III., c. 1, 1696-7.

An Act for importing and coining Guineas and Halfe-Guineas.

Whereas by an Act made in the First Session of this present Parliament entitled An Act for taking off the Obligation and Encouragement of coining Guineas for a certain time therein mentioned itt is enacted that from the second day of March in the year of our Lord One thousand six hundred ninety five until the First day of January then next following there shall not bee any obligation of receiving into His Majesty's Mint or Mints to be coined any Gold whatsoever nor shall the officers of His Majesty's Mint bee obliged to coin any Gold within the time aforesaid for any person whatsoever and that the Recompenses appointed by the Statute made in the Eighteenth Year of the Reign of King Charles the Second and other subsequent Statutes for Encouragement of Coinage shall bee applied to the use of the Silver Mint And it is also thereby further enacted That from and after the said Second Day of March until the said First day of January it shall not bee lawful for any Person or persons whatsoever to import Guineas or Halfe-Guineas into this Kingdom upon any pretense whatsoever upon forfeiture of the said Guineas or Half-Guineas. And whereas the reason of making the said Act was occasioned by the High and unusual Price of Guineas which might in the end be very prejudicial to the Subject But the said Price of Guineas being now reduced to or near the Standard and sundry persons being desirous to coin Gold and also to import great Quantities of Guineas and Halfe-Guineas which will be very beneficial to the Trade and Commerce of this Kingdom. For the Encouragement whereof be it enacted by the Kings most Excellent Majesty by and with the Advice and Consent of the Lords Spiritual and Temporal and Commons in Parliament assembled and by the authority of the same that the said Act and every clause matter and thing therein contained (other than what relates to the recompenses by the said Act appointed to be applied to the Silver Mint and what concerns the Royal African Company) be and are hereby repealed and utterly made void to all intents and purposes and that all and every Person and Persons may freely import into this Kingdom Guineas and Halfe-Guineas as they might or usually did before the making the said Act prohibiting the same.

And be it further enacted by the Authority aforesaid That the Master and Worker and other Officers of His Majesty's Mint in the Tower of London shall on or before the Tenth day of November One Thousand six hundred ninety six prepare and set apart one or more Mill or Mills Press or Presses with other conveniences to be in the first place employed in the Coinage of Gold which shall be brought thither by any Person or Persons Native or Foreigner to be received in coined and delivered out in such manner course and order as by the aforesaid Statute made in the Eighteenth year of King Charles the Second is directed and appointed so that the course in Coinage of Gold and Silver be kept in distinct Accounts and not interfere one with another either in receiving or delivering out of his Majesty's said Mint and that such coining and delivering out Gold in a distinct course according to the time of bringing in the same although there be silver remaining there uncoined shall not be interpreted any undue preference to incur any Penalty in point of delivery of money coined. Anything in the said Statute of the Eighteenth of King Charles the Second or other Statute to the contrary thereof notwithstanding.

No. 9.

ACTION OF THE TREASURY TOUCHING THE CURRENCY OF THE GUINEA AT TWENTY-TWO SHILLINGS, 1697.

[*Parliamentary Return, March 12, 1830.*]

Copy of Letter from the Board of Treasury to Sir Robert Howard, dated October 25th, 1697.

Sir,

The Lords Commissioners of His Majesty's Treasury desire you to signify to the Tellers in the receipt of Exchequer, that they receive Guineas at 22s. each, pursuant to the advertisement in The Gazette of Thursday last.

(Signed) WM. LOWNDES.

Copy of Advertisement inserted in The Gazette, dated from Monday, October 18th, to Thursday, October 21st, 1697 :

WHEREAS in the Gazette of the 11th instant, notice was given (amongst other things), That Guineas would be received at 21s. 6d. a-piece (with a discount and interest therein mentioned) for loans only. The Lords Commissioners of His Majesty's Treasury being informed, that by occasion thereof, a difficulty is arisen in taking Guineas for His Majesty's revenues and taxes, are therefore pleased hereby to give notice, that it was intended but that all receivers of taxes and public revenues should receive Guineas for the same to His Majesty's use, at the rate they did before the said advertisement was published.

No. 10.

LETTER OF THE COMM'RS. OF EXCISE TOUCHING THE RATING OF THE GUINEA IN 1694-6.

[*MS. Treasury Papers, vol. 55, No. 10.*]

To the Right Honble. the Lords Comm^{rs}. of his Maties Treary.

The comm^{rs}. of his Maties. Revenues of Excise humbly represent unto yo. Lo^{pps}

That between Christmas 1694 and Ladyday 1696 severall of the Collectors of Excise in their collections received Guineas and other Species of Gold Coyne att severall rates then currant which they could not putt off att the rates att which they received the same. Whereby they have been att a loss which they have prayd us to allow them on their respective Accounts And to that purpose have made their respective Affidavits of their respective losses by receipt of the said Species of Gold they so received, and that they have made no advantage to themselves thereby. A list of which respective Collectors Names with the quantities of Gold soe received and the loss they have sustained thereby is hereto annext amounting to the same of L506. 8. 9. Wherefore wee humbly pray your Lo^{pps} Warrant for our

allowing the collectors their respective loss in the said list mentioned on the respective collectors accounts to be passed by Us.
All which is most humbly submitted to yo. Lo[rps].

Excise Office
London
July 22: 1698.

Fran. Parry.
William Strong.
I. Danvers.
P. Medows.
Jno. Everard.

(Indorsed) "Agreed."

No. 11.
JOHN LOCKE AND THE RATIO OF 15.* TO 1.

A.

ORDER OF REFERENCE TO THE COUNCIL OF TRADE ON THE QUESTION OF LOWERING THE GUINEA.

At the Council-chamber at Whitehall the eighth day of September 1698. Present their Excellencies the Lords Justices in Council.

It having been represented to their Excellencies the Lords Justices in Councill that the value of Guineas at two and twenty shillings each is very Prejudicial to the trade of this Kingdom, and particularly to the Importation of Silver Bullion. Their Excellencies taking the said Matter into consideration are pleased to order that this matter be referred to the Councill of Trade, who are to send for such Merchants and others as they shall think fit and having spoken with them to Report their opinion to this Board as soon as conveniently they can, what they conceive their Excellencies may fitly do in the matter.

B.

REPORT SIGNED BY JOHN LOCKE ON LOWERING THE GUINEA.

[*From the Journal of the House of Commons.*]

Veneris, 10° *die Februarii*, 10 *Gulielmi Tertii.*

Ordered, That the Commissioners of Trade do lay before this House, such observations as they have made, in relation to the difference of value of Gold and Silver.

(P. 511.) Mr. Blaithwaite, from the Commissioners of Trade, according to order, presented the House a copy of a representation relating to the Difference in value of Gold and Silver: And the Title therefore was read: The said Representation is as followeth: viz:

(A copy.) To their Excellencies the Lords Justices:

May it please your Excellencies. *Sept.*

In obedience to your Excellencies Order in Council dated the 8th of this Month, that we should take into consideration the Value of Guineas, as they are now current at 22^s, and the prejudice which had been represented to your Excellencies to arise from thence to the trade of this Kingdom, and particularly in the Importation of Silver Bullion; and that having spoken with merchants and other fit persons, we should report to your Excellencies our opinion thereupon, and what we conceive your Excellencies may fitly do in the matter: we have accordingly spoken with several eminent merchants, and other persons, whom we thought most capable to give us information therein; and thereupon must humbly report.

That the merchants and others, we have consulted thereupon are generally agreed, that the Importation of Gold, occasioned by our overvaluing it in the currency of guineas at 22^s is a prejudice to this Kingdom in our Trade; and an occasion that so much silver as the Value of the Gold so imported is worth, hath been either carried out of England, or hindered from coming in; and that we cannot expect any Silver Bullion, from Spain or elsewhere, should be imported and coined here, whilst we put so great an over-value upon Gold; because it is easy for merchants to know the value of both, in all Places where they deal, and exchange their Silver for Gold; and most certain, that they will only import hither to be coined, what makes most for their own advantage.

But besides their Opinion, the thing demonstrates itself, for it is certain, That Gold in Holland, from whence the greater Part, of what has been lately coined here been brought over to us, is about Six per cent cheaper than it is here; that is to say, The same Quantity of Gold that will yield here at the Mint a Sum equivalent to One Hundred ounces of Silver will there be bought for less than 94 ounces of the same Silver; and from thence it evidently follows, That whoever imports Gold, gains Six per cent. here more than if he imported Silver to be coined, and carries away for it, either so much of our silver or, at least, so much of our Commodities as that Six per cent amounts to: which is both ways alike prejudicial to this Kingdom. That this over value of Guineas draws Gold in upon us, the Mint is an unquestionable Evidence; when from the first of May last, to the 12th of this present September have been coined 250713 Guineas but in Silver only 72,866L. 0s. And it is also observable that the Silver so coined has been only some Remain of our clipped and hammered Money and not foreign Bullion imported: nor can it be hoped, that this course of coinage, now in the Mint, viz.: The Coinage of Gold in a much greater proportion than silver, should alter; but that it will be continued on to the exportation of our silver, and very great loss to this Kingdom in trade, so long as gold here shall have the value of 22s. sterling for a Guinea.

The Prejudice arising from hence to Trade and the advantage that may be expected from the fall of Guineas, are also more particularly observed to us by Merchants, from the rate of exchange. For the course of exchange between England and Holland, having of late by the importation of so much gold from thence been brought considerably lower than the Par, the consequence of which is, that we pay so much more for everything we bring from thence, and receive so much less for everything we send thither; that course has ever since Your Excellencies Commands to us to make Inquiry into this Matter, by the spreading of the Rumours and expectation of some Change, already received an Alteration of about one per cent to our Advantage; and it is not doubted, but as the Price of Guineas shall be more certainly reduced towards their true value, the Exchange will rise proportionately. This being the state of the Matter, we are humbly of Opinion that it is necessary, Guineas in their common currency be brought down to 21s. 6d. at least; And further humbly conceive that Your Excellencies may fitly do it by giving directions, That the officers of the Receipt of his Majesty's Exchequer and all other, the Receivers of His Majesty's Revenue, do not take them at a higher rate. This appears to us the Most Convenient way; because it may, at all times, be a ready and easy remedy, upon any further variation that shall happen in the world in the Price of Gold; or even in case this now proposed Lowering of Guineas should not prove sufficient: For it being impossible, that more than one Metal should be the true Measure of Commerce; and the world by common Consent and Convenience, having settled that Measure in Silver; Gold as well as other

Metals, is to be looked upon as a Commodity, which varying in its Price as other Commodities do, its Value will always be changeable; and the fixing of its value in any Country; so that it cannot be readily accommodated to the course it has in other neighbouring Countries will be always prejudicial to the Country which does it. The Value of Gold, here at the price of 21s. 6d. a Guinea, in proportion to the Rate of Silver in our Coin, will be very near as fifteen and one half to one; the value of Gold in proportion to Silver, in Holland and Neighbouring Countries, as near as can be computed, upon a Medium, is as fifteen to one; so that by bringing down the Guineas to 21s. 6d. Gold will not here be brought to so low a Price as in our Neighbouring Countries; Nevertheless, we are humbly of Opinion that the Abatement of Sixpence in the Guinea will be sufficient to stop the present disproportionate Importation of gold; because the Charge for Insurance, Freight, Commission, and the like, will eat up the Profit that may then be made thereby, and hinder that Trade; but if, contrary, to our Expectation, this Abatement should prove too small Guineas may by the same easy Means be lowered, yet farther, according as may be found expedient.

All of which, nevertheless, is most humbly submitted.

Ph. Meadows.
John Pollexfen.
John Locke.
Abr. Hill.

Whitehall,
22 September 1698.

C.

ORDERS TO THE GOVERNMENT OFFICERS NOT TO TAKE GUINEAS FOR MORE THAN 21s. 6d.

[*Parliamentary Return, March* 12, 1830.]

Letters addressed by the Board of Treasury to the following Boards or Persons.

Agents for Taxes.
Commissioners of Excise.
„   Glass Duty.
„   Customs.
Auditor of the Receipt.

Copy of various Letters from the Board of Treasury to the following Boards and Persons : viz. :

Agents for Taxes.

Gentlemen :

The Lords Commissioners of His Majesty's Treasury direct you to write to the respective Receivers of the Taxes, not to take any Guineas that are not yet collected at more than One-and-twenty Shillings and sixpence each Guinea, and that they be very careful upon this occasion that no fraud be committed against the King or the country, for that they may expect a narrow scrutiny will be made into their respective behaviours in this matter.

Dated 15th February 1698.   (Signed) WM. LOWNDES.

To THE RECEIVER-GENERAL OF CUSTOMS.
          OF THE POST OFFICE.
          OF THE STAMP OFFICE.

Receiver-General Customs :

Sir :—

The Lords Commissioners of His Majesty's Treasury direct you not to take any Guineas that are not yet collected at more than Twenty-one Shillings and six pence each Guinea, and that you be very careful upon this occasion that no fraud be committed against the King or his Subjects, for that you may expect a narrow scrutiny will be made into this matter. Dated and Signed the same.

Mr. Montague,

Sir :—

The Lords Commissioners of His Majesty's Treasury desire you to signify to the Four Tellers not to take any Guineas to the King's use at more than Twenty-one shillings and sixpence each Guinea, and that they be very careful upon this occasion that no deceits be committed against the King or any of His Subjects, for that they may expect a narrow scrutiny will be made into their respective fidelities in this matter.

Dated 16th February, 1698.

          Signed the same.

No. 12.

INSTANCES OF CONTRADICTION BETWEEN DIFFERENT STATEMENTS IN LOCKE'S WRITINGS ON MONEY.

I quote from "SOME CONSIDERATIONS OF THE CONSEQUENCES OF THE LOWERING OF INTEREST AND RAISING THE VALUE OF MONEY. In a letter sent to a Member of Parliament 1691. The second edition corrected. London. Awnsham and John Churchil 1696. [Second Title.] SEVERAL PAPERS RELATING TO MONEY INTEREST AND TRADE ETC. writ upon several occasions, and published at different Times, by Mr. John Locke." [On the reverse page.] "Licensed Nov. 27, 1691. Ja. Fraser": and from " FURTHER CONSIDERATIONS CONCERNING RAISING THE VALUE OF MONEY Wherein Mr. Lowndes Arguments for it in his late Report concerning an Essay for the Amendment of the Silver Coins, are particularly examined. The second edition corrected. London A & J Churchill 1695. Dedicated to Right Hon. Sir John Sommers Kt. Lord Keeper, etc.

The following extract is from the Essay entitled "Short Observations on a Printed Paper Intituled, For encouraging the Coining Silver money in England, and after for keeping it here" in "Some Considerations," the volume first above-named. (The paging is from the 12mo ed. 1696.)

"The Silver being the measure of commerce, 'tis the quantity of Silver that is in every piece he receives, and not the Denomination of it which the Merchant looks after and values it by." (Page 16.) And, later, "men in their bargains contract not for denominations or sounds, but for the intrinsic value."

Compare these assertions with the following, which quite refutes them, namely :—" And our bargains for Commodities as well as all other Contracts being made in Pounds Shillings and Pence, our clipt money retains amongst the people (who knows not how to count but by Current Money) a part of its legal value, whilst it passes for the satisfaction of legal contracts as if it were lawful money." (P. 96, " Further Considerations, etc.")

The latter is pure fact; the former a broad statement which includes in part what *is* and a part of what *ought to be*, but is *n't* in certain cases.

In the Essay " Of Raising our Coin," in " Some Considerations etc," after setting forth the prevalent instability of ratio as a reason why Gold should not be made a Measure [unit] like Silver, he says, page 168 —

" What then ? (will you be ready to say) would you have gold kept out of England ? Or being here, would you have it useless to Trade ? and would there be no Money made of it ? I answer, quite the contrary. 'Tis fit the Kingdom should make use of the Treasure it has.

'Tis necessary your *Gold should be coin'd*, and have the King's stamp upon it to secure men in receiving it, that there is so much gold in each piece . . . .

The Gold Money so coined will never fail to pass at the known Market rates as readily as any other species of your Money."

Three pages later, page 171, in the same paper, he says—

" That it is the interest of every country that all the current Money of it should be of one and the same metal; that the several pieces should be all of the same alloy and none of a baser mixture and that the standard once thus settled should be inviolably and immutably kept to perpetuity."

Here is apparently a glaring conflict. Gold money coined and never failing to pass as readily as any other species of your Money, and yet a Single Silver Standard with all the current Money of one and the same metal !

There is, however, a mode of reconciliation of the two statements which reduces the inconsistency within manageable limits. Say instead of " all the Current Money " all the Money which is compulsory Legal Tender between individuals, and you state what, I imagine, was in Locke's mind when he wrote the passage. The rest of the contradiction must be due to haste. There is no allusion to the existing Statute of Free and Gratuitous Coinage of both Silver and Gold, or to the fact that the Guinea was unquestioned Legal Tender (by the Terms of the Mint Indenture) for 20 shillings. It is evident that the paper was put forth in the heat and haste of controversy.

The following is another instance of the change of tone between 1691 and 1695.

In " Some Considerations" p. 9, I find :

"The Standard once settled by public authority the quantity of Silver established under the several denominations I humbly conceive should not be altered till there were an absolute necessity shown of such a change, which I think can never be."

In " Further Considerations," page 7, Locke says—

" In coined Silver or *Money* there are these three things which are wanting in other Silver. 1. Pieces of exactly the same weight and fineness. 2. A stamp set on those pieces by the publick authority of that Country. 3. A known denomination given to these pieces by the same authority."

The reader will observe that the " denomination" embraces the idea of the legal character given to Money.

On page 22, summing up the preceding argument, he says :

" 4 That Money differs from uncoin'd Silver, only in this, that the quantity of Silver in each piece of Money is ascertained by the stamp it bears which is set there to be a publick voucher of its weight and fineness."

So in the argument he expressly makes a vital point which he omits in the summing up, namely : the " known denomination given to these pieces by the same authority."

No. 13.

A PRIVATE LETTER OF JOHN LOCKE,

In which the Recoinage is Mentioned.

Oates, 30th March, 1696.

Mr. Locke to Mr. Molyneux.

The Business of our Money has so near brought us to Ruin, that, till the Plot broke out, it was every Body's talk, every Body's uneasiness. And because I had play'd the Fool to print about it, there was scarce a Post wherein Somebody or other did not give me fresh Trouble about it. But now the Parliament has reduced Guineas to two and twenty Shillings apiece after the 10th Instant, and prohibited the receipt of clip'd Money after the 4th of May next.

The Bill has passed both Houses, and, I believe will speedily receive the Royal Assent.

Though I can never bethink any Pains, or Time of mine, in the Service of my Country as far as I may be of any Use: yet I must own to you, this, and the like Subjects, are not those which I now relish, or that do, with most Pleasure, employ my thoughts.

. . . .

(*From Locke's Works, folio ed., vol. iii.*)

No. 14.

MEMOIRS OF THE GREAT RE-COINAGE.

BY HOPTON HAYNES, ESQ., THE KING'S ASSAY MASTER (1700).

The following are brief extracts from a MS. in the British Museum, entitled as follows:—

"Brief memoires relating to the silver and Gold coins of England, with an account of the corruption of the hammer'd monys, and of the reform by the late grand coynage at the Tower, and the five country mints, in the years 1696, 1697, 1698, and 1699. By Hopton Haynes, Esq., Assay Master of the Mint. 1700." *Lansd. MS.* 801, *ff.* 54-64.

ACCOUNT OF THE PROVISIONS IN PARLIAMENT TO REMEDY Yᴱ ILL STATE OF Yᴱ COIN.

ANNO 1695.

The confusion and distraction in all receipts and payments by the Guineas and Clipt mony come to that pitch that nothing lesse than recoyning all the hammerd Silver monys and reduceing the Guineas could remedy the generall disorders: and the people grew so weary of this greivance, that our Ennemys abroad depended upon a new Revolution, and their Partizans here were in great hopes that some disorders would happen thereupon; but to their great mortification they found, after all their utmost essays to corrupt the loyalty of the people, that they remain'd inflexible in their allegiance and affection to the King; His Gouvernment and martial genius had purchas'd him the Universal love of his people ; & every body knew where to charge all our miserys, and publick misfortunes; and plac'd all their hopes of relief in some expedient to be found out in y^e ensuing Session of 169$\frac{5}{6}$. As soon as the King was return'd from abroad he was fully and particularly inform'd of the very ill state of the Coin, and the universall complaint and generall uneasinesse of his Subjects on that Account.

The Lords of the Treasury who had for some time before consider'd this matter wherein they were particularly concern'd were prepared to debate it in Parliament and to propose their Expedient to the House for redressing a greivance that was become intolerable. And divers Members of both Houses took some pains likewise in inquireing into the State of the Coin, and considering what measures were fitt to be pursued att their next meeting ; & many of 'em receiv'd it as an instruction, from the Country Corporations wch they represented, to take a particular care in remedying the ill state of the Silver mony.

The generall Mischiefs that were allready felt and the fatall consequences that must have attended a delay in reforming it, allarm'd the whole Kingdom & entirely convinc'd the Members of both Houses of the necessity of begiñing the Session with this important debate.

Every body without doors was inspir'd with an unusuall zeale for the publick on this occasion, which produced a world of papers containing Proposalls to the Parliam^t for amending the Silver coins, providing funds for ye warr, reviving the publick credit, and supplying the necessitys of our Inland trade.

Some of which Papers I doubt not were of good use afterwards to diverse Gentlemen in their Parliamentary debates ; M^r. Lowndes his Memorial was well received by the publick. But what M^r. Locke had written about ye Coin was in very great esteem with every Judicious Reader ; for he expos'd the delusion of raising the value of our monys, and very much contributed to the preservation of ye legal weight & purity of 'em which some persons mightily endeavoured to change. The Kingdom was oblig'd to that very worthy Gentleman, for the pains he took to serve his Country yet the affair was of that moment and generall concern that no privat person could perhaps foresee all that was proper to be done to restore the Coin and our creditt to their ancient Standard.

The King himself would not undertake to remedy the ill state of the Coin by his meer Prerogative; but, as ye wisest of his Predecess^{rs} had don before him thought fitt to advise with his Parliament about it; and was pleas'd at the opening of the winter Session the 23 November 1695 after other weighty matters to tell 'em in his Speech, That he could not but take notice of the great difficultys wee lay under by *Reason of the ill state of the Coin, the redresse of which might prove a further charge to the Nation, but 'twas a matter of such generall concern, and of so very great importance, that he thought fitt to leave it entirely to the consideration of his Parliament.*

The following excellent admonition from the close of the Chapter will be recognized by some eyes as having a peculiar appropriateness, when applied to a very different time to that which the author had in view:—

Which by the way may be an Instruction to the Gent'lmen who in 1695-6 so zealously espoused the keeping up of ye Guineas, at 28 to 30s. a piece and treated all such, particularly the then Chancelour of the Exchequer, and some other Members who saw the fatall consequences of it, and endeavour'd to reduce 'em to their just value, as Enemys to their Country; but notwithstanding this ill treatment and many other aspersions, this good service to the Kingdom was effectually don; and the good Patriots, who did all they could to hinder it, have ever since reaped the Advantage of it, as well as their Neighbours, and stand equally obliged with the whole Nation to those worthy Gentlemen who did it without 'em and very much against their will.

No. 15.
MONETARY REPORTS (1701—1702) SIGNED BY SIR ISAAC NEWTON.

Printed from Manuscripts found in the Tower Mint[1] and in the Public Record Office.

A.

[*MS. Mint Records, Vol. vii., p. 25.*]

To the Right Hon'ble, the Lords Comm'rs of His Ma'ts Trea'ry:

May it please your Lordships

The great value put upon French and Spanish pistoles in England has made them of late flow plentifully hither above all other sorts of Gold especially the French pistoles which are better seized and coined and less liable to be counterfeited and by consequence of more credit than the Spanish. For pistoles pass among us for 17s. 6d. apiece whereas one with another they are worth but about 17s. 1d. at the rate that guineas of due weight and alloy are worth 21s. 6d. In France by an edict of May last a pistole (marked or not marked) passes for 13 livres or 3 14-17 ecus that is for 17s. 2 8-17d. reckoning an ecu worth 4s. 6d. according to the reputed par of Exchange and so much may pistoles be worth here if allowance be made for the lightness of our money by wearing.

About four years ago by the English putting too great a value upon Scotch money the northern borders of England were filled with that money and Scotland with ours the Scots making about eight or nine per cent profit by the Exchange until your Lordships were pleased to put a stop to the mischief. The case being now the same (but of much greater consequence) in the course of exchange between English money and pistoles by the overvaluing of pistoles to the nation's loss, we thought it our duty to present it to your Lordships in order to such a remedy as your Lordships shall think fitt.

We presume also to lay before your Lordships that the great demand of silver for exportation in trade has raised the price of bullion above

---

[1] I am indebted to the friendly courtesy of Mr. Fremantle for the privilege of examining these Records.

that of silver monies 3d. or 4d. and sometimes 6d. or 7d. per ounce, whereas monies ought to be of as great or greater value than bullion by reason of the workmanship and certainty of the standard and this high price of bullion has not only put an end to the coinage of silver but is a great occasion of melting down and exporting what has been already coined.

All which is most humbly submitted to your Lordships great wisdom.

Mint Office, January 20, 1701.

J. STANLEY.
Is. NEWTON.

B.

[*MS. Mint Records.*]

TO THE RIGHT HON'BLE. THE LORDS COMM'S OF HIS MAJESTY'S TREA'RY:

May it please your Lordships

In obedience to your Lordships order we have made enquiry whether the Publick Receivers of money do pursue the intent of the Act of Parliament in cutting all counterfeit money offered to them in payments, and do find that tis observed in the Exchequer the Custom House the Excise and in the Stamp Office. But upon enquiry into the practice of the Bank of England we are informed that the receivers there have orders only to refuse counterfeit money but not to cutt it for fear of disobliging those who bring their money to be lodged there and who might otherwise remove it to the goldsmiths where they are sure to be better treated.

We are also credibly informed that the Receivers General in the several countys for the Land Tax, the Dutys on Glass Windows, and on Births Marriages, &c. do not cut the counterfeit money offered them in payments which may be one great reason why the trade of counterfeiting is more practised in the country than in towne and we are humbly of opinion that the trade of counterfeiting money would be in a greate measure prevented if all publick receivers of money were required to putt a stop to the currency of it by cutting it as they are obliged by Act of Parliament.

All wch is humbly submitted by

J. STANLEY.
Is. NEWTON.

C.

[*MS. Treasury Papers, Vol. lxxvi., No. 36.*]

TO THE RT. HON'BLE THE LORDS COMM'RS OF HIS MAJ'TIES TREASURY:

May it please yo' Lord'ps

By the late edicts of the French King for raising the monies in France, the proportion of gold to that of silver being altered, I humbly presume to give your Lord'ps notice thereof. By the last of those edicts the Lewis d'or passes for fourteen livres and the ecus or French crown for three livres and sixteen sols. At wch rate the Lewis d'or is worth 16s. 7d. sterling supposing the ecus worth 4s. 6d. as it is recconed in the course of exchange and as I have found it by some assays. The proportion therefore between gold and silver is now become the same in France as it has been in Holland for some years. For at Amsterdam the Lewis d'or passes for nine guilders and nine or ten styvers wch in our money amounts to 16s. 7d. and it has past at this rate for the last five or six years.

At the same rate a guinea of due weight and allay is worth 1li. 00s. 11d.

In Spain gold is recconed (in stating Accompts) worth sixteen times its weight in silver of the same allay, at wch rate a guinea of due weight and allay is worth £1 2s. 1d., but the Spaniards make their payments in gold and will not make their payments in silver without an abatement. This abatement is not certain but rises and falls accordingly as Spain is supplied with gold or silver from the Indies. Last winter it was about 5 per cent.

The state of the money in France being unsettled, whether it may furnish a sufficient argument for altering the proportion of the values of gold and silver monies in England is most humbly submitted to yo'r Lord'ps great wisdome.   Is. NEWTON.

Mint Office, Sept. 28, 1701.

(Indorsed) Mr. Newton's Memorial concerning the proportion of gold to silver in value.

D.

[MS. Treasury Papers, Vol. lxxx., No. 105.]

To the Rt. Hon'ble Sidney Lord Godolphin, L'd High Treasurer of England:

May it please your Lord'p

According to your Lord'ps direction we have examined the values of several forreign coyns & endeavoured to inform ourselves of the values of gold in proportion to silver in several nations and considered the ways of preserving the coyn. And by the accompts we have met with gold is higher in England then in France by about 9 *l.* or 10*d.* in the guinea then in Holland by 11*d.* or 12 pence in the guinea, then in Germany and Italy by 12*d.* in the guinea or above. In Spain and Portugal gold is higher then in England by about 11*d.* in the guinea ffor the great quantity of silver coming from the West Indies has brought down the price of silver in all Europe in proportion to gold & principally in Spain where the bullion first arrives. The low price mends the market and thereby carries silver from Spain into all Europe and from all Europe to the East Indies & China, the merchants bidding more for it then it goes for among the natives. In Spain the merchants advance about six p cent. or above for silver: att which rate a guinea is worth about 21*s.* 3½*d.* & sometimes less. In England they advance 3*d.* or 4*d.* per ounce, and at the rate of 3*d.* per ounce advance a guinea is worth but 20*s.* 6 1-6*d.*

Gold is therefore at too high a rate in England by about 10*d.* or 12*d.* in the guinea, & this tending to the decrease of the silver coyn we humbly conceive that our way of preserving this coyn is to lower the price of gold suppose by taking 6*d.*, 9*d.* or 12*d.* from the price of the guinea so as that gold may be of the same value in England as in the neighbouring parts of Europe. France has set us an example for in the last war when the lewidor was raised there to 14 livres the ecu was raised only to 72 sols but it is now raised to 76 sols tho' the lewidor be raised only to 14 livres as before so that gold in respect of silver is lower in France now then in the last war in the proportion of 76 to 72 that is by above 13½*d.* in the guinea.

The liberty of melting forreign monies into ingots in private shops and houses for exportation gives opportunity of melting down the money of England for the same purpose ffor restraining of wch a law might be useful against exporting any Ingots of Silver melted down in England except in a publick Office to be appointed or erected for that purpose.

The law by barring the exportation of forreign silver after it is coyned prevents the coynage thereof because the Merchant cannot afterwards export it & tends to discourage the importation of this silver into England because the Merchant can make no use of it whilst it stays here in the form of Bullion. The bringing of silver to the market of England & the turning it into money should rather be encouraged as the proper means of encreasing the coyn, silver being more apt to stay with us in the useful form of money then in the useless form of Bullion. If the merchant might export what he coynes some part of what he coyns would be apt to be laid out here, And this liberty may be allowed him after some such manner as is described in the scheme hereinto annexed.

The licensing the exportation of Bullion whilst the exportation of the money is prohibited makes silver worth more uncoyned then coyned and thereby not only stops the coynage but causes the melting down of the money in private for exportation. For remedying this mischief it maybe perhaps better on the contrary to prohibit the exportation of Bullion and license that of money and whenever the money is in danger to license the exportation of so much money only as shall from time to time be coyned out of forreign Bullion.

The safety and encrease of the coyn depends principally on the ballance of trade be against us the money will be melted down and exported to pay debts abroade & carry on trade in spight of laws to the contrary, and if the ballance of trade be for us such laws are needless & even hurtfull to trade. If trade can be so ordered that no branch of it can be detrimental to the nation the money will be safe ffor wch end luxury in forreign commodities should be checkt and the exportation of our own commodities encouraged. If a law were made & well executed against trading with more gold & silver by any Merchant or Company of Merchants then in certain proportions to the value of the goods exported, such an Addition to the Act of Navigation might put Merchants upon searching out sufficient ways of vending our commodities abroad & as we humbly conceive be more effectual for preserving the coyn then the absolute prohibition of the exportation thereof.

As for the alteration of the standard we are humbly of opinion that if the value of the several species to be thereafter coyned be diminished without changing the denomination it will occasion the melting down & recoyning the species already coyned for the profit that may be made thereby. And if the value be encreased the Merchants and people will value their goods by the old money already coyned in wch they are to be paid and the new money of greater value (if any shall be coyned) will be pickt out for exportation and the Importer who coyns it will lose the overvalue to the discouragement of the coynage and in payments made by sale to forreigners the nation will also lose the over value.

But if it be proposed to retain the value of the several species or quantity of fine silver therein & only alter the allay, we are humbly of opinion that if small money which by continual use weares awaye fast & is apt to be lost, were coyned of coarse allay as is done in several countries abroad provided it were well coyned to prevent counterfeiting, such money would weare longer & be less apt to be lost than the small money now in use. By small money we understand Groats Three-pences, Twopences, and pence, unless the penny by reason of its smallness should be made of copper.

All wch is most humbly submitted to yor Lordps great wisdome.

Mint Office, 7 Jul. 1702.
        J. STANLEY.
        ISC. NEWTON.
        JN. ELLIS.

(Indorsed)   Report of the Officers of the Mint about the preservation of the Coyne.

(In pencil)   All in the hand-writing of Sir Isaac Newton, 7 July, 1702.

[The accompanying tables, showing " the values of several forreign coynes," are here omitted. The tables, like the following paper on the value of Gold, are stated in the Calendar to be in Newton's hand. Report C. is in the same hand.]

E.

THE VALUE OF GOLD IN PROPORTION TO SILVER IN SEVERAL PARTS OF EUROPE.

[*MS. Treasury Papers, Ditto.*]

The Ecu of France goes there for 3 livres 16 sols and by the weight and assay is worth 4s. 6d. English and thence the Livre is worth 1s. 2·21d. The Lewid'or goes there for 14 livres, which amount to 16s. 6·94d. English. At wch rate a Guinea is worth 20s. 8¼d. For as 17s. 2·8d. (the value of an unworn Lewidor in England according to the annexed Table) is to 16s. 6·94d. (the value of the same in France) so is 21s. 6d. (the value of an unworn Guinea in England) to 20s. 8¼d.

By the French Kings Edict of 17 Sept 1701 the Mark of fine Gold is valued at 494 livres 6 sols 4 deniers & the mark of fine silver at 32 livres 16 sols 7 deniers. According to which proportion a Guinea of just weight & fineness is worth 20s. 8¼d. in English silver money of just weight & fineness.

The Ducat is coyned every where in Germany & some northern countries adjoining of the same weight & fineness excepting that the Hungary Ducats are more certainly of full value. It is coyned for two old Rix dollars of the Empire or nine shillings English & usualy goes at that rate or within two or three styvers more or less, whereas in England it is worth 9s. 6.3d. But if the Rixdoller be of a lower value, as are the Rixdollers of Holland, Flanders Danemark & some other places, the Ducat may go for two Rix dollers & 6. 8 or 10 styvers or above.

In Holland the Guilder or Floren is of equal value with 20.82d. English & the styver is 1d. 041 as may be collected from the said Table. And there the Ducat goes usually for 5 Guilders & about 5 styvers, that is in our money for 9s. 1.3d. at which rate a Guinea is worth 20s. 6¼d.

The Lewidor goes in Holland for 9 Guilders & about 9 styvers or 16s. 4¼d. At which rate a Guinea is worth 20s. 5¼d.

In the Countries of the Electors of Brandenburg Saxony Hannover

& Dukes of Zell Brunswick, Lunenburg, Wolfenbuttel & some other places are coyned Guilders of one & the same value by consent of the Princes, tho of various allays. This Guilder consists of 16 Gute Groshes or 24 Marien Groshes & 46 Marien Groshes are accounted the value of an old Rixdoller or 4s. 6d. English. So that a Guilder is worth 2s. 4¼d. or thereabouts. By the Table it is worth 2s. 4 1-7d. according to the weight & assay. Now a Ducat goes in the countries above mentioned for 3½ Guilders or 8s. 9 3-7d. & sometimes for two or three Groshes more. If it be valued at 9s. a Guinea at that rate will be worth 20s. 4d.

In the same countries a Lewidor is valued at 7 Guilders or thereabouts, that is at 16s. 5d. At which rate a Guinea is worth 20s. 5¼d.

At Hamborough the Ducats goes for two Dollars & about 8 or 9 sols lubs. or sols of Lubec. This Doller is three Marks lubs that is 48 sols lubs, recconing 16 sols to a mark. But the Cross Doller wch is worth 4s. 4.91d. goes for 52 sols lubs & therefore the other Doller which goes but for 48 sols lubs is worth only 4s. .084d. or thereabouts. The Marks & sols lubs are at Hamborough accounted double to the Marks & sold Dans or of Danemark & the four Mark piece or Crown of Danemark goes at Hamborough for two Marks lubs & by the assays of several pieces is worth 2s. 8.4d. as in the Table. And at this rate three marks lubs are worth 4s. 0.6d. English. This is the value of the common Hamborough Doller & two Dollers & nine sols lubs (the value of the Ducat) are 8s. 10.4d. At wch rate a Guinea is worth 20s. 0¼d.

At Dantzick Gold is very scarce. Their Guilder consists of 30 Grosh, & the Bank Doller wch is worth about 4s. 6d. goes for three Guilders 23 Grosh: Whence the Guilder is 14½d. The Ducat is there valued at about 7 Guilders 12 Grosh; or two Bank Dollers wanting four Grosh, that is at about 8s. 10.09d. And at this rate a Guinea is worth 19s. 11¼d.

At Geneva the Hungary Ducat was lately valued at two Ecus & 2 or 3 sols of ffrance, that is at 9s. 2d. or 9s. 3d. At which rates a Guinea is worth about 20s. 9¼d. Then also the Lewidor was lately valued at 3½ Ecus of France or 16s. 10½d. At which rate a Guinea is worth 21s. 0½d. But Gold was lately higher in France then at present, wch might raise the price of Lewidors at Geneva. For there the Spanish Pistole was valued only at 3⅐ Ecus or 16s. 6d.

2. At Genoa the Croistat goes for 7½ lires & by assay is worth

6s. 6¼d. & therefore the Lire of Genoa is 10½d. And there the Pistole is valued at 17½ lires that is 15s. 3¼d.

1. At florence and Legorn the silver Ducat goes for 7 lires & by assay is worth 5s. 4.57d. & therefore the lire of those places is 9.224d. And there the Pistole of Italy goes for 20 lires or 15s. 4½d. & the Lewidor & Spanish Pistole for between 20 & 21 lires.

At Rome, Florence, Legorn Bullogne & Ancona (a city upon the Gulph of Venice) three Julios make a Teston & the Teston by assay is worth 1s. 6.21d. & thence the Julio is 6.07d. Ten Julios make the Escudi or Ecu of Rome, but I cannot yet procure that piece of money for an assay. At florence three Julios are two lires & 10½ Julios make the Ducat, and thence the Julio is 6.15d. Now in those cities the Pistole of Italy goes for 30 Julios or 15s. 4½d. & the Spanish Pistole for 31 Julios or 15s. 10.65d. supposing the Julio 6.15d.

At Bologne & Ancona the Sequin of Venice goes for 18 Julios or 9s. 2.7d. & the Hungary Ducat for 17 Julios or 8s. 8.55d.

If the Ducat of Venice whose value is set down in the Table, be that Ducat, as I am told wch goes now at Venice for 6 lires 4 sols de Piccoli the Lire of Venice will be 6.52d. And there the Hungary Ducat wch goes for 16 lires will be worth 8s. 8.32d. & the sequin of Venice which goes for 17 lires will be worth 9s. 2.84d. & the Pistole of Venice wch goes for 28 lires will be worth 15s. 2.56d.

At Millain the Piece of eight went lately for 5 lires 17 sols & the Philip or Silver Ducat for 6 lires, so that the Philip is to the Piece of eight (or 4s. 6d.) as 40 to 39 & therefore is worth about 4s. 7 5-13d. This piece, as I am informed goes at Venice for 8½ lires & therefore the sequin wch goes at Venice for 17 lires is there worth 9s. 2 10-13d. as before.

At Naples the Ducat of silver is worth 3s. 4.43d. and there the Pistole, as I am informed goes for 45 Carlins or 4½ Ducats that is for 15s. 2d.

By all wch gold seems to be lower in Italy then in France, the Spanish Pistole being every where worth less then 16s. At wch rate the Guinea is worth less than 20s.

In Spain the Pistole is recconed at four pieces of eight or 18s. which is 9.2d. more then in England. And in Portugal the Moeda is recconed at ten Crusados or 27s. 7.1d. wch is 14d. more then in England. At wch rates a Guinea is worth 22s. 5½d. in Spain & 22s. 5d. in Portugal.

In these recconings standard Gold is valued in England at 4li p ounce as Goldsmiths value it for the melting pot. The standard value is 3li 19s. 8½d., at wch rate about ⅞ths of a penny are to be added to the value of the Guinea in forreign Countries.

J. Stanley.
Is. Newton.
Js. Ellis.

Mint Office, 7 Jul. 1702.

(Indorsed) Proportions of Gold to Silver abroad.

F.

Proposals for Preserving & Encreasing the Silver Coin of this Kingdom.

(MS. Treasury Papers, Ditto.)

All Silver exported and design'd for Exportation except fforeign Money to be examined & enter'd in ye Mint & for that End upon its first arrival at London, to be brought to ye Mint by ye Owner & Two or more other Witnesses, who shall there prove ye importation upon Oath. And such of ye said Silver as is not yet in ye Ingot, to be there melted down into Ingots, the Mercht paying 1d. p pound for ye melting & these Ingots & all other Ingots of ye Silver above mention'd shall at ye choice of ye Merchant be coin'd into moneys or mark't with a stamp provided in ye Mint for that purpose. And ye Master of ye Mint (if desired) shall give ye Merchant an Indented Ticket certifying to ye Weight of ye Moneys coyn'd out of ye said fforeign Silver & ye time of ye coynage thereof: which Ticket shall be cut out of a Book provided in ye Mint & be enter'd in the same Book.

Ingots not mark't with ye Mint Stamp may not be Exported nor carry'd on Board any Ship, nor bought or sold, but may be brought to ye Mint for encreasing the Coin, excepting that Ingots of fine Silver may be sold by Refiners to Silver Smiths, Wyerdrawers, & such other Artificers as manufacture ye same. This law now obtains in France by an Edict of March was a Twelve-month for preventing ye melting down of ye moneys.

The Merchants upon delivering ye Mint Tickets at ye Custom House may within a year after ye Coynage of the Moneys mention'd therein by warrant of ye Commissioners of ye Customs upon a day appointed in ye Warrant, Ship for Exportation, the said Moneys, or ye same weight of like moneys or any part thereof & also any Ingots wch have ye Mint Stamp upon them & any forreign Moneys & the Customer shall enter ye same and file ye Tickets.

All Silver English Moneys before shipping for Exportation to pay 1½d. p ounce Troy at the Custom House for ye charges of assaying, melting & Coyning ye same which Duty shall be kept apart with ye Duty already granted for Encouragement of Coynage & therewith paid unto ye Exchequer and thence imprest to ye Mr of ye Mint for ye same uses.

Penalties on them who counterfeit ye Mint Stamp or ye Mint Tickets or Shipp off Silver not licens'd, or without paying ye duty or upon any other day then that appointed in ye Warrant or under any other name than that of ye true Owner, or buy or sell unmark'd Ingots or knowingly bring Silver to ye Mint to be Mark't or Coin'd or fforeign which is not fforeign.

Such a Law would Enable ye Officers of ye Mint to understand ye State of ye Money with respect to Trade. It would render Trade freer than at present. It would save the Merchant ye trouble of attending with his Bullion and Witnesses at Goldsmith's Hall & Guildhall after he has melted it at ye Refiners or Goldsmiths. It would Check ye melting down of Her Majesty's moneys for Exportation or for sale to Goldsmiths, much better than ye laws do at present. It would encrease ye Coynage in her Ma'ts Mint & decrease ye Indian Manufacture of coyning or Bullion in Ports where ye Company have not a Mint of their own for which Coynage ye Indians receive of us a large Seigniorage. It would be profitable to ye Merchant by ye use of his Gold & Silver when turned into Money before Exportation. It would encrease our Coin as well by ye Merchants Money running amongst us, till Exportation, as by what is not exported within ye year. It would be of great Credit to ye Nation by ye Merchants exporting their Gold & Silver in ye form of English money, to be current in fforeign Nations and thereby make us appear abroad more rich & potent than We do at present. And all this would be done without any new charge to ye Government. And if ye Governmt should pay the charge of Coynage, or any part thereof, it would be pay'd by one part of ye Nation to another part thereof wthout loss to ye whole.

Mint Office, 7 Jul. 1702. J. STANLEY,
IS. NEWTON,
JN. ELLIS.

No. 16.

AN ORDER IN COUNCIL TOUCHING THE CURRENCY OF LOUIS D'ORS AND PISTOLES.

[*Parliamentary Return, March* 12, 1830.]

Copy of the Order of the 5th February 1700-1, respecting the Value at which the Louis d'Or and Spanish Pistole were to be received as part of the Current Coin of the Realm.

AT THE COURT AT KENSINGTON.

The 5th February, 1700.

Present: The King's Most Excellent Majesty in Council.

It having been this day represented to His Majesty in Council, That certain pieces of Gold in French and Spanish Coin, called Louis d'Ors or Pistoles, do pass and are accepted in payment in this kingdom, at the rate of seventeen shillings and sixpence a piece, which is near sixpence more than the real value; His Majesty, taking the same into His Royal consideration, and being desirous to prevent the damage that may accrue to His good Subjects by the great quantity of such French Louis d'Ors and Spanish Pistoles which have of late been and may hereafter be imported into this Kingdom, in case the said Louis d'Ors or Pistoles should continue to be received for more than the intrinsic value. His Majesty, with the advice of his Privy Council, is therefore pleased to Order, as it is hereby Ordered, That notice be given in the Gazette, that the said French Louis d'Ors and Spanish Pistoles be not hereafter received for more than seventeen shillings a-piece.

JAS. BULLER.

A true copy,
Council Office, Whitehall,
9 March, 1830.

No. 17.

MINUTE OF ORDERS TO THE OFFICERS OF THE MINT, FEB. 12, 1700-1.

[*MS. Mint Records.*]   February 12th, 1700.

Present { The Warden and Master.

Upon the Notice given in the Gazett by Order of the King and Councill not to take French and Spanish Pistols for more than 17s it being found that the merchants and Goldsmiths brought great Quantities of them to be coyned into Guineas and desired a speedy dispatch in Order to answer their Bills, it was resolved that the Master should make use of all the   of the Mint for the more speedy circulation amounting to £9,700.

Ordered for the greater help to the Importers that Gold should be melted three times a week and paid out Mondayes Wednesdayes and Frydayes to continue dureing the Great Importation of Gold.

No. 18.

SIR JAMES STEUART AND ADAM SMITH ON THE ENGLISH STANDARD.

Extract from " An Inquiry into the Principles of Political Economy," by Sir James Steuart, of Coltness, Bart.

(Vol. II., Chap. viii. page 337.)

It is absurd to say that the standard of Queen Elizabeth has not been debased by enacting that the English Unit shall be acquitted with 113 grains of fine Gold, as it would be to affirm that it would not be debased from what it is at present by enacting that a pound of butter should everywhere be received in payment for a pound sterling, although the pound sterling should continue to consist of 3 ounces, 17 pennyweights, and 10 grains of standard Silver, according to the statute of 43 Elizabeth. I believe in this case most debtors would pay in butter. . . . .

(Chap. viii., pages 337-8.)

From what has been said, it is not at all surprising that the pound sterling should in fact be reduced nearly to the value of the Gold. Whether it ought to be kept at this value is another question, and shall be examined in its proper place. All that we here decide is, that the coining the pound troy into 65 shillings would restore the proportion of the metals, and render both species common in circulation.

(Chap. xi., pages 353-4.)

[METHOD FOR RESTORING THE MONEY UNIT TO THE STANDARD OF ELIZABETH, AND THE CONSEQUENCES OF THIS CHANGE.]

I come now to the proposal of restoring the standard to that of the statute of Elizabeth, which is in other words the same with what has been proposed in bringing down the guineas to 20 shillings; except that it implies a new Coinage of all the Silver specie and of all the old Gold. Nothing is more easy than to execute this reformation.

1. The first step is to order all Coin, Gold and Silver, coined preceding a certain year, to pass by weight only.

2. To preserve the mint price of Silver as formerly, at 5s. 2d. the ounce, and to fix that of Gold at £3 14s. 2½d.

3. To order the pound troy standard Silver to be coined as formerly, into 62 shillings, and the pound of Gold into 44½ guineas.

4. And last of all to order these guineas to pass for 20 shillings.

Thus the standard is restored to the value of the Silver by the statute of Elizabeth; the metals are put at within a mere trifle of the proportion of 1 to 14½; all the coin in the kingdom is brought to standard weight; no profit will be found in melting or exporting one species preferably to another; exchange will answer, when at par, to the real par (when rightly calculated), of either Silver or Gold, with nations, such as France, who observe the same proportions, and the pound sterling will remain attached to both the Gold and Silver as before.

Extract from Smith's " Wealth of Nations."

(Book I., Chap. v.)

In England, therefore, and for the same reason, I believe, in all other modern nations of Europe, all accounts are kept, and the value of all goods and of all estates is generally computed, in Silver; and when we mean to express the amount of a person's fortune, we seldom mention the number of guineas, but the number of pounds sterling which we suppose would be given for it.

No. 19.

BIOGRAPHICAL NOTICE OF LORD LIVERPOOL.

It may serve the reader's convenience if I present here a brief outline of Lord Liverpool's career. I gather the following statements from various sources apparently worthy of confidence, but do not vouch for them from independent investigation.

Charles Jenkinson (1727-1808) was M.A. Oxford in 1752—where he wrote a poem on the death of the Prince of Wales. Later he wrote for the "Monthly Review," and in 1756 published a dissertation on the formation of a national guard; and in 1758 a discourse on the "Conduct of the Government of Great Britain in respect to Neutral Nations during War."

This paper was a defence of the course of the Government, which had lately seized some Dutch vessels. It was translated into various languages in Europe, and seems to have brought the author a pension. He presently appeared in politics as a *protégé* of Lord Bute, entered Parliament, and became Under-Secretary of State in 1761; Secretary of the Treasury, 1763; Member of the Board of Admiralty, 1766; Lord of the Treasury, 1767-1773; Member of the Privy Council, 1773; Vice-Treasurer of Ireland, 1775; Clerk of the Pells of Ireland, 1775-1808; Secretary of War, 1778-1782; President of the Board of Trade, 1784-1801; Chancellor of the Duchy of Lancaster, 1786-1802; Baron Hawkesbury, 1786; succeeded to Baronetcy as Seventh Baronet, 1789; Earl of Liverpool, 1796; subsequently Collector of the Customs-Inwards of the Port of London.

He compiled and published, in 1785, an important collection of Treaties.

At the outset of his career he identified himself with the party known as "The King's Friends," and is understood to have been the leading spirit of that System of the "Interior Ministry" or "Double Cabinet," which Burke attacked in his "Thoughts on the Present Discontents." He was generally believed to be the chief political adviser of George III., and the course of the government toward the American Colonies has been ascribed to his secret influence.

The following extract from an early page of the "Treatise on the Coins of the Realm" in a Letter to the King will indicate the occasion of its appearance.

After describing the necessity and success of the general recoinage of the Gold coins—upon his advice, in 1774—he proceeds as follows:—

"A difficulty then existed, and continues to exist, which must necessarily be removed, before any plan can be adopted for the improvement of the Silver Coin. I have already observed, that Gold and Silver, in reference to each other, are estimated at your Majesty's Mint at a different value or price, than these metals are generally sold for at the market. As long as this difference subsists, both these metals will not be brought in a sufficient quantity to the Mint to be coined: that metal only will be brought which is estimated at the lowest value with reference to the other; and Coins of both metals cannot be sent into circulation at the same time without exposing the public to a traffic of one sort of Coin against the other; by which the traders in money would make a considerable profit, to the great detriment of Your Majesty's subjects. And this mischievous practice, and the frauds committed in carrying it on, are the more to be apprehended in this country, where the Mint is free;— that is, where every one has a right to bring Gold and Silver to the Mint to be converted into Coin, not at the charge of the person who so brings it, but of the public: for since the 18th Charles II., ch. 3, the charge of coining Gold and Silver has been borne by the public, and, contrary to the practice of most other countries, no seigniorage has been taken. To prevent this evil it is necessary to determine whether there must not be a standard or superior Coin, made of one metal only; and whether the Coins made of other metals must not be made and take their value with reference to this standard Coin, and become subservient to it—and, in such case, of what metal this standard Coin, to which the pre-eminence and preference are to be given, should be made. These are delicate and very difficult questions, which require great consideration. Many persons of acknowledged abilities and great authority have entertained different opinions on this subject. I will not at present farther disclose my sentiments upon it, as a considerable portion of what I intend to write will be employed in the discussion of these questions; and I wish that the opinion which I have formed should appear to be the result of the reasons I shall offer, and of the facts which I shall state:—conscious that any opinion I may deliver cannot derive any weight from my single judgment in opposition to the respectable authorities from which I am forced, on this occasion, to differ.

"No farther measure was adopted for the improvement of the Coins of the realm, and particularly of the Silver Coin, though so very defective, for more than twenty years; when, in consequence of an address of the House of Commons, recommending a new Copper Coinage, Your Majesty was pleased, by Your Order in Council of the 7th Feb., 1798, to appoint a Committee, who were to take into consideration the state of the Coins of this kingdom, and the present establishment and constitution of Your Majesty's Mint; and to propose such improvements, in both these respects, as might appear to them to be necessary. Your Majesty was also pleased to insert my name among those members of Your Privy Council who were to form this Committee. Having had some experience in a business of this nature, and having occasionally reflected upon it, I ventured to open to the Committee, at their first meeting, the mode in which I thought they should proceed in the execution of Your Majesty's commands; and I suggested the principles, which, in my opinion, ought to be adopted for the further improvement of the Coins of this realm. The Committee made some progress in their enquiries on this extensive and difficult subject; and, in conformity with the wishes of the House of Commons, they established the principles, on which the Copper Coin should in future be made;—and a certain quantity of Coins, made according to these principles, was sent into circulation, very much to the satisfaction of Your Majesty's subjects:—but obstructions were raised, which prevented the completion of this measure."

No. 20.

REPORT of the Lords of the Committee of Council, appointed to take into Consideration the State of the COINS of this Kingdom, and the present Establishment and Constitution of His Majesty's Mint, to His Royal Highness the PRINCE REGENT; dated the 21st May 1816.

(L. S.)

AT THE COUNCIL CHAMBER, WHITEHALL,

the 21st of May 1816;

BY the Right Honourable the Lords of the Committee of Council, appointed to take into Consideration the State of the COINS of this Kingdom, and the present Establishment and Constitution of His Majesty's Mint.

HIS MAJESTY having been pleased, by His Order in Council of 7th February 1798, to direct this Committee to take into Consideration the State of the Coins of this Realm, and the present Establishment and Constitution of His Majesty's Mint; the Committee, in discharge of their duty, have already submitted to His Majesty, their opinions on some of the points so referred to them.

A new Mint has, at their recommendation, been erected, and furnished with a most complete and extensive Coining Apparatus, including all the modern improvements; and in a Representation to Your Royal Highness in Council, of 6th March 1815, this Committee suggested several Alterations in the Establishment and Constitution of His Majesty's Mint; which Your Royal Highness was graciously pleased to approve; and which will, it is presumed, render that Establishment more efficient.

These preliminary steps having been completed, the Committee have availed themselves of the return of General Peace, to resume the consideration of the important subject referred to them, which the unusually high Prices of the precious Metals, and other circumstances arising out of a state of War, had obliged them to suspend; and they now take leave humbly to represent to Your Royal Highness, that an immediate Coinage of Gold and Silver Monies, would be of great public benefit:

But that if Your Royal Highness should be pleased to give directions for carrying the same into effect, they do not conceive it would be advisable to make any Alteration, either in the Standard, Weight, or Denominations of the Gold Coins. The Committee are however of Opinion, that it should forthwith be proposed to Parliament, to pass an Act declaring the Gold Coin alone to be the Standard Coin of this Realm; and that the Silver Coins are hereafter to be considered merely as representative Coins, and to be a legal tender only in Payment of Sums not exceeding Two Guineas.

The Committee do not think it necessary to state to Your Royal Highness the Reasons which have led them to recommend that the Gold Coin alone should be declared to be the Standard Coin of the Realm, because they humbly conceive that such a Declaration by Parliament would in truth be merely in confirmation of a Principle, already established by the universal consent and practice of His Majesty's Subjects, and which appears to be in great measure recognized by the Act of 38 Geo. III. chap. 59.

With respect to the Silver Coins, of which an immediate supply appears to be more indispensably necessary for the public convenience; the Committee are of opinion, that no alteration should be made either in the Standard of Fineness, or in the Denominations of the Coins; but they think it will be advisable to diminish the Weight of the Pieces, in order to prevent a recurrence of those inconveniences which have hitherto arisen from the melting of the new and perfect Silver Coins as soon as they have appeared in circulation, for the purpose of converting them into bullion, in which state they have generally been more valuable than as Coin: The Committee are therefore of opinion, that it should be proposed to Parliament to authorize His Majesty to direct, that in all future Coinages of Silver, Sixty-six Shillings (and other Coins in proportion) shall be struck from each Pound Weight Troy of Standard Silver, instead of Sixty-two.

It has hitherto been the practice in His Majesty's Mint to return to those who import Silver for the purpose of having it converted into Coin, a quantity of Coin equal in weight to the quantity of Standard Silver so imported, the expense of Coining being borne by the Public. So long as the Silver Coins were considered to be the Standard Coin of the realm, this Principle appears to this Committee to have been a wise one, and they conceive that it should still be adhered to in respect of the Gold Coin, which is now to be declared the Standard Coin of the Realm; but the Committee are of opinion that the charge of coining the Silver Coins, as well as a small allowance for Seignorage, ought to be deducted; and that His Majesty should be authorized to direct the Master of His Mint to retain Four Shillings out of each Pound Weight Troy of Silver Coin, hereafter to be coined, for the charge of Brassage and Seignorage, and that the Money received for the same, should be applied to the Public Service in discharge of the interest of the Sum expended in the erection of the new Mint, and in defraying the general Expenses of the Mint Establishment. In thus stating the number of Pieces to be struck from each Pound of Silver, and the amount of the Sum to be deducted from Brassage and Seignorage, the Committee have, to the best of their judgment, endeavoured to fix on such a Rate as will on the one hand be sufficiently high to protect the new Coins, by a small increase of their nominal Value, from the danger of being melted down and converted into Bullion when the Market Price of Silver rises, while on the other, it will, they trust, not be found to be so low as to afford any encouragement to the issue of counterfeit Coin if the Market Price of Silver should fall.

Should Your Royal Highness think fit to adopt the Plan which the Committee have thus recommended, they think it would be advisable that a Sum of not less than £2,500,000 in Silver Coin should actually be coined, before any issue of new Coin takes place; viz. £2,000,000 for the use of *Great Britain*, and £500,000 for the use of *Ireland*.

It will, however, be necessary, before any further progress can be made in the execution of a New Silver Coinage, on the above principles, that the legal prohibitions against coining any Silver Coins of the Realm, or altering the Weight of such Coins, arising out of the Acts of 18 Charles II. ch. 5. 7 & 8 William III, ch. 1. sec. 1 & 2. 14 Geo. III. ch. 42. sec. 1. 38 Geo. III. chap. 59. sec. 2. should be repealed; and with this view, the Committee take leave to recommend, that in the Bill to be proposed to Parliament, provision should be made for the removal of those prohibitions. When that shall have been effected, the Committee will proceed humbly to recommend to Your Royal Highness, the Regulations which they conceive will be necessary with respect to the time and mode of calling in the Silver Coins now in currency; as well as with respect to the Allowance (if any) to be made hereafter for reasonable wear, in each denomination of the proposed New Silver Coins. The Committee think it right however now to state, as their opinion, with respect to the Silver Coins at present in Circulation, that it should be proposed to Parliament to authorize His Majesty, whenever He shall see fit to call in such Silver Coins, to direct that all such Pieces as shall be judged by the Officers of the Mint to have been actually coined in His Majesty's Mint, should be received by Tale, and that the holders of the same should receive in Return an equal Value by Tale of the New Silver Coins.

No. 21.

THE PROCLAMATION OF THE NEW CURRENCY, 1817,

By His Royal Highness THE PRINCE OF WALES,

REGENT of the United Kingdom of Great Britain and Ireland, in the Name and on the Behalf of HIS MAJESTY.

A PROCLAMATION.

GEORGE P. R.

WHEREAS by an Act passed in the Fifty-sixth Year of His Majesty's Reign intituled "An Act to provide for a new Silver Coinage, and to regulate the Currency of the Gold and Silver Coin of this Realm," the Master and Worker of His Majesty's Mint in London was authorized and empowered to coin or cause to be coined Silver Bullion into Silver Coins, consisting of Crowns, Half-Crowns, Shillings, and Sixpences, of the Standard of Eleven Ounces and Two Pennyweights of fine Silver and Eighteen Pennyweights Alloy to the Pound Troy; and in Weight after the Rate of Sixty-six Shillings to the Pound Troy: And whereas in virtue of the Powers so given a Coinage of Half-Crowns, Shillings, and Sixpences, at the Rate of Sixty-six Shillings to the Pound Troy, and of the Standard of Fineness above mentioned; every such Half-Crown Piece having for the Obverse Impression the Head of His Majesty, with the Inscription "Georgius III. Dei Gratia," and the Date of the Year, and for the Reverse the Ensigns Armorial of the United Kingdom, contained in a Shield surrounded by the Garter, bearing the Motto, "Honi soit qui mal y pense," and the Collar of the Garter, with the Inscription "Britanniarum Rex Fid: Def:" with a newly invented Graining on the Edge of the Piece; every such Shilling and Sixpenny Piece having for the Obverse Impression the Head of His Majesty, with the Inscription "Geor. III. D. G. Britt: Rex. F. D." and the Date of the Year, and for the Reverse the Ensigns Armorial of the United Kingdom, contained in a Shield surrounded by the Garter, bearing the Motto "Honi soit q mal y pense," with a newly invented Graining on the Edge of the Piece; has been completed, Part of which has been delivered for the Use of His Majesty's Subjects, and the Remainder thereof is now ready to be delivered for the Use of His Majesty's Subjects: We have therefore in the Name and on the Behalf of His Majesty, and by and with the Advice of His Majesty's Privy Council, thought fit to issue this Proclamation: And We do hereby ordain, declare, and command, that the said Pieces of Silver Money shall from and after the Day of the Date of this Our Proclamation, be current and lawful Money of the Kingdom of Great Britain and Ireland, and shall pass and be received as current and lawful Money of the said Kingdom: that is to say, such Half-Crown Pieces as of the Value of Two Shillings and Sixpence, such Shilling Pieces as of the Value of One Shilling, and such Sixpenny Pieces as of the Value of Sixpence, in all Payments and Transactions of Money.

> Given at the Court at Carlton House, the First Day of March One thousand eight hundred and seventeen, in the Fifty-seventh Year of His Majesty's Reign.

> God save the King.

By His Royal Highness THE PRINCE OF WALES,

REGENT of the United Kingdom of Great Britain and Ireland, in the Name and on the Behalf of HIS MAJESTY.

A PROCLAMATION.

GEORGE P. R.

WHEREAS We have thought fit to order that certain Pieces of Gold Money should be coined, which should be called "Sovereigns or

Twenty Shilling Pieces," each of which should be of the Value of Twenty Shillings, and that each Piece should be of the Weight of Five Pennyweights Three Grains $\frac{2741}{5000}$, Troy Weight of Standard Gold, according to the Weights approved of and confirmed by Us in Council, in pursuance of an Act made in the Fourteenth Year of His Majesty's Reign, intituled "An Act for regulating and ascertaining the Weights to be made use of in weighing the Gold and Silver Coin in this Kingdom;" And We have further thought fit to order that every such Piece of Gold Money, so ordered to be coined as aforesaid, shall have for the Obverse Impression the Head of His Majesty, with the Inscription "Georgius III. D. G: Britanniar. Rex. F. D." and the Date of the Year; and for the Reverse the Image of St. George armed sitting on Horseback encountering the Dragon with a Spear, the said Device being placed within the ennobled Garter, bearing the Motto "Honi soit qui mal y pense," with a newly invented Graining on the Edge of the Piece: And whereas Pieces of Gold Money of the above Description have been coined at His Majesty's Mint, and will be coined there, in pursuance of Orders which we have given for that Purpose: We have therefore, in the Name and on the Behalf of His Majesty, and by and with the Advice of His Majesty's Privy Council, thought fit to issue this Proclamation; and We do hereby, in the Name and on the Behalf of His Majesty, ordain, declare, and command, That the said Pieces of Gold Money so coined, and to be coined as aforesaid, shall be current and lawful Money of the Kingdom of Great Britain and Ireland, and shall be called "Sovereigns or Twenty Shilling Pieces," and shall pass and be received as current and lawful Money of the United Kingdom of Great Britain and Ireland; and every of such Pieces shall pass and be received as of the Value of Twenty Shillings of lawful Money of Great Britain and Ireland in all Payments whatsoever.

>Given at the Court at Carlton House, the First Day of July One thousand eight hundred and seventeen, in the Fifty-seventh Year of His Majesty's Reign.
>
>God save the King.

From Appendix D, 7, 8, to Evidence taken upon the Committee on the Royal Mint, 1837.

HISTORICAL MATERIAL—MISCELLANEOUS.

No. 22.
CONTRACTION IN 1818-1822.

The Effects of Resumption in Gold by Contraction of Paper Issues.
1818-1822.

Extract from Minutes of Evidence taken before the Committee on the Bank of England Charter, June 8, 1832.

Examination of J. Horsley Palmer, Esq.

No. 809.

Question. Are there any means of compelling the bank to provide a sufficient quantity of Gold?

Answer. The bank has only the means of obtaining an increased quantity if it be deemed desirable by contracting its issues, thereby creating a scarcity of Money and consequent fall in prices.

Extract from a paper on variations of prices and value of currency since 1782. "Journal of the Statistical Society," 1865, p. 294, by Prof. W. Stanley Jevons.

VARIATIONS OF AVERAGES OF PRICE.
[On a scale of 100; the prices of 1782-'83 affording this basis being assumed to be 100.]

Year.	Gold.	Paper.
1810	142	161
1811	136	147
1812	121	148
1813	115	149
1814	114	153
1815	109	132
1816	91	109
1817	117	120
1818	132	135
1819	112	117
1820	103	106
1821	94	......
1822	88	......
1823	89	......

No. 23.

ALEXANDER BARING (LORD ASHBURTON) ON THE SILVER AND GOLD STANDARD IN ENGLAND.

[Mr. Baring's evidence given before the Committees for Coin in 1828 was reprinted in Washington in 1830, in an appendix to a work on Gold and Silver, which deserved to make an epoch, although in fact it failed to do so.

I allude to the Report of Mr. S. D. Ingham, Secretary of the Treasury. In it was foreshadowed a "conventional agreement between the nations desiring to use both Gold and Silver as Standards of value fixing the same relative values." The reader will find this Report in the Document of the Conference of 1878.]

PARLIAMENTARY PAPER.—COIN.

(Extract from Minutes of Evidence taken before the Committee for Coin, at the Board of Trade, April 26, 1828.)

ALEXANDER BARING, Esq., M.P.—Examined.

Q. Is it your impression that it is possible and desirable to maintain in this country a silver currency as a legal tender, founded on the proportion of silver to gold established in the currency of France, or something very near it; at the same time that we maintain our present silver currency, which is obviously not in that proportion, and that there would be an advantage in that system?

A. I have always thought so, and certainly think so still. I have no doubt about it.

Q. Would you execute that by issuing silver coin of the same denominations as the present silver coin, but of a different standard, or by confining it to a silver coin of a new denomination?

A. It is quite clear that, if it were desired to have a silver coinage, all of the same weight and quality, the present silver coinage must be called in entirely; but I can see no difficulty whatever in the coexistence of a silver coinage as a legal tender, in the proportion, or nearly the proportion, now existing in France, with the present silver coinage remaining as a token, and provided the limitation continues as to the amount: with this precaution, I feel quite confident there can be nothing to prevent those two silver coinages existing together.

Q. Would you put them under the same denomination?

A. No, I think I would not. You might take one of two plans; you might either call in the present silver currency, and put the whole on the same footing, which would be a considerable expense, and I think an unnecessary one, or you might continue the silver now out, which now exists as a token silver coinage. There would be then the present gold coin and the new silver coin as legal tenders, and as they would not be interfered with by the token coinage, and as there is a considerable profit on the coining the latter, it might be continued as a measure of economy, and as a means, in some degree, of defraying the expenses of the Mint. When any additional token coinage should be wanted, I do not see any objection to keeping the shillings and sixpences and half-crowns as at present. In that case, I should propose that the 5s. pieces should be called in, and that the silver coin for legal tender should be confined to crown pieces; or, if it should be preferred, for the purpose of making a decimal division of the pounds, 2s. pieces might be substituted. In that case you might leave the few 5s. or 2s. pieces is not material, only, that if you make them 5s. pieces, then you would have to call in the 5s. token pieces which are at present out.

Q. The circulation of the country would consist of a silver coinage of tokens, being of a legal tender only to a limited amount; and a silver coinage being a legal tender to an unlimited amount; and a gold coinage?

A. Exactly so.

* * * * * *

Q. Supposing we were to adopt precisely the proportions of the French Mint, would not the result probably be the same as in France, namely, that silver would become the bulk of our metallic currency, and that gold would be in use only for those purposes for which it was more convenient; and that, in consequence, the diffusion of gold, which is now concentrated in this country, would be more equable over the civilized countries of the world?

A. Undoubtedly, if you were to take the same proportions. I do not see any single reason why exactly the same result should not take place, with this single difference, the extent of which I am not able to calculate; that this country partially rejecting gold as its tender, the effect would be to reduce to some extent the value of gold over the rest of the world. There is no doubt that, when this country returned to payments in specie, supposing we wanted from £15,000,000 to £20,000,000 of gold, for instance, and that, to that extent, there was a demand on the rest of the world for gold, gold got an increased value from that circumstance. If you make silver a large proportion of your currency, and still more if you were to make it the bulk or the whole of your currency, silver would gain something in value over gold. A free concurrent circulation of the two metals in all countries would certainly keep the proportions of each to the other most equable, and have little other ground for fluctuations than such as may arise from the charges of producing them. At present these fluctuations are more affected by changes in the wants of the gold or silver circulating countries than by any other cause.

Q. The result would be that silver would rise in value over the continent, as we claimed a larger proportion?

A. Yes.

Q. Does not the preference given to gold in the French currency arise from silver being over-valued?

A. Undoubtedly.

Q. Supposing both gold and silver coin made legal tenders in this country, and that the proportions rather favoured gold as a legal tender, would not the advantage of a double standard, such as it exists in France, be obtained, without our disturbing the existing mode of our currency; that is, with the advantage of retaining gold as the bulk of it, and silver as an aid to it; just as in France, silver is the currency and gold the aid?

A. This might certainly be easily done; by a very slight difference we could make gold the ordinary and habitual currency, and silver the auxiliary, which would come in aid on an emergency; the variation in France is seldom above a tenth per cent.; it sometimes runs up to a quarter per cent. It has been, I am told, something higher on particular occasions; when the Bank of England was running all over the continent for gold, this was the case; I believe, also, at another time, for the service of the peninsula; now and then, from casual circumstances, one metal gets preferred. If Russia goes to war in a distant part, she does it always with gold. At the present time, gold has been bought up to a large extent for this purpose, but unless any disturbing causes of this description arise, a very slight difference of one tenth or one fourth per cent. would determine the use of one metal or another.

Q. As they are liable to vary in their relative proportions, would it not be a difficulty attending such a system, that we should have frequently to re-adjust the proportions?

A. In using the two metals, one of two courses must be taken—either to leave them to chance, and to give to the debtor the advantage of the option, as was the case under the old system, or to fix at once which is to be your standard, and to adjust at given periods your other metal to it. If you want the advantages of the fixity of standard of one metal with the facilities and conveniences of two, you must take this latter course. I gave this opinion when the questions of currency were brought before Parliament, and I see no objection to it now. This system of occasional adjustment has been practised in France, and in these matters practical experience is worth all the theories of mere speculation. It is quite clear that, without this occasional adjustment, you may lose the benefit of the double standard, which is only to be preserved by keeping the value of gold and silver coins within a fraction of each other. Nobody can say how their value may vary according to the varying cost of their production, and as it is the duty of the State to see justice done between all debtors and creditors through the kingdom, I should prefer the principle of adjustment to leaving the result of their contracts or engagements to greater hazard.

No. 24.

THE RESTORATION OF SILVER BEFORE THE BANK OF ENGLAND IN 1828.

MINUTES OF EVIDENCE BEFORE COMMITTEE FOR COIN.

QUERIES given in Writing to the Governor and Deputy-Governor of the Bank of England.[1]

1st. WHETHER, in the opinion of the Bank, it be desirable that there should be established and maintained in this country, at the same

[1] Mr. Samuel Drew and Mr John Horsley Palmer.

time that we maintain the existing silver currency, a silver currency as a legal tender, the value of which should bear to gold nearly that proportion which is established in France, say about 15½ to 1?

Whether, if such an arrangement be desirable, it would be preferably effected by issuing silver coin of the same denomination, but of a different standard from the present, or by confining it to silver coin of a new denomination?

Whether the existence of such a silver currency would have the effect of forcing gold out of circulation, either occasionally or permanently?

In what manner does the Bank of England think that the existence of such a silver currency would operate on their transactions?

Would it afford them security against combinations which might be made to their prejudice?

Would it afford them means of more readily rectifying the foreign exchanges?

Would it enable them to provide with less difficulty for periods of panic or distress; and would it in any degree facilitate their procuring, when necessary, supplies of gold from abroad?

2. Whether the Bank of England has any objection to making advances on deposits of silver at a very low rate of interest, in the same manner as is now done by the Bank of France on deposits of gold?

Whether such a measure would in their view be advantageous, as affording convenience or security to the Bank or to the Public?

Whether their opinion of such an arrangement would be altered, if on such deposits of silver, notes or receipts were to be issued by the Bank, not payable in gold, but payable in portions of the silver deposited?

3. Whether the Bank consider any and what advantages likely to result from reverting to the system formerly established by law, that of making silver by weight a legal tender to any amount, the value of such silver being either fixed in relation to gold, or such value depending on the market price, as published in the Gazette in the week or month preceding the tender?

In replying to the three preceding queries, the Bank will bear in mind that the object is to retain gold as the bulk of the currency, and to have silver as an aid to it.

4. Whether there be in the country, at the present moment, a

sufficiency of coin for the purposes of the ordinary transactions which, in a country where paper forms so large a portion of the circulation, coin is necessarily applicable, and to provide for the deficiency which may be occasioned by the withdrawal from circulation of the small notes of the country bankers?

ANSWERS to the foregoing QUERIES.

1. PROVIDED there be sufficient silver currency in the country for the small payments, there does not appear to the Bank to be any advantage in the proposed addition of silver, as a general legal tender, from the great difficulty of retaining gold as the bulk of the currency under such an arrangement.

If such an arrangement were adopted, it appears to the Bank that it would be preferable to confine all the silver coin to one denomination, and not to issue silver coin of the same denomination as the present, of a different standard.

Whenever the state of the foreign exchanges might give gold a higher value, or when it might bear a higher agio, in foreign countries than in this, so far out of its relative value to silver as 15¼ to 1, thereby affording a profit to the exporter, the gold would leave this country for those parts of Europe where it might be more valuable.

For the reason given in answer to the first query, the Bank are of opinion, that the proposed general legal tender of silver would not materially operate upon their transactions.

It does not appear that it would afford to the Bank any security against combinations made to their prejudice, nor would it enable the Bank more readily to rectify the foreign exchanges, nor to provide with less difficulty for periods of panic; neither does it appear to the Bank that it would facilitate their procuring, when necessary, supplies of gold from abroad.

2. There does not appear to be any material objection to the Bank making advances on deposits of silver for limited periods, at a low rate of interest, which might afford convenience to the public, when the state of the foreign exchanges materially operated upon the demand and price of silver in the market. The Bank are of opinion, that notes or receipts payable in silver only would not be negotiable, as the same could not be received for deposits made with the Bank.

3. The Bank can see no advantage in reverting to the former system, of making silver by weight a legal tender to any amount; and they are further of opinion, that a varying scale of value in any metal intended to be used as a legal tender, cannot be otherwise than prejudicial in its effect upon all contracts. The payment by weight was formerly almost, if not entirely, nugatory.

In replying to the three first questions, the Bank have borne in mind, that the object is to retain gold as the bulk of the currency.

4. In answer to the fourth query, the Bank can only advert to the quantity of coin in their possession, and that issued by them since 1st January 1821, which, together with the silver issued from the Mint since 1816, induces the Bank to believe that there is a sufficiency of coin for the ordinary transactions of the country, and also to provide for the withdrawal from circulation of the small notes of the country bankers.

No. 25.

SILVER DISCUSSION IN 1837.

Extract from the Evidence before the Select Committee on the Royal Mint, 1837.

Questions by Joseph Hume, Esq., M.P., Chairman; Answers by Mr. Haggard, Head of the Bullion Office of the Bank of England.[1]

2474. Are you acquainted generally with the bullion market in London?—We have a great deal pass through our hands, more than any other.

2475. What, in your opinion, would be the effect of the Mint having in possession gold or silver coin to deliver to merchants having bullion to coin, so that the exchange might be made in the course of a week from the period of delivering it?—I consider that the Bank of England are bound to keep coin, because their notes are payable in cash, and the Bank ought to be the regulators of the coinage; they ought to be regulators of the quantity of bullion coined, for bullion is more valuable for mercantile purposes than coin.

[1] Mr. Wm. Debonaire Haggard entered the Bank of England, 1805; head of the Bullion Office, 1833; retired 1856; died 1866.

2476. The question was, what would be the effect on the price of bullion if merchants could carry smaller quantities to the Mint direct than can now be coined, instead of sending it to the Bank or the bullion merchants?—The effect would be, that the public would coin when it was profitable to them, and not otherwise; and therefore your circulation might be deficient or it might be over done, because they do not coin with reference to the quantity wanted by the people, but to the profit that arises upon the coinage.

2477. Would a facility given to merchants to carry that bullion in small quantities to the Mint for coinage tend to raise the price of bullion in the London market?—Certainly not; the fact is this, the public are not allowed to coin silver, they are only allowed to coin gold. The price fixed by the Bank is 3*l*. 17*s*. 9*d*. for the purchase of gold; the profit between coining and that price is only 1½*d*.; therefore it is hardly worth their while to coin, because the profit is not sufficient.

2478. Is there never a greater difference than 1½*d*. an ounce in the price the Bank gives to the seller and what it receives from the Mint? —I believe it is in consequence of the public having the privilege of coining at the Mint that the Bank gives 3*l*. 17*s*. 9*d*. an ounce, when at this moment I have not the least doubt they might buy it for 3*l*. 17*s*. 6*d*.

2479. That observation relates to gold?—To gold.

2480. Suppose the same facility to be given to the coinage of silver, and supposing silver to be equally pure as gold without a seinorage, what effect would that have on the silver bullion market?—It would affect the prices; the public would coin for profit, and never coin without.

2481. Would the price of silver in that case be more steady than it has hitherto been?—I should say yes, if made a legal tender.

2482. You think it would not produce any great change?—No: because at present our silver is 10 per cent. seinorage.

2483. But supposing the seinorage removed?—Then if they could buy the metal of the foreigner cheap, they would coin it dear; at least they would get a good price for it; if it was dearer than your standard of value, then there would be no coinage. Now, if it is left to the Bank, the public have the privilege of bringing their bank notes to the Bank, and getting cash when they please; and whether the price be 3*l*. 17*s*. 9*d*. or 3*l*. 17*s*. 10½*d*., the Bank must coin.

2484. That is with regard to gold?—Even with the silver it would be the same.

2485. What is the greatest variation in the price of gold that you have known since 1816?—In 1825 to 1828 we purchased a large quantity of gold at 3*l.* 17*s.* 6*d.* In 1828 Mr. Rothschild brought a large quantity of gold from Paris, took it to the Mint and coined it into sovereigns; he then brought those sovereigns to the Bank, and made them pay equal to 3*l.* 17*s.* 10½*d.* for them, merely to put down, in the coffers of the Bank. In consequence of that, I have no doubt that the Bank, to prevent the public coining, offer the price of 3*l.* 17*s.* 9*d.* per ounce, in any quantity and at all times, without reference to demand or supply.

2486. Then since 1828 the Bank price has remained fixed at 3*l.* 17*s.* 9*d.*?—Yes, for purchase, and 3*l.* 17*s.* 10½*d.* for sale.

2487. Now what is the greatest variation in the price of silver in your recollection?—It is a very extraordinary circumstance, that at this present time, if silver was to be made the standard of value, I should recommend that the standard should be coined at the rate of Queen Elizabeth's time; that 62*s.* of standard silver should be coined out of the pound troy, instead of 66*s.*, which is the present rate. Some of our coin is 7½ per cent. worse by wear at the present moment.

2488. Were all Elizabeth's silver coin 62*s.* to the pound?—I forget whether the whole of it was, but I think it was.

2489. What variations have taken place in the coinage of silver since then?—Only from 62*s.* to 66*s.*

2490. When did it begin?—It began in 1816; the alteration took place then, by Lord Liverpool's recommendation.

2491. Why would you recommend that now, in case of a change?—Because it would not be cheating the public; it would be a fair remuneration for the price of the manufactured coin, brassage, and the expense of the Mint.

2492. Then it is your opinion that silver, if made a tender, should be coined with simply a brassage, for the expense of coining, added?—That would give a per-centage to the Mint; it would be most desirable to keep a reserve fund to make the coin, when light, a proper weight.

2493. What do you reckon the price of silver?—At present?

2494. Yes.—It is not quite 5*s.*

2495. What is the greatest variation you have ever known from that price?—At the time of the cash restriction, I think I recollect 7s. 6d. an ounce; but since that it has hardly ever varied from 5s. to 5s. 0½d.

2496. Are you able to form an opinion what the exact proportion between the value of gold and silver should be?—According to a calculation that I have made, it would be about 15 to one, as near as possible.

2497. On what ground do you make that calculation?—I calculate that the exchanges with France would then be about 25 francs; it is now 25 francs and 30 cents., I believe.

2498. And why would you make that difference between France and us?—Taking all the other countries as one, it seems to be the best proportion you can make between gold and silver; but you cannot always keep that due proportion; the foreign exports will affect the exchanges; if silver was fixed and the other free, you never would have your circulation disturbed, as it is at present.

2499. Are you able to state whether, since the two extensive houses for exchange have been established, within the last 10 or 15 years, the price of bullion remains more on a par in the different states of Europe than formerly?—I should say so, decidedly; and as we get more civilized, that will be still more the case; if you overtrade, you are sure to get the precious metals back again, because it is the par of your goods.

No. 26.

SIR ROBERT PEEL ON THE STANDARD OF VALUE.

May 6th, 1844.[1]

Sir Robert Peel's best-known statement on the standard of value is contained in his speech in the House of Commons on the Bank Charter Act of May 6th, 1844. He expressed himself as follows:—

"Now, I fear, there is not a general agreement on those fundamental principles—that there is still a very material difference of opinion as to the real nature and character of the Measure of Value in this country. My first question, therefore, is, What constitutes this measure of value?

---

[1] I take the following from Mr. R. H. Inglis Palgrave's Memorandum on "Currency and Standard of Value in England." (3 Rep. R. Com. on Depression of Trade, p. 321.)

What is the signification of that word 'a Pound,' with which we are all familiar? What is the engagement to pay a 'Pound'? Unless we are agreed on the answer to these questions, it is in vain we attempt to legislate on the subject. *If a 'Pound' is a mere visionary abstraction*, a something which does not exist either in law or in practice, in that case one class of measures relating to Paper Currency may be adopted; but if the word 'Pound,' the common denomination of value, *signifies something more than a mere fiction*—if a 'Pound' means *a quantity of the precious metals of certain weight and certain fineness*—if that be the definition of a 'Pound,' in that case another class of measures relating to Paper Currency will be requisite. Now, the whole foundation of the proposal I am about to make rests upon the assumption that, according to practice, according to law, *according to the ancient monetary policy of this country*, that which is implied by the word 'Pound' *is a certain definite quantity of gold with a mark upon it to determine its weight and fineness*, and that the engagement to pay a Pound means nothing and can mean nothing else than the promise to pay to the holder, when he demands it, *that definite quantity of gold*. What is the meaning of the 'Pound' according to the ancient monetary policy of this country? The origin of the term was this:—In the reign of William the Conqueror, a pound weight of silver was also the pound of account. The 'Pound' represented both the weight of metal and the denomination of money. By subsequent debasements of the currency a great alteration was made, not in the name, but in the intrinsic value of the Pound sterling; and it was not until a late period of the reign of Queen Elizabeth that silver, being then the standard of value, received that determinate weight which it retained without variation, with constant refusals to debase the standard of silver until the year 1816, *when gold became the exclusive standard of value*. The standard of silver was fixed about 1567; but in 1717 *the value of the guinea was determined to be 21s.*; and, *for a certain period*, both gold and silver constituted the *mixed standard of value*. In the year 1774, it being then enacted that no legal contract *should be discharged in silver for any sum of more than 25l., gold became substantially the measure of value*, and so it continued to be legally and practically until 1797, when that fatal measure for restricting cash payments by the bank was passed, and parties were enabled to issue, at their discretion, Paper Money not convertible into coin at the will of the bearer. From 1797 to 1810, public attention was not much directed to this important subject; but in 1810, men of sagacity observed that the exchanges had been for a considerable period unfavourable to this country—more unfavourable than could be accounted for by the balance of trade, or the monetary transactions of the country. A Committee was appointed to inquire into the subject, and opinions, not really novel, but at that time very startling, were enounced, to the effect *that the 'Pound' meant, in fact, nothing else than a definite quantity of the precious metals,* and that those who promised to pay a Pound *ought* to pay that quantity." . . . . . .

"Now, no one contends that there is or can be an absolutely fixed and invariable standard of value. No one denies that the value of gold, with reference to all commodities, excepting gold itself, may be subject to slight variations. But what other substance is not more subject to variations in value than the precious metals? What other substance possessing intrinsic value will not also be in demand as an article of commerce? It is because gold is an article of commerce, because there are no restrictions upon its export or its import, that you can at all times depend upon such a supply of gold for the purposes of coin as may be sufficient for the wants of this country. The precious metals are distributed among the various countries of the world in proportion to their respective necessities, by *laws of certain, though not very obvious operation, which, without our interference, will allot to our share all that we require.* Some entertain the apprehension that we may be drained of all our gold in consequence of a demand for gold from foreign countries either for the payment of their armies in time of war, or in consequence of sudden and unforeseen demand for foreign coin for our own internal consumption. It is supposed that gold, being an article in universal demand, and having at all times and in all places an ascertained value, is more subject to exportation than anything else. But the export of gold, whether coin or bullion, is governed by precisely the same laws by which the export of any other article is governed. Gold will not leave this country, unless gold be dearer in some other country than it is in this. It will not leave this country, merely because it is gold, nor while there is any article of our produce or manufacture which can be exported in exchange for foreign produce with a more profitable return. If gold coin be in any country the common medium of exchange; or if the promissory notes which perform, in part, the functions of gold coin, are at all times, and under all circumstances, of equal value with gold, and are instantly convertible into gold; there are causes in operation which, without any interference on our part, will confine within known and just limits the extent to which gold can be exported. There may, no doubt, be temporary pressure from the export of gold, even when it is confined within those limits; but none for which you may not provide, none to which you would not be subject, in a higher degree, probably, were any other standard of value adopted in preference to gold. I have thus stated the grounds which justify the conclusion, that, according to the ancient monetary policy of the country, according to the law, according to the practice that prevailed at all times, excepting during the period of inconvertible paper currency, a certain quantity of the precious *metals*, definite in point of weight and fineness, has constituted, and ought to constitute, the measure of value." . . . . . .

" It must, at the same time, be admitted that it would be quite consistent with that principle to adopt some other measure of value than that which we have adopted. *It would be consistent with that principle to select silver instead of gold as the standard,—to have a mixed standard of gold and silver, the relative values of the two metals being determined,*—to dispense with gold coin altogether, and regulate the amount of paper currency by making it convertible only, according to the proposal of Mr. Ricardo, into gold bullion of a given minimum amount. I trust, however, this House will adhere to the present standard,—will resolve on the maintenance of a *single standard, and of gold as that standard*. All great writers on this subject, Sir William Petty, Mr. Locke, Mr. Harris, and Lord Liverpool, have been decidedly *in favour of a single, in preference to a double standard*. Mr. Locke, indeed, was of opinion that silver ought to be the standard, but there appears *good ground to doubt the soundness of that opinion ;* and there are, at any rate, the most cogent reasons, since gold has been for a long course of years the standard in this country, for the continued maintenance of it. They are well stated in the admirable Treatise on Coins, written by the first Lord Liverpool. In that treatise a system of coinage is recommended which is in exact conformity, both in point of principle and detail, with the system which we have adopted. Lord Liverpool observes :—

" ' After full consideration of this extensive, abstruse, and intricate subject, I humbly offer to Your Majesty as the result of my opinion,

" ' First. That the coins of this Realm, which are to be the principal measure of property and instrument of commerce, should be made of one metal only.

"'Secondly. That in this kingdom the gold coins only have been for many years past, and are now, in the practice and opinion of the people, the principal measure of property and instrument of commerce.

"'It has been shown that, in a country like Great Britain, so distinguished for its affluence and for the extent of its commercial connexions, the gold coins are best adapted to be the principal measure of property; in this kingdom, therefore, the gold coin is now the principal measure of property and standard coin, or, as it were, the sovereign archetype by which the weight and value of all other coins should be regulated. It is the measure of almost all contracts and bargains; and by it, as a measure, the price of all commodities bought and sold is adjusted and ascertained. For these reasons the gold coin should be made as perfect, and kept as perfect, as possible.

"'Thirdly. It is evident that where the function of the gold coins as a measure of property ceases, there that of the silver coin should begin; and that where the function of the silver coins in this respect, ceases, there that of copper should begin; it is clear, therefore, that so far only these silver and copper coins should be made legal tender and no further, at least not in any great degree: and it follows that the coins, both of silver and copper, are subordinate, subservient, and merely representative coins, and must take their value with reference to the gold coins according to the rate which the sovereign sets upon each of them.'

"These are, in fact," Sir Robert Peel continued, "the principles which regulate our present coinage. We have a single standard, and that standard gold,—the metal which was practically the standard for many years previously to the suspension of cash payment. The silver coin is a mere token, auxiliary and subordinate to the gold coin; the ounce of silver being now coined into 66s. instead of 62s., and silver coin not being a legal tender for any greater sum than 40s."—Speech on Bank Charter, House of Commons, May 6, 1844.

No. 27.

MONETARY TREATIES IN THE PAST.[1]

In all cases where communities which severally have maintained an independent Coinage System have come into union with each other, or into subjection one to another, a conflict of Coinages must naturally ensue, and the settlement of such conflict must naturally offer analogies both with the jarring of the Money Systems of independent nations and with that Monetary pacification which is the aim of international monetary contract.

For instance, the monetary arrangements arising out of the consolidation of the Roman Empire, or, later, out of that of the royal power of France and that of the United Kingdom of Great Britain, must offer such analogies, while the partial and desultory coinage legislation of the Holy Roman Empire of the German Nation in past centuries, and in its turn the speedy monetary unification of the new German Empire of to-day, would offer similar points of resemblance and of instruction.

A list of Treaties is presented herewith: which, however, so far as earlier times are concerned, must be regarded as merely tentative: for, in view of the novelty of the investigation, it is not improbable that the list is incomplete, if not, indeed, incorrect. Treaties of the German States which formerly formed part of the old German Empire stand distinct from acts which bear a character more decidedly international.

To guard against misunderstanding, an important distinction must be observed. The possible future monetary treaty of the chief Western Powers, contemplated by the advocates of the policy adopted by the United States in the law of February 28, 1878, under which the Conference was convoked, differs in an essential point from treaties of which history offers an example. Such treaties have, it is believed, invariably had for their object a Fusion of Currencies or Mutuality of Legal Tender; the Coins struck in one country were to receive legal currency in another; and this interchangeability of Coin was the main object of the treaty.

[1] Reprinted from the Document of the Monetary Conference of 1878.

This general object may have implied the purpose, or carried with it the result, that a certain metal or certain metals should become or remain material of Coinage in the contracting countries, and may have included the obligation of each party to maintain by appropriate laws the Legal-Tender character of such coined metal. But it was the coining and not the metal: it was the subdivision and the stamping of the material, and not the material itself, that offered the motive of the contract.

This happened very naturally because, until lately, the status of both Gold and Silver was regarded as fixed. It appears to have been taken for granted, perhaps unconsciously, but in any case by general consent, that the two metals would remain Money ; that they would retain an international currency as material for Money sufficient to guarantee their general status. Gold might be excluded here from Legal-Tender, and there Silver might be ostracized, but there was no combined effort to exclude Silver, and the nations which would not admit Gold as Legal-Tender furthered its use as a Trade Coin.

On the other hand, the advocates of the policy now proposed necessarily regard the material, not the stamping of its subdivisions.

The object of this policy would be fully met by a Treaty which should merely guarantee the equality of the metals before the law. Under such a Treaty the contracting parties might each retain undisturbed their national Coins ; their mutual engagement would relate merely to the use of the two metals as full Legal-Tender at the same ratio. Full-Legal-Tender power is to be appropriately secured by each contracting country to its *own Coins*. In making Coins, uniform freedom should be granted to the private individual to have metal coined, and it is desirable that the same charge, or absence of charge, for Coinage, should obtain in the contracting nations.

An examination of the History of the Coinage Confederations hereafter mentioned, will reveal that their disadvantages or deficiencies arose either, 1st, from this extra-national legal currency of Coins, which was their primary object ; or, 2nd (when they contemplated the concurrent use of the two metals), from an extra-federal demand for Gold at Silver-price higher than that assigned to the metal in the Federal Coinage System.

These disadvantages which inhered in all European Monetary Unions actually formed, are believed to be excluded from that which the United States has proposed to the nations for discussion. It is not essential, nor is it an important practical object of this policy, that extra-national legal currency of Coins should be included in the contract, while the Union contemplated is so large that, so far as probabilities can be calculated, its tranquillity could not, under any circumstances which this generation is warranted in anticipating, be disturbed by an extra-federal demand for Gold.

LIST OF TREATIES.

GERMAN STATES.

Coinage Union of the Four Electors of the Rhine, fifteenth century.

Coinage and Customs Union of the same, seventeenth century.

Coinage "Correspondenz" of the various Districts of the Empire, sixteenth, seventeenth, and eighteenth centuries.

Coinage Agreement (*Recess*), of Zinna, 1677; Electors of Saxony; Electors of Brandenburg; joined by the House of Brunswick-Lüneburg.

Coinage Union of Leipzig, 1690; Elector of Saxony; Elector of Brandenburg; House of Brunswick-Lüneburg.

Coinage Treaty of Vienna, September 21, 1753; Austria; Elector of Bavaria.

Coinage-Union-Treaties of Frankfort, February 22, 1765, and of Worms, January 19, 1766, of the Electors of Mainz, Treves, and the Palatinate Landgrave of Hesse-Darmstadt, and Free-City Frankfort.

In some of the various treaties which established and regulated the GERMAN TRADE AND CUSTOMS UNION are to be found provisions affecting the reciprocal acceptance of coins.

COINAGE TREATY OF MUNICH, August 25, 1837. (Bavaria, Würtemberg, Baden, Hesse, Nassau, and Frankfort.)

COINAGE TREATY OF DRESDEN, July 30, 1838. (States of the German Customs Union.)

COINAGE TREATY OF MUNICH, March 27, 1845.

MONETARY CARTEL: for punishment of all crimes against the prerogative of coining and of issuing paper money. Karlsruhe, October 21, 1845. (Prussian Customs-Union); Prussian Customs-Union, February 19, 1853.

COINAGE TREATY OF VIENNA, January 24, 1857. (Formed in pursuance to Art. 9 of the Treaty of Karlsruhe, July 19, 1853, by Austria, the Principality of Lichtenstein, and the States which were parties to the Treaty of Dresden, July 30, 1838.) Austria, Prussia, Bavaria, Saxony, Hanover, Würtemberg, Baden, Electorate of Hesse, Grand Duchy of Hesse, Grand Duchy of Saxony, Oldenburg, Saxe-Meiningen, Saxe Coburg and Gotha, Saxe Altenburg, Brunswick, Nassau, Anhalt-Dessau-Köthen, Anhalt-Bernburg, Schwarzburg-Sondershausen, Schwartzburg-Rudolstadt, Lichtenstein, Waldeck and Pyrmont, Reuss older line, Reuss younger line, Schaumburg-Lippe, Lippe, Landgraviate of Hesse, The Free City of Frankfort.

THE LATIN UNION.

MONETARY TREATY OF PARIS, December 23, 1865. France, Belgium, Switzerland, and Italy. Took effect August 1, 1866. Ratified, by Italy, June 2, and July 21, 1866; by Belgium, July 21, 1866; by Switzerland, 1866; and by France.

The Accession of Greece to the Treaty took place April 10-22, 1867; of Roumania, April 14, 1867; of the States of the Church, June 18, 1866.

Supplementary Treaty of January 30, 1874. Belgium, France, Italy, Switzerland.

Supplementary Declaration of February 5, 1875.

Supplementary Declaration of February 3, 1876.

Supplementary Declaration, 1877.

Treaty of Renewal of the Treaty of 1865, November 5, 1878.

Treaty of Renewal, etc., 1885-1886.

FRANCE AND AUSTRIA.

PRELIMINARY MONETARY TREATY OF PARIS, July 3, 1867. France and Austria.

THE SCANDINAVIAN UNION.

MONETARY TREATY OF DECEMBER 18, 1872. Sweden and Denmark.

Supplementary Treaty of May 27, 1873.

Treaty of Accession of Norway, to the latter Treaty, October 16, 1875.

No. 28.

CERTAIN STATE PAPERS RELATING TO THE POLICY OF MONETARY UNION, 1878, 1881, 1882.

CONFERENCE OF 1878.

(From the Document of the Conference, page 213.)

Extract from the Report of the American Commission.

At the second session, on the 16th August, the Commissioners of the United States submitted the two following propositions:

I.

It is the opinion of this Assembly that it is not to be desired that Silver should be excluded from Free Coinage in Europe and the United States of America. On the contrary, the Assembly believes that it is desirable that the Unrestricted Coinage of Silver, and its use as Money of Unlimited Legal Tender, should be retained where they exist, and, as far as practicable, restored where they have ceased to exist.

II.

The use of both Gold and Silver as Unlimited Legal Tender Money may be safely adopted:

First—By equalizing them at a relation to be fixed by international agreement: and

Secondly—By granting to each metal, at the relation fixed, equal terms of Coinage, making no discrimination between them.

The following third proposition was prepared and held in reserve, awaiting the development of the views of the Conference:

III.

The Delegations here present agree to recommend to their respective governments that, by the free coinage of silver at a relation to be agreed upon, or provisionally, through extended coinage upon government account and the accumulation of silver bullion in public treasuries, they make a concerted effort to restore silver to its function as money of full power.

At no time during the further proceedings did the interest of our mission appear to require the presentation of this proposition.

At the seventh and concluding session, on the 29th of August, the following reply to the propositions submitted by the Delegates of the United States was offered on behalf of the majority of the European Delegates:

The Delegates of the European States represented in Conference wish to express their sincere thanks to the Government of the United States of America for having procured an international exchange of opinion upon a subject of so much importance as the monetary question.

Having maturely considered the proposals of the representatives of the United States, they recognize:

I.

That it is necessary to maintain in the world the monetary functions of Silver as well as those of Gold, but that the selection for use of one or the other of the two metals, or of both, simultaneously, should be governed by the special position of each State, or group of States.

II.

That the question of the restriction of the Coinage of Silver should equally be left to the discretion of each State, or group of States, according to the particular circumstances in which they may find themselves placed, and the more so, in that the disturbance produced during the recent years in the Silver market has variously affected the monetary situation of the several countries.

III.

That the differences of opinion which have appeared, and the fact that even some of the States which have the Double Standard find it impossible to enter into a mutual engagement with regard to the free coinage of Silver, exclude the discussion of the adoption of a common ratio between the two metals.

Contemporaneously with the presentation of this paper, individual expressions of opinion were offered by several of the Delegations, which may be seen in the journal accompanying this report.

To this declaration of the European Delegates, the Delegates of the United States rejoined with the following statement of their views, with which the formal proceedings of the Conference terminated :

In response to the address of the representatives of the European States, the representatives of the United States desire, on their part, to express their thanks to the European States for accepting their invitation and consulting with them upon a subject of so much importance.

The representatives of the United States regret that they cannot entirely concur in all that has been submitted to them by a majority of the representatives of the European States.

They fully concur in a part of the first proposition, viz., that " It is necessary to maintain in the world the monetary functions of Silver as well as those of Gold," and they desire that ere long there may be adequate co-operation to obtain that result.

They cannot object to the statement that " the selection for use of one or other of these two metals, or of both simultaneously, should be governed by the special position of each State ;" but if it be necessary to maintain the monetary functions of the two metals as previously declared, they respectfully submit that special positions of States may become of secondary importance.

From so much of the second proposition as assigns as a special reason for at present restricting the Coinage of Silver "that the disturbance produced during the recent years in the Silver market has differently affected the monetary situation of the several countries," they respectfully dissent, believing that a policy of action would remove the disturbance that produced these inequalities.

In regard to the third and last proposition, they admit that " some of the States which have the Double Standard," or, as they prefer to say, use both metals, " find it impossible to enter into a mutual engagement for the free Coinage of Silver."

They, as representatives of the United States, have come here expressly to enter into such an engagement. The difficulty is not with them, and, wherever it may be, they trust it may be soon removed. They entirely concur in the conclusion drawn from this state of the case that it " excludes the discussion of the adoption of a common ratio between the two metals" if the nations are not ready to adopt a policy to uphold it. We remain upon ours; the European States upon theirs.

R. E. FENTON.
W. S. GROESBECK.
FRANCIS A. WALKER.
S. DANA HORTON.

CONFERENCE OF 1881.

(From the Document of the Conference, page 502.)

Mr. EVARTS, on behalf of the Delegates of France (Magnin, Dumas, De Normandie, and Cernuschi), and of the United States of America (Evarts, Thurman, Howe, and Horton), read the following Declaration:

The Delegates of France and of the United States, in the name of their respective Governments, make the following Declarations:

1. The depreciation and great fluctuations in the value of Silver relatively to Gold, which of late years have shown themselves, and which continue to exist, have been, and are, injurious to commerce and to the general prosperity, and the establishment and maintenance of a fixed relation of value between Silver and Gold would produce most important benefits to the commerce of the world.

2. A convention, entered into by an important group of States, by which they should agree to open their mints to free and unlimited coinage of both Silver and Gold, at a fixed proportion of weight between the Gold and Silver contained in the monetary unit of each metal, and with full legal tender faculty to the money thus issued, would cause and maintain a stability in the relative value of the two metals suitable to the interests and requirements of the commerce of the world.

3. Any ratio, now or of late in use by any commercial nation, if adopted by such important group of States, could be maintained; but the adoption of the ratio of $15\frac{1}{2}$ to 1, would accomplish the principal object with less disturbance in the monetary systems to be affected by it than by any other ratio.

4. Without considering the effect which might be produced toward the desired object by a lesser combination of States, a convention which would include England, France, Germany, and the United States, with the concurrence of other States, both in Europe and on the American continent, which this combination would assure, would be adequate to produce and maintain throughout the commercial world the relation between the two metals that such convention should adopt.

Resolution for an Adjourned Meeting.

The Conference, considering that in the course of its two sessions it has heard the speeches, declarations and observations of the delegates of the States hereinafter enumerated;

Germany, Austria-Hungary, Belgium. Denmark, Spain, The United States, France, Great Britain, British-India, Canada, Greece, Italy, The Netherlands, Portugal, Russia, Sweden, Norway and Switzerland;

Considering that the declarations made by several of the delegates have been in the name of their governments;

That these declarations all admit the expediency of taking various measures in concert, under reservation of the entire freedom of action of the different governments;

That there is ground for believing that an understanding may be established between the States which have taken part in the Conference;

But that it is expedient to suspend its meetings;

That, in fact, the monetary situation may, as regards some States, call for the intervention of their Governments, and that there is reason for giving an opportunity at present for diplomatic negotiations;

Adjourns to Wednesday, 12th April, 1882.

PROPOSED CONFERENCE OF 1882.

Copy of an Identical Note sent to the Powers by the Governments of France and of the United States, March 31, 1882.

PARIS, *March* 31, 1882.

The International Monetary Conference which was convened at Paris last year, upon the invitation of France and of the United States, and in which the Government of   was represented, adjourned to meet the 12th of April, 1882.

In making this decision at the session of July 8, 1881, the Delegates anticipated that, before the date thus fixed, the Governments represented in the Conference would be able to prepare solutions of the questions involved, with a view to the conclusion of an international convention, the terms of which should be discussed and determined by the Conference.

This anticipation has been, in part, realized. From all the information which has been received, it appears that in a large number of States the question has continued to be the subject of earnest consideration and that various plans have been under discussion, with the object either of re-establishing the free coinage of silver money, or of restoring to the metal silver its proper international value by enlarging its use as coin. Up to the present time, however, these investigations do not appear to have produced conclusions sufficiently positive to serve as a basis for formal deliberations of the Conference.

Hence, in the opinion of the Government of the United States, in conformity with the view entertained by various other Governments, notably by those of Germany, Holland, and Italy, there would be no sufficient advantage in re-opening the discussions of the Conference at present.

In this situation, the Governments of the United States and of France are of opinion that it would be desirable to defer the convocation of the Conference, subject to a determination, on the part of the States interested, of the date for its re-assembling, the same to take place within the present year.

BY THE SAME AUTHOR.

SILVER AND GOLD, and their Relation to the Problem of Resumption. (Cincinnati: Robert Clarke & Co., 1876.) [Presented as a printed deposition to the Monetary Commission of 1876.] New edition, January, 1877; with Appendix containing—
The Laisser faire theory and Iwan Poreschkow, &c., &c., and reprint of
An Address to Congress against the Bland Bill, Dec., 1876.

Monetary Malaria, or the Health of Nations, 1877.

THE MONETARY SITUATION. (Cincinnati: Robert Clarke & Co., May, 1878.) Containing also as Appendix papers on the Prussian Anti-Silver Theory, and its origin in an historical error.—General Restoration of Silver, a condition precedent to successful cancellation of paper money (1877). A Vindication of the Practicability of Bimetallic Union (1877).

SPEECHES IN THE MONETARY CONFERENCE OF 1878, and Documents presented — In "Procès-Verbaux," or Report [original in French] of the Proceedings of the Conference, etc. (Paris: Imprimerie Nationale, Nov. 1878, folio.) Ditto in English Translation in DOCUMENT OF THE CONFERENCE OF 1878. (Washington: Government Printing Office, July, 1879. 918 pp., 8vo. & 4to.) This volume comprises also the two following Titles.

HISTORICAL MATERIAL FOR THE STUDY OF MONETARY POLICY (518 pp.). Consisting chiefly of documents illustrating the monetary history of France, England and the United States (of which many are printed for the first time from MSS., and others for the first time translated), compiled and edited as a partial DOCUMENTARY HISTORY OF MONETARY POLICY; and—

CONTRIBUTIONS TO THE STUDY OF MONETARY POLICY (125 pp.). Consisting of Historical and Doctrinal Essays and a Bibliography of Money.

Sir Isaac Newton and England's Prohibitive Tariff upon Silver Money: an open letter to Prof. W. S. Jevons. (Cincinnati: March, 1881.)

La Monnaie et la Loi. Traduction par Emile de Laveleye. (Paris: Guillaumin et Cie., May, 1881.)

Das Geld und das Gesetz nebst Rede uber das Interesse der Vereinigten Staaten an der Silberfrage. Uebersetzung Von E. Koch. (Köln: Heimann, August, 1881.)

DISCOURS PRONONCÉS ET DOCUMENTS PRÉSENTÉS DANS LA CONFÉRENCE MONÉTAIRE INTERNATIONALE DE 1881.—In Procès-Verbaux. (Paris: Imprimerie Nationale, August, 1881, folio.) (Also separate edition, 72 pp. folio.) Ditto in English Translation: Report of Proceedings of Conference of 1881. Blue-Book. (London: Spottiswoode, September, 1881, folio), and Published by department of State (Washington: November, 1881); also in German Translation. Published by German Government. (Berlin: 1882.)

THE POSITION OF LAW IN THE DOCTRINE OF MONEY, and other papers. (London: 1882.)

SILVER AS AN INTERNATIONAL QUESTION. An Address to Congress: being a letter written in response to a request to Hon. A. H. Buckner, of Missouri, Chairman of the Committee of the House of Representatives on Currency and Banking. (Washington: Privately printed, February, 1885. 15 pp.)

REASONS FOR SUSPENDING SILVER COINAGE. An Address delivered in response to the invitation of the Executive Committee of the NATIONAL COMMERCIAL CONVENTION, at its meeting in Atlanta, Georgia, May 21, 1885. Also Extracts (7 pp.) reprinted by the New York Board of Trade and Transportation, July, 1885.

Ought the National Banking System to be abolished? (*North American Review*, September, 1885. 3 pp.)

THE INTERNATIONALITY OF THE SILVER QUESTION. An Address prepared at the invitation of the Executive Committee of the American Bankers' Association, for its meeting at Chicago, September 24, 1885. (Bankers' Pub. Assoc., New York, 1885.)

A CHAPTER ON MONETARY POLICY. (*North American Review*, December, 1885. 11 pp.)

SILVER: AN ISSUE OF INTERNATIONAL POLITICS. An Address to Congress, March, 1886. (Cincinnati: R. Clarke & Co., 1886.)

THE BANKING COMMUNITY AND THE SILVER QUESTION. An Address delivered at the Annual Convention of the American Bankers' Association, Aug. 21, 1886, at Boston. (In Report of Convention, American Bankers' Pub. Assoc.)

SILVER BEFORE CONGRESS IN 1886. (*Quarterly Journal of Economics*, first number. Boston: George H. Ellis, October, 1886. 31 pp.)

www.ingramcontent.com/pod-product-compliance
Lightning Source LLC
Chambersburg PA
CBHW021152230426
43667CB00006B/367